First World War

and Army of Occupation

War Diary

France, Belgium and Germany

25 DIVISION
Divisional Troops
South Wales Borderers
6th Battalion Pioneers
24 September 1915 - 31 May 1918

WO95/2238/2

The Naval & Military Press Ltd
www.nmarchive.com
Published in association with The National Archives

Published by

The Naval & Military Press Ltd

Unit 10 Ridgewood Industrial Park,

Uckfield, East Sussex,

TN22 5QE England

Tel: +44 (0) 1825 749494

www.naval-military-press.com

www.nmarchive.com

This diary has been reprinted in facsimile from the original. Any imperfections are inevitably reproduced and the quality may fall short of modern type and cartographic standards.

Contents

Document type	Place/Title	Date From	Date To
Heading	WO95/2238/2 6 Battalion South Wales Borders (Pioneers)		
Heading	6th Bn Sth Wales Bord'rs (Pioneers) Sep 1915-May 1918 To 30 Div Troops		
Heading	25th Division 6th S. W. Borderers Vol I Sept 15-June 19		
War Diary	Aldershot	24/09/1915	24/09/1915
War Diary	Havre	25/09/1915	26/09/1915
War Diary	Choques Ham-En-Artois	27/09/1915	27/09/1915
War Diary	Le Sart	28/09/1915	29/09/1915
War Diary	Le Bizet	30/09/1915	30/09/1915
Heading	25th Division 6th S. W. Borderers Vol 2 Oct 15		
War Diary	Le Bizet	01/10/1915	04/10/1915
War Diary	Oosthove Farm	05/10/1915	31/10/1915
Heading	25th Division 6th S. W. Borderers Vol: 3 Nov 15		
War Diary	Oosthove Farm	01/11/1915	30/11/1915
Heading	25th Div 6th S. W. Borders Vol. 4 Dec 1915		
War Diary	Oosthove Farm	01/12/1915	31/12/1915
Heading	6th. South Wales Borderers (Pioneers) January 1916		
Heading	6th S. W. Borders Vol: 5 Jan 1916		
War Diary	Oosthove Farm	01/01/1916	21/01/1916
War Diary	Rouge Croix	22/01/1916	31/01/1916
Heading	6th. South Wales Borderers (Pioneers) February 1916		
Heading	6 Bn. S. Wales Border 25 Div. Vol 6 Feb 1916		
War Diary	Rouge Croix	01/02/1916	26/02/1916
War Diary	Armentieres	27/02/1916	29/02/1916
Heading	6th. (S) Battalion S. W. Borderers, (Pioneers) By. Lt. Col E. V. O. Hewett.		
Heading	6th. South Wales Borderers (Pioneers) March 1916		
Heading	6 S W B Vol 7 March 1916 25 Div		
War Diary	Armentieres	01/03/1916	06/03/1916
War Diary	Dickebusch	07/03/1916	12/03/1916
War Diary	Haute-Avesnes	13/03/1916	16/03/1916
War Diary	Tilley les Hernville	17/03/1916	31/03/1916
Heading	6th. South Wales Borderers (Pioneers) April 1916		
War Diary	Tilley les Hermville	01/04/1916	21/04/1916
War Diary	Neuville St Vaas	22/04/1916	30/04/1916
Heading	6th. South Wales Borderers (Pioneers) May 1916		
War Diary	Neuville St Vaas	01/05/1916	06/05/1916
War Diary	Neuville St Vaast	07/05/1916	31/05/1916
Miscellaneous	Cr 25 O.C. 6th S. W. B.	14/05/1916	14/05/1916
Heading	6th. South Wales Borderers (Pioneers) June 1916.		
War Diary	Bois De Bray	01/06/1916	01/06/1916
War Diary	Villers Chatel	02/06/1916	12/06/1916
War Diary	Bouzincourt	13/06/1916	24/06/1916
War Diary	Pierregot	25/06/1916	30/06/1916
Heading	6th Battn. The South Wales Borderers. July 1916		
War Diary	Senlis	01/07/1916	03/07/1916
War Diary	Bouzancourt	04/07/1916	07/07/1916
War Diary	Aveluy Wood Albert	08/07/1916	10/07/1916

War Diary	Albert	11/07/1916	20/07/1916
War Diary	Aveluy Von	21/07/1916	21/07/1916
War Diary	Bus les Artois	22/07/1916	24/07/1916
War Diary	Beausart	25/07/1916	30/07/1916
Heading	To H.Q. "A" 25th Division Herewith please find War Diary for this Battn: for month of August.		
War Diary	Reaussart	01/08/1916	09/08/1916
War Diary	Authie	10/08/1916	14/08/1916
War Diary	Lealvillers	15/08/1916	17/08/1916
War Diary	Martinsart Wood	18/08/1916	27/08/1916
War Diary	Aveluy	28/08/1916	31/08/1916
Heading	6th. South Wales Borderers (Pioneers) September 1916.		
War Diary	Aveluy	01/09/1916	06/09/1916
War Diary	Acheux	07/09/1916	09/09/1916
War Diary	Amplier	10/09/1916	10/09/1916
War Diary	Feinvillers	11/09/1916	11/09/1916
War Diary	Longvillers	12/09/1916	24/09/1916
War Diary	Amplier	25/09/1916	25/09/1916
War Diary	Acheux Wood	26/09/1916	29/09/1916
War Diary	Aveluy	30/09/1916	30/09/1916
Heading	6th. South Wales Borderers (Pioneers) October 1916.		
Heading	To. Headquarters 25th: Div: A.		
War Diary	Aveluy	01/10/1916	22/10/1916
War Diary	Contay	23/10/1916	23/10/1916
War Diary	Candas	24/10/1916	29/10/1916
War Diary	Eecke	30/10/1916	31/10/1916
Heading	6th. South Wales Borderers (Pioneers) November 1916.		
Heading	To H.Q. 25th: Div: "A"		
War Diary	Mont De Cats	01/11/1916	02/11/1916
War Diary	Oosthove Farm	03/11/1916	30/11/1916
Heading	6th. South Wales Borderers (Pioneers) December 1916		
Miscellaneous	Headquarters, "A" 25th. Division.	01/01/1917	01/01/1917
War Diary	Oosthove Farm	01/12/1916	31/12/1916
Heading	War Diary of 6th Bn. S. Wales Bdrs. Jany to Decbr. 1917.		
Heading	To H.Q. 25th: Div: A		
War Diary	Oosthove Farm	01/01/1917	31/01/1917
War Diary	Oosthove Farm	01/02/1917	25/02/1917
War Diary	Thieushouk	26/02/1917	01/03/1917
Heading	To, Headquarters, "A" 25th Division.	01/04/1917	01/04/1917
War Diary	Thieushouk	02/03/1917	12/03/1917
War Diary	Le Nieppe	13/03/1917	19/03/1917
War Diary	Swarthenbrock Area	20/03/1917	22/03/1917
War Diary	Neuve Eglise	23/03/1917	31/03/1917
War Diary	Neuve Eglise	01/04/1917	09/04/1917
War Diary	Neuve Eglise Enlist	10/04/1917	19/04/1917
War Diary	Neuve Eglise Area	20/04/1917	29/04/1917
War Diary	Swartenbruck	30/04/1917	30/04/1917
Heading	To, Headquarters, 25th. Division "A"	01/06/1917	01/06/1917
War Diary	Swartenbruck	01/05/1917	14/05/1917
War Diary	Neuve Eglise Area	15/05/1917	31/05/1917
Heading	To H.Q. 25th: Div: A	30/06/1917	30/06/1917
War Diary	Neuve Eglise Area	01/06/1917	24/06/1917
War Diary	Wippenhoek	25/06/1917	27/06/1917
War Diary	Ouderdom	28/06/1917	30/06/1917
War Diary	Ouderdom	01/07/1917	20/07/1917

War Diary	Steenvoorde Area	20/07/1917	28/07/1917
War Diary	Ouderdom	29/07/1917	30/07/1917
War Diary	Belgian Chateau	31/07/1917	31/07/1917
Heading	25th: Div: A		
War Diary	Belgian Chateau	01/08/1917	12/08/1917
War Diary	Devonshire Camp	13/08/1917	16/08/1917
War Diary	Eecke Camp	17/08/1917	19/08/1917
War Diary	Oudezeele	20/08/1917	21/08/1917
War Diary	Belgian Chateau Area	22/08/1917	22/08/1917
War Diary	Pioneer Camp	23/08/1917	25/08/1917
Heading	25th: Div: A		
War Diary	Pioneer Camp	01/09/1917	09/09/1917
War Diary	Halifax Camp	10/09/1917	11/09/1917
War Diary	Caestre Area	12/09/1917	12/09/1917
War Diary	Wittes	13/09/1917	13/09/1917
War Diary	Francquehem	14/09/1917	30/09/1917
Heading	25th: Div: "A"		
War Diary	Francquehem	01/10/1917	05/10/1917
War Diary	Annezin	06/10/1917	06/10/1917
War Diary	Beuvry	07/10/1917	31/10/1917
Heading	25th: Div: A.		
War Diary	Beuvry	01/11/1917	23/11/1917
War Diary	Bomy	24/11/1917	30/11/1917
Heading	25th: Div: 'A'		
War Diary	Coyecques	01/12/1917	01/12/1917
War Diary	Monchy Cayeux	02/12/1917	04/12/1917
War Diary	Courcelles	05/12/1917	05/12/1917
War Diary	Be Aulen Court	06/12/1917	08/12/1917
War Diary	Fremicourt	09/12/1917	31/12/1917
War Diary	Fremicourt	01/01/1918	31/01/1918
War Diary	Fremicourt	01/02/1918	11/02/1918
War Diary	Achiet Le Grand	12/02/1918	28/02/1918
Heading	6th Battalion South Wales Borderers. (pioneers) March 1918		
War Diary	Achiet-Le Grand G.2.d.5.5	01/03/1918	05/03/1918
War Diary	Achiet-Le-Grand	06/03/1918	12/03/1918
War Diary	Favreuil	13/03/1918	20/03/1918
War Diary	Sapignies Etc.	21/03/1918	28/03/1918
War Diary	Pernois	28/03/1918	30/03/1918
War Diary	Romarin	31/03/1918	31/03/1918
Heading	6th S. W. B.		
Miscellaneous	Report On Operations Of 6th S. W. Borderers (Pioneers)	28/03/1918	28/03/1918
Miscellaneous	C Company.		
Miscellaneous	D Company.		
Miscellaneous		30/03/1918	30/03/1918
Heading	Report on Operations by "D" Company 6th S. W. B. 25th March.		
Miscellaneous	Report On Operations Carried Out By "D" Coy. 6th. Bn. South Wales Borderers On 25th. Insatnt.		
Map	Sketch To Accompany Report Of D Coy Operations On 25th Inst.		
Heading	6th Battalion The South Wales Borderers Pioneers April 1918		
War Diary	Romarin	01/04/1918	09/04/1918
War Diary	Wippinhoek	09/04/1918	16/04/1918

War Diary	Godewaersvelde	17/04/1918	21/04/1918
War Diary	Flamatinghe	22/04/1918	25/04/1918
War Diary	Proven	26/04/1918	29/04/1918
War Diary	Lies Ciseaux	30/04/1918	30/04/1918
Miscellaneous	Operation carried out by 6th. Bn. So. Wales Borderers (Pioneers) between 9th. and 15th. April 1918	27/04/1918	27/04/1918
War Diary	Les Ciseaux	01/05/1918	04/05/1918
War Diary	Wylder	05/05/1918	11/05/1918
War Diary	Vezilly	11/05/1918	24/05/1918
War Diary	Magneux	25/05/1918	26/05/1918
War Diary	Loisy En Brie	31/05/1918	31/05/1918
Miscellaneous	Report Of Operations Carried Out 6th Bn. South Wales Borderers (Pioneers) between 26th and 31st May 1918.		
Miscellaneous	Report On Movement Of Transport 25.5.18 to 31.5.18		
Miscellaneous	Reference Map Soissons 1-100,000.	01/06/1918	01/06/1918

WO/95/2238/2

6 Battalion South Wales Borderers (Pioneers)

25TH DIVISION
DIVL TROOPS

6TH BN STH WALES BORD'RS
(PIONEERS)
SEP 1915-MAY 1918

TO 30 DIV TROOPS

P/ 25th Division)

121
6997

6th S. W. Borderers

Vol I
Sept. 15
|
June '19

I.S.
1 page

Army Form C. 2118.

Instructions regarding War Diaries and Intelligence Summaries are contained in F. S. Regs., Part II. and the Staff Manual respectively. Title pages will be prepared in manuscript.

WAR DIARY

6th Battn South Wales Borderers (Pioneers)

~~INTELLIGENCE SUMMARY.~~

From 24th Sept (Erase heading not required.) 1915

Place	Date	Hour	Summary of Events and Information	Remarks and references to Appendices
ALDERSHOT	24/9	3 AM 1st train	The Battn proceeded by 3 trains (consisting of one [illegible]) from the Government Siding 1st train Col Hewett 2nd train Capt Mayor 3rd train Major Samuda in charge. Arrival Southampton to time and Battn assembled in shed by 7.30 am. Embarked for HAVRE at 6 pm Personnel in EMPRESS QUEEN, transport with 6 officers and 126 other ranks in the ARCHIMEDES. Strength of Battn 30 officers 963 other ranks, 110 animals 24 wagons, limbers & carts. Escorted by four Destroyers, calm crossing.	[initials]
HAVRE	25/9	8 A.M.	Battn disembarked 8 am and proceeded to Rest Camp No 5 (distance 3 miles) Regt Transport arrived in Camp 3 pm (2 Heavy Draught Horses cast and replaced by Remount Depot,	[initials]
HAVRE	26/9	8 AM	Battn paraded and marched to Gare Marchandise where it entrained at 11.30 and departed 12 noon for LONGUEAU. During the journey orders were received at different times to proceed to ABBEVILLE, LE BASSET, BOURGETTE but finally arrived at CHOQUES where it detrained	Reference Maps
CHOQUES / HAM-en-ARTOIS	27/9	11.45 am	at 11.45 am and marched to BUSNES. Here orders were received to proceed to HAM en ARTOIS where it billeted for the night (distance 7 miles) 1 man admitted to Hospital at St VENANT.	[initials] HAZEBROUCK 5A [initials]
Le SART	28/9	9 am	Battn left HAM at 9 am for Le SART arriving there 3 pm (having been delayed by the Div Artillery en route) and was billeted by 3.30 pm (distance 10 miles) During the afternoon I received orders to act for G.O.C. 74 Bde and forward all units of the 25 Divn in vicinity to destination. Orders were issued accordingly to all concerned i.e. Transport 8th & 9th L.N. Lancs, 11th Lanc Fusiliers + 13 Cheshires. 75 Field Ambulance, O.C. 110 Field Artillery Bde. O.C. 195 & 199 Coys A.S.C., OC Details 25 Div Headquarters. My Battn to march to neighbourhood of STRAZEELE and MERRIS. (1 man admitted to Hospital at MERVILLE.	BELGIUM. [initials]
Le SART.	29/9	7.30 am	At 5 am orders arrived from H.Q. 25 Div to detail all units to move cancelling our night orders; Orders issued accordingly my Battn to march to Le BIZET one mile N of ARMENTIERES. Battn marched 7.30 am via MERVILLE, ESTAIRES, PONT de NIEPPE, arriving Le BIZET at 2.30 pm. Weather very stormy, cold N.W. wind with heavy rain. Arranged billets in Bed Factory and surrounding houses. Reported in person to Adv. H.Q. 25 Division at NIEPPE (distance marched 15 miles) 1 man admitted Hospital at MERVILLE.	[initials]
Le BIZET	30/9		Day devoted to Drying & cleaning kit. Machine gun detachments and Bomb throwers (i.e. grenadiers) exercised. German Artillery registered at times on village	[initials]

[signature] Lt Col

Col. 6th South Wales Borderers (Pioneers)

25th Division

121
7608

6th S. W. Borderers:
Vol 2

Oct 15

2S
4 pages

Army Form C. 2118.

Instructions regarding War Diaries and Intelligence Summaries are contained in F. S. Regs., Part II. and the Staff Manual respectively. Title pages will be prepared in manuscript.

WAR DIARY
6th South Wales Borderers (Pioneers)
INTELLIGENCE SUMMARY.
From 24 Sept (Erase heading not required.) 1915

Place	Date	Hour	Summary of Events and Information	Remarks and references to Appendices
BIZET ?			? Armentières	
Le BISET	1. Oct		Transport moved W of ARMENTIERS Road. M.G and Bombers commenced, Billets cleared and Vets + Engineers prepared for baths. C.O. visited all trenches on front to be held by 25 Division.	[signature]
"	2 "		3 Cos working W of Le RUAGE, North of HOUPLINES. One Co night work (night 2-3) at same place.	[signature]
"	3 "		2 Cos working W of Le RUAGE, 2 Cos working W of Le RUAGE (night 3-4) Pte COLES, "C" Co shot by a sniper. Working parties shelled (Pte ~~[struck out]~~ COLES buried in Military burial ground at HOUPLINES - N. side of FRELINGHIEN Road) At 4 pm Batt received orders to move to OOSTHOVE Farm (2 miles N of NIEPPE) taking over billets vacated by the 11 Cheshires. C.O. attended Bombing experiments at School of Grenadiers TERDESHAM. Batt settled in new billets by 8 pm	[signature]
"	4 "		2 Cos working PARK AVENUE and STATION AVENUE. B+C Cos resting. C.O. visited working parties and arranged following days work.	[signature]
OOSTHOVE Farm	5.		4 Cos (less 1 Platoon resting) working on trenches at NARNIANS and PARK Avenues. Resting Platoon clearing billets and improving washing accomodation and latrines.	[signature]
"	6th		Cos working at improving Communication trenches of PARK, KENT, LONG and STATION AVENUES. A Co Road making South of Le CHEER. C.O. visited all work and in conference with CRE arranged tally of work for future. G.O.C. 25 Division inspected Billet area and expressed approval ~~of~~ improvements made since arrival of Batt.	[signature]
	7		Batt working as yesterday C.O. & 2 i/c Command visited all work. Resting Platoon employed repairing roofs of barns where damaged by shell fire, draining, erecting extra washing & latrine accomodation and generally clearing up as it was a dry sunny day.	[signature]

2353 Wt. W2544/1454 700,000 5/15 D. D. & L. A.D.S.S./Forms/C. 2118.

Instructions regarding War Diaries and Intelligence Summaries are contained in F. S. Regs., Part II. and the Staff Manual respectively. Title pages will be prepared in manuscript.

WAR DIARY or INTELLIGENCE SUMMARY.

6th Batt South Wales Borderers (Pioneers).

(Erase heading not required.)

Army Form C. 2118.

Place	Date	Hour	Summary of Events and Information	Remarks and references to Appendices
OOSTHOVE FARM	8th	F.W.	Working parties as on 7th. 2 Reserve Platoons to Baths at NIEPPE remainder cleaning and improving an yesterday. C.O. visited working parties.	
"	9th		Orders received from H.Q. 25 Div to re-distribute detail 2 Cos for work with the 74 Bde, 1 Co to the 75 and 1 Co the 76 Bdes to commit technical work. CRE 25 Div & C.O. met G.O.C. II Corps and visited the 76th Bde Area. Orders as noted yesterday carried out. C.O. and 2 in Command visited work.	
"	10th		Working parties as yesterday, but now B Co was bombed but suffered no casualties. Service of Preparation at 4 pm. Completed sandbagging magazine. Lecture on 1st Aid and fitting gas helmets.	
"	11th		Working parties as yesterday, at 11 am withdrew C & D Cos from work on fire trenches as notice of bombardment was issued. These Cos were employed road making in subsidiary line. Lecture to resting Platoons on 1st Aid and adjusting & securing gas helmets.	
"	12th		Working Parties. A & C Cos PLUEGSTEERT, B Co 75 Bde Area, D Co 74 Bde Area. Resting Platoons lecture on 1st Aid and fitting & securing gas helmets. Repairing shops of [illegible] completed.	
"	13th		Working Parties as yesterday with exception of A Co which was employed making trenches for Bomb School at Divisional H.Q. resting Platoons lecture & cleaning up. Section of German trenches in front of 74 Bde [illegible] at 2 am D Co was withdrawn.	
"	14		A & C working at THE MOATED FARM, FORT BOY and ST. IVES. B Co constructing trenches for Bombing School. D Co firing trenches 93. All Cos bathed at time. C.O. visited A B & C Cos.	

Instructions regarding War Diaries and Intelligence Summaries are contained in F. S. Regs., Part II. and the Staff Manual respectively. Title pages will be prepared in manuscript.

Army Form C. 2118.

WAR DIARY
6th South Wales Borderers (Pioneers)
INTELLIGENCE SUMMARY.

(Erase heading not required.)

Place	Date	Hour	Summary of Events and Information	Remarks and references to Appendices
OOSTHOVE FARM	15/10	—	A + C Cos at work on THE MOATED FARM, Fort BOYD and St. IVES Trenches, D Co trench 93 B Co continuing trenches for Bombing School, C.O. visited B & D Cos 2 in Command A. C. & D Cos Regt Bombers, Lewis & [illegible] finished 10 men per Co to be daily trained in Bomb throwing [illegible] any men in M.D.	
"	16	—	Work as yesterday. C.O visited Trenches of 50 Division South of ARMENTIERES	
"	17	—	Work as yesterday. No work after Dinner for which working parties returned to Billets. Church Parade 3.30 pm	
"	18	-	A + C Cos Moated Farm, Fort BOYD and Trenches 122-123, B Co H.Q. Bombing School Trench, D Co trench 63 C.O. visited A. B & C Cos, 2 in Command D Co.	
"	19	-	A & C Cos Holiday, but employed putting up Recreation Hut. B Co H.Q. Bombing School Trench, D Trench 63 2nd in command visited D. Co – C.O. visited B. Co	
"	20	"	A Co work on Trenches 122-123, B Co Bombing School, C Co Moated Farm and Fort Boyd D Co Trench 63. C.O. visited D & B Cos. 2 in Command A. & C.	
"	21	"	A. C. + D. Cos as yesterday B on trenches at Convent. No 6-17070 Pte R. Jenkins A Co Killed in action trench 123 and buried in cemetery next 1st Monmouth L.I. Cemetery. C.O. visited ABC Cos 2 in Command A + C.	

2353 Wt. W2544/1454 700,000 5/15 D. D. & L. A.D.S.S./Forms/C. 2118.

Instructions regarding War Diaries and Intelligence Summaries are contained in F. S. Regs., Part II. and the Staff Manual respectively. Title pages will be prepared in manuscript.

WAR DIARY
or
INTELLIGENCE SUMMARY.
(Erase heading not required.)

Army Form C. 2118.

Place	Date	Hour	Summary of Events and Information	Remarks and references to Appendices
OOSTHOVE FARM.	22		As for yesterday. C.O. visited C & D 2 i C. A + B Cos.	
"	23		As for yesterday. Men in billets erected a Recreation and Drying Hut: and improved drainage of farm. C.O. visited D Co. 2 i C. A. & C.	
"	24.		A Co 1 Platoon H.Q. Battle Centre 3 Platoons French 120. C Co Moated Farm, B Convent, D French 93. Church Parade 9.30 cancelled on account of rain. Resting Sections ordered to join Cos for work in future. C.O. visited A. B & C. Cos 2 i C. D Co.	
"	25		As yesterday excepting A. Co which rested. Heavy rain all day, [illegible]. Arranged as far as possible for braziers for drying mens clothing. C.O. visited C. 2 i C. D Co.	
"	26		Work. A Co 1 Platoon constituting H.Q. Battle Centre 1 Platoon work on billets drainage and [illegible]. 2 Platoons A Co and B Co at Convent. C Co MOATED FARM, D Co Schools French 93. 2 i Command visited B Co. C.O. visiting all R.E. yards for Material.	
"	27		Work as yesterday C.O. visited A & C Cos [illegible] the Division. [illegible]	
"	28		Work as yesterday C.O. visited D & B Cos 2 i Command A & C.	
"	29		Work as yesterday 2 i C visited D & B Cos No. 6-17545 Pte G. Coombes B. Co killed.	
"	30		Work as yesterday C.O. visited A & C Cos 2 i C. D Co. No 6.14452 Pte L. H. Clarke C. Co. killed. No 6-17170 Pte E Davis wounded.	
"	31.		Work as yesterday C.O. visited A C & B Cos 2 i C. D Co. Lounge Kitchen started and all men [illegible] during the evening.	

2353 Wt. W2544/1454 700,000 5/15 D. D. & L. A.D.S.S./Forms/C. 2118.

25th Division 1.

121/7631

Q

6th S.W. Borderers

Vol: 3

Nov. 15

3. S.
5 pages

Instructions regarding War Diaries and Intelligence Summaries are contained in F. S. Regs., Part II. and the Staff Manual respectively. Title pages will be prepared in manuscript.

Army Form C. 2118.

WAR DIARY or INTELLIGENCE SUMMARY.

6th South Wales Borderers (Pioneers)

(Erase heading not required.)

Place	Date	Hour	Summary of Events and Information	Remarks and references to Appendices
OOSTHOVE FARM	1 Nov	A Co	Work as yesterday. Latrines + wash houses being built. Château windows repaired with canvas and roofs of Observation Post and other Turrets.. Coy definitely allotted to Brigade and receive orders direct from same. 1 Coy bathing R.C.D. then have from the remainder of day in billets. Very wet day and mud terrible.	
"	2.		A Co trench 121-D, B Co trench 109, C Co MOATED FARM and FORT BOYD, D Co trench 90-94. C.O. visited B & C, 2 i/c Command A. Co, all trenches shelled during the day – rain.	
"	3		Work as yesterday. C.O. visited A & C Cos, 2 i/c Command D Co. Germans shelled fairly vigorously at ST YVES the area in which A & C are working. A very regrettable accident occurred during the afternoon on the Bombing Field, which led to the wounding of 9 men of the Batt. A thrower slipped and dropped his bomb. 2nd Lieut S. EVANS who was in charge of the training exhibited great courage, judgement and prompt action by rushing to the bomb which he picked up and threw towards the Pit. Unfortunately the fuse was [illegible] (being set for 5 seconds) that it burst in the air, thus wounding the men taking shelter behind the throwing parapet. Had not 2nd Lieut EVANS acted as he did many more men would have been hit, as the bomb fell within a few feet of the [illegible] when the man dropped it. The following men were wounded. No 6-17571 Pte A. G. HAMMOND. Seriously No 6-14093 Lcpl J. H. TARRANT No 6-17611 Cpl J. H. POPE, No 3-10822 Pte A. CRANE, No 3/19893 Pte S. FREEMAN, No 6-17155 Pte E. FRENCH, No 6-17025 Pte W. JOHN, No 6-17256 Pte W. C. BOAST, and No 6/17931 Pte D. HOPKINS. All slightly wounded. Very wet day and trenches a flow of mud. 2 bridges in places. Many of the dug outs caving in	

Instructions regarding War Diaries and Intelligence Summaries are contained in F. S. Regs., Part II. and the Staff Manual respectively. Title pages will be prepared in manuscript.

WAR DIARY
or
INTELLIGENCE SUMMARY.
(Erase heading not required.)

Army Form C. 2118.

Place	Date	Hour	Summary of Events and Information	Remarks and references to Appendices
OOSTHOVE FARM	4/11		A Co bathing and work on billets. B Co [illegible] 109, C Co [illegible] 121-122, D Co [illegible] 90. This day, pitched tents for reception of C Co, their barn being condemned as unsanitary. Turning [illegible] of huts and making the kitchen.	[illegible]
"	5/		A Co working on 120 & 124, [illegible], B [illegible] 109, C [illegible] 121.122, D Co [illegible] 90-94. Men in billets employed in pitching Tents & drawing [illegible] for C. Co Camp when they evacuate the Barn. [illegible] place being completed and [illegible] turned & repaired. No 6/16990 Pte F. BUSTIN and No 6/17424 Pte G.F. MORGAN of B Co wounded.	[illegible]
"	6/		Work as yesterday. Battn gave a concert at Soldiers Club NIEPPE, it was well patronized by [illegible] and reported to be a successful performance. C.O. visited 74 Bde Area. 2 i C. 7 Bde Area	[illegible]
"	7/		Work as yesterday (half holiday) Communion service 2.30 pm [illegible]	[illegible]
"	8/		Work as yesterday C.O. visited PLOEGSTEERT Area 2 i Command D Co. No 6/17155 Pte G. MILLER killed in action, No 6/17457 & Pte No 6/16900 J MORRIS wounded in action. The [illegible] MOAT E C. Co Camp completed & Camp ready for reception. Transport lines slowly being completed. Lack of bricks cause of delay.	[illegible]
"	9/		Work as yesterday C.O. visited A Co, 2 i Command 7th Bde Area. No 6/17058 L/Cpl F. WILKINSON, No 6/16412 Pte L. DAVIES and No 6/19051 Pte E. WOOLGAR wounded in action	[illegible]
"	14/		Work as yesterday 2 i Command visited II Bde Canadian Area No 6/17560 Pte L. BROWN. D Co wounded in action. C. Co moved into Tents.	[illegible]

2353 Wt. W2544/1454 700,000 5/15 D. D. & L. A.D.S.S./Forms/C. 2118.

Army Form C. 2118.

Instructions regarding War Diaries and Intelligence Summaries are contained in F. S. Regs., Part II. and the Staff Manual respectively. Title pages will be prepared in manuscript.

WAR DIARY
or
INTELLIGENCE SUMMARY.
(Erase heading not required.)

Place	Date	Hour	Summary of Events and Information	Remarks and references to Appendices
OOSTHOVE FARM	11th Nov		Work as yesterday. C.O. visited III Bde Canadian Div. No 6/17240 Pte W. H. WRIGHT to be awarded a citation. Information received that No 6/17571 Pte HAMMOND died in Hospital No 8 Clearing Casualty Station on the 8th from injuries received in the bombing accident on the 3 inst. Machine gun Detachments under the Brigade to Harbour.	[illegible]
"	12/-		Work as yesterday. Very wet stormy day. In future no entry of daily visits of C.O. & 2nd in Command will be made. These officers will daily visit all working parties of the Battn then. ~~C.O. moved into Tent.~~	[illegible]
"	13		Work as yesterday	[illegible]
"	14		Work as yesterday, commenced building huts for C.O. MO & LO were employed. Bright fine & sunny day, heavy frost.	[illegible]
"	15		Work as yesterday weather as yesterday. No 6/16990 Pte F. BUNTIN died in 23 General Hospital ETAPLES from Tetanus after wound received 5/11/-	[illegible]
"	16		Work as usual. Fine day. From 9-4 the guns of the 2nd Division and 1st Canadian Division bombarded the German lines, without reply.	[illegible]
	17		Bombardment resumed at midnight 16-17 and continued until 3 am when a small party of Canadians raided a German salient killing 30 and capturing 12 of the enemy. These prisoners established the identity of the troops opposed to us	[illegible]
	18		Work as usual, when remaining in billets erecting huts and thatching the roofs as a disguise against aerial observation. From 2 - 3 pm OOSTHOVE FARM was fairly heavily shelled with 8 & 6 inch HE. Men in billets were ordered out to the previously selected spots for cover but the following casualties occurred.	

Army Form C. 2118.

Instructions regarding War Diaries and Intelligence Summaries are contained in F. S. Regs., Part II. and the Staff Manual respectively. Title pages will be prepared in manuscript.

WAR DIARY
or
INTELLIGENCE SUMMARY.

(Erase heading not required.)

Place	Date	Hour	Summary of Events and Information	Remarks and references to Appendices
OOITHOVE FARM	17/[illegible]		No 6/16547 Pte D. R. JONES killed No 6/16836 L/Cpl W. HOPE, No 6/17039 Pte G. HOULSTON No 6/16757 Pte W. J. SHEPHERD, No 6/17036 1st L/Cpl C. W. JONES, No 6/17051 Pte A. BROWN, and No 6/17227 Pte W. HONEYWELL wounded.	
			The men behaved well under rather trying circumstances for young troops. The men of the transport returned and led away the heavy horses from the enclosure of the Farm buildings, and the sentry on the Magazine No 6/16806 Pte J. DAVIES ~~JAMES~~, the archway alongside of which was shattered by a shell, remained at his post until relieved. One transport horse was killed.	
			2nd Lieut T. SIDDLE transferred to the Base for duty at ETAPLES. M. G. Detachment returned from the line.	[illegible]
	18		Work as usual. Huts turned and [illegible] with [illegible] to disguise them and a new Magazine commenced 300 yds to S of Farm. and the shelter ditch to E drained as far as possible in order to afford shelter from shell fire. A few shells fired at Farm but no hits.	[illegible]
			D. Coy ordered to proceed to TILLEUL Farm and there be billeted tomorrow.	
	19		Work as usual, cold raw day. D. Coy moved to TILLEUL Farm. No 6/17036 1st L/Cpl C. W. JONES died from ~~injuries~~ wounds received on the 17th.	[illegible]
	20		Work as usual, fine but cold, two new huts erected. From 8–10 pm Farm shelled but none came near. 20 Belgians employed on Drainage scheme.	[illegible]
	21		Work as usual. 1 Platoon D Co to Farm opposite GUNNERS FARM	
	22		Work as usual. C. O. visited 75 line & inspected new billets of D. Co.	[illegible]

Instructions regarding War Diaries and Intelligence Summaries are contained in F. S. Regs., Part II. and the Staff Manual respectively. Title pages will be prepared in manuscript.

WAR DIARY
or
INTELLIGENCE SUMMARY.
(Erase heading not required.)

Army Form C. 2118.

Place	Date	Hour	Summary of Events and Information	Remarks and references to Appendices
[illegible] FARM.	23		Work as usual.	
"	24		Work as usual. As now all in billets, tents returned to O.O. [illegible] with the exception of a few (6) retained for the accommodation of Scabies patients. The Regtl M.O. mentions this trouble and hopes to have the Battn free from it in a few days. Heavy bombardment by both sides during day. C.O. visited [illegible] and inspected MOATED FARM.	[signature]
"	25		Work as usual. No 6/16950 Pte T. MORRIS reported died 12/11/15 of wounds received 8/11/15. No 6/17566 Pte L.H. BROWN reported died 16/11/15 of wounds received 10/11/15. No 6/19715 Pte T. HUGHES reported died 17/11/15 of cerebro-spinal Meningitis.	[signature]
"	26		Work as usual No 6/17153 Pte W.R. PANTING Killed in action. No 6/17491 Pte P. BROWN wounded in action. Divisional Baths completed.	[signature]
"	27		Work as usual No 6/19380 Pte J.S. CARTER died in hospital of bronchitis	[signature]
"	28		Work as usual No 6/17419 Pte A. HARLEY wounded in action	[signature]
"	29		Work as usual A. Co furnished detachments of 20 men to MOATED FARM and 10 men to Fort BOYD for work. Capt ~~[illegible]~~ FRANCIS to FOSSE LE BERRE there to [illegible] and check the work of [illegible] up to the Forts OXFORD and BERKS	[signature]
"	30		Work as usual. Proposal as far as possible shelter for men in billets in the event of being shelled and arranged at conference of Coy Commanders the necessary action to take. No 6/17224 Pte H. JONES wounded in action.	[signature]

2353 Wt. W2544/1454 700,000 5/15 D. D. & L. A.D.S.S./Forms/C. 2118.

25th Div (Pioneers)

6th S. W. Borderers
Vol: 4
Dec. 1915

121/7928

Instructions regarding War Diaries and Intelligence Summaries are contained in F. S. Regs., Part II, and the Staff Manual respectively. Title pages will be prepared in manuscript.

Army Form C. 2118.

WAR DIARY or INTELLIGENCE SUMMARY.

(Erase heading not required.)

6th South Wales Borderers Pioneers

Place	Date	Hour	Summary of Events and Information	Remarks and references to Appendices
OOSTHOVE FARM.	Dec 1		Work as usual to Noon at which hour all working Parties returned to Billets on account of bombardment of German lines at FACTORY FARM by 25th Div Artillery in conjunction with the Canadian 1 Div RA. C & A Coys on return employed digging shell slits about billeted area.	[illegible]
"	Dec 2		Work as usual. C.O. visited all detached working parties billets and arranged for the work to be carried on. At 9.30 pm Division called C.O. up reporting mine exploded under parapet of Trench 99 in 74 Bde area. One Co to be sent tomorrow morning at 3 am. C. Co detailed for this duty.	[illegible]
"	3		Work as usual. C. Co transferred from 7[illegible] Bde area to 74th. The [illegible] Platoon of D Co did excellent work entrenching mine crater, the latter [illegible] being on duty for the first part of 36 hours. Crater was 60 ft in diameter and about 10 ft of parapet blown in. 11 men of 9th L.N. LANCS. hurt. C Co sent 2 platoons at 4.30 pm for work on crater, these to be relieved by 2 Platoons of same Company at midnight 3-4. C.O. visited 74 & 75 Bde areas and visited crater & [illegible] shattered parapet of trench 99. All trenches in terrible condition owing to wet, support trenches very bad.	[illegible]
"	4		Work as usual C.O. visited all detachments	[illegible]
"	5		Work as usual Lt H.C. DAVIES to Hospital. threatened appendicitis. All M.D. were employed in repairing PAVÉ FRUET and building magazine for [illegible] cutters & [illegible]. Night work discontinued on crater trench 99.	[illegible]
"	6		Work as usual, road making. Lieut L.G. BLOMFIELD to Hospital (heart) No 6/16963 L/Cpl W. JAMES wounded in action	[illegible]

2353 Wt. W2544/1454 700,000 5/15 D. D. & L. A.D.S.S./Forms/C. 2118.

Instructions regarding War Diaries and Intelligence Summaries are contained in F. S. Regs., Part II. and the Staff Manual respectively. Title pages will be prepared in manuscript.

WAR DIARY
or
INTELLIGENCE SUMMARY.
(Erase heading not required.)

Army Form C. 2118.

Place	Date	Hour	Summary of Events and Information	Remarks and references to Appendices
OOSTHOVE FARM	7 Dec		Work as usual. Billets of Battn inspected by G.O.C. II Army. He congratulated the Battn upon the good work that it was doing, and expressed approval of arrangements of area especially the Drying Room and Recreation Hut. No 6/16751 Pte A. TERRY wounded in action	[illegible]
"	8		Work as usual. C.O. visited detachments in 9th Div area weather mild and wet.	[illegible]
"	9		Work as usual No 6/17556 Pte H. WILLIAMS slightly wounded in action [illegible]	[illegible]
"	10	"	Work as usual, Platoons scattered on different tasks No 6/17114 Pte J. COOMBES and No 6/17505 Pte F. FREEMAN wounded in action	[illegible]
"	11		Work as usual. Party employed in repairing holes caused by shells in the Le BIZET — NIEPPE Road. Very heavy rain whole country flooded	[illegible]

DEEDS THAT WON THE D.S.O. AND MILITARY CROSS.

~~[illegible] Dec~~ 5-2-1915

The King has been pleased to approve of the appointment of the undermentioned officers to be Companions of the Distinguished Service Order, in recognition of their gallantry and devotion to duty in the field:—

Evans, Temp. 2nd Lt. Stuart, 6th S. Wales Borderers.

For conspicuous gallantry on November 2 in France.

During bombing practice a man who was about to throw a five-second English ball grenade slipped, and the grenade was knocked from his hand. Three or four seconds had elapsed when Second Lieutenant Evans picked up the grenade and threw it towards the trench. It was due to his cool bravery and presence of mind that several lives were not lost, and that many men were not seriously injured.

Place	Date	Hour	Summary of Events and Information	Remarks and references to Appendices
	12		Work as usual. Fine Day. ~~LE TOUQUET [illegible]~~ Captain and Adjutant F. CARTER resigned Adjutancy and returned to England owing to ill health. 2nd Lt L.C.L. DEANE appointed Adjt.	[illegible]

2353 Wt. W2544/1454 700,000 5/15 D. D. & L. A.D.S.S./Forms/C. 2118.

Instructions regarding War Diaries and Intelligence Summaries are contained in F. S. Regs., Part II. and the Staff Manual respectively. Title pages will be prepared in manuscript.

WAR DIARY
or
INTELLIGENCE SUMMARY.
(Erase heading not required.)

Army Form C. 2118.

Place	Date	Hour	Summary of Events and Information	Remarks and references to Appendices
OOSTHOVE FARM	Dec 13		Work as usual. LE TOUQUET salient heavily bombarded. Fine day	[illegible]
"	14		Work as usual	
"	15		Work as usual heavy bombardment by our artillery of different points in enemy position	[illegible]
"	16		Work as usual quiet day mild.	[illegible]
"	17		Work as usual quiet day mild & foggy	
"	18		Work as usual 2nd Lieut. T. G. RANDOLPH. attached to R.E. for roads and Drainage work. mild & foggy	[illegible]
"	19		Work as usual. 2nd Lt Jenkins and 4 M.G. & team to 7 Bde for duty in the trenches	
"	20		Work as usual. [illegible] very heavily shelled at the Convent from 2-3, no casualties	[illegible]
"	21		Work as usual. 2 Platoons II to transferred from 74 to 75 Bde areas. Wet & foggy day. very quiet all day scarcely any firing	[illegible]
"	22.		Leave for 6 days clear at home over & above travelling commenced at rate of 13 all ranks per day. Work as usual. Forts FOSSE la BARRE, BERKS and OXFORD by now repaired. The Parapets had to be rebuilt, drainage made good, foot-boards laid and dug outs rebuilt. Old Magazines filled down and new ones built. No 17546 Cpl Francis (A Co) superintending the work of these forts in a capable manner. Trench 127 rebuilt and M.G. emplacement built up. St. IVES AVENUE timbered and dug outs made in right sector. Forts BOYD and MOATED FARM nearly completed.	[illegible]

Instructions regarding War Diaries and Intelligence Summaries are contained in F. S. Regs., Part II. and the Staff Manual respectively. Title pages will be prepared in manuscript.

WAR DIARY
or
INTELLIGENCE SUMMARY.
(Erase heading not required.)

Army Form C. 2118.

Place	Date	Hour	Summary of Events and Information	Remarks and references to Appendices
OOSTHOVE FARM	Dec 23		Work as usual. Communicating trench in rear of Crater (trench 123) completed. Two Bombing Posts made on lip of Crater and fire steps in rear. Dug outs made at RESERVE FARM, AMEN CORNER and BACHELORS WALK (completed revetting & duck boards) Parapet repaired and M.G emplacement made in Trench 123. mild wet day EEL PIE Fort and HUNTERS AVENUE shelled 11.30–12.30 midday.	
	24		Work as usual mild wet day. Lt Jenkins and Machine Gun Detachment returned from Trench Duty (5 days) with 7th Bde.	
	25		G.O.C. sanctioned a Holiday. All detachments were permitted to join their Coys for the day. Quiet day and fine. Men had good Xmas dinners & ½ lb plum pudding per man from Newspaper Fund afforded much pleasure also receipt of Xmas Day mails. C. Co gave a concert in the evening in big barn. 2nd Lieut B.S. MARSHALL joined Batt and posted to C. Co.	
	26		Work as usual remainder (2 Platoons) of D Co transferred for work to 75 Bde area. mild day.	
	27		Work as usual. C.O. inspected all detachments. Usual work [illegible] on Fort FOSSE LE BARRE, OXFORD and BERKS. At 2.30 our Trench Mortars bombarded the BIRDCAGE. Germans at 3 pm retaliated destroying and setting fire to N E corner of Fort BOYD. No 6/17095 Pte G. LEWIS wounded. No 6/17294 1c Cpl T. MARSHALL showed presence of mind and pluck in getting his detachment out of Fort, during the bombardment, to cover of parapet to E of Fort.	
	28		Work as usual. 2nd Lt E.C. AMOS wounded. fine mild day.	

WAR DIARY *or* **INTELLIGENCE SUMMARY**

(Erase heading not required.)

Army Form C. 2118

Instructions regarding War Diaries and Intelligence Summaries are contained in F. S. Regs., Part II. and the Staff Manual respectively. Title Pages will be prepared in manuscript.

Place	Date	Hour	Summary of Events and Information	Remarks and references to Appendices
OOSTHOVE FARM	Dec 29		Work as usual.	
"	30		Work as usual. 2nd Lt JENKINS and M.Gun [illegible] with 7th Bde. [illegible] RESERVE FARM [illegible] completed. HARRIANS AVENUE completed. Work on ESSEX LANE. CRATER [illegible] Listening and Bombing Posts completed. No 6/16847 Sergt. G. STANTON wounded	
"	31st		Work as usual – Fine mild day.	

1875 Wt. W593/826 1,000,000 4/15 J.B.C. & A. A.D.S.S./Forms/C. 2118.

25th. DIVISION

6th. SOUTH WALES BORDERERS
(PIONEERS)

J A N U A R Y   1 9 1 6.

25th D.

6th S. W. Borderers
Vol: 5
Jan 1916

5S.
4 pages

Instructions regarding War Diaries and Intelligence Summaries are contained in F. S. Regs., Part II. and the Staff Manual respectively. Title Pages will be prepared in manuscript.

WAR DIARY ~~or~~ ~~INTELLIGENCE SUMMARY~~

6th South Wales Borderers (Pioneers)

(Erase heading not required.)

Army Form C. 2118

Place	Date	Hour	Summary of Events and Information	Remarks and references to Appendices
OOSTHOVE FARM	1916 1 Jan		Work as usual. Trench 123, Sentry box completed. St YVES AVENUE very exposed so work discontinued. PROWSE POINT drained. Lack of material delays work. Trenches 122 & 123, sites for gunboxes made. MOATED FARM, E Parapet and Parados completed. FORT BOYD Flying traverse and bridge traverse at N entrance completed. Damage caused by bombardment being repaired.	[signature]
"	2 Jan		work as usual. 1 platoon B Coy started work in trench 120	CS.
"	3 Jan		work as usual. Ptes 6/16957. G. Thomas, 6/17367. D Richards 6/17317 A Walters - A Coy. slightly wounded while working on St Yves avenue. a lot of shelling - very clear day.	CS.
	4 Jan		work as usual. B Coy started work repairing NORFOLK AVENUE.	CS
	5 Jan		B & D Coys working as usual. A & C Coys each supplied 100 men to be put through a gas test at NIEPPE. a lecture was given first by chemical officer to all troops, then the gas was turned on into a short piece of covered in trench, each man passing through in single file. The length of time actually in gas was only about 1 minute & no one felt any effect. an NCO of C Coy was employed on a special duty in the trench & had to remain in it for 20 minutes & he also felt not the slightest effect. Afternoon road repairing for these Coys.	CS.
	6 Jan		work as usual. dull windy day. PLOEGSTEERT WOOD shelled a lot during the morning.	CS.

1875 Wt. W593/826 1,000,000 4/15 J.B.C. & A. A.D.S.S./Forms/C. 2118.

Instructions regarding War Diaries and Intelligence Summaries are contained in F. S. Regs., Part II. and the Staff Manual respectively. Title Pages will be prepared in manuscript.

6th S. Wales Bdrs (Pioneers)

WAR DIARY
or
~~INTELLIGENCE SUMMARY~~
(Erase heading not required.)

Army Form C. 2118

Place	Date	Hour	Summary of Events and Information	Remarks and references to Appendices
OOSTHOVE. FARM.	7 Jan.		Work as usual. Very quiet day.	
	8 Jan.		Work as usual excepting for 75 men of B and D Coys who were ordered to attend a gas test at NIEPPE. They were sent back late after waiting some hours as the gas expert could not come. After dinner these men were employed by their O.C. Coys.	CS. CS.
	9 Jan		Work as usual, except 75 men each from B & D Coys who underwent the gas test referred to above. Clear day. More shelling than usual. After dinner drill in putting on gas helmets & doubling about in them.	CS.
	10th		Work as usual very quiet day	
	11th		Work as usual No 6/19158 Pte H. THOMAS wounded. Enemy active. PLOEGSTEERT, The BREWERY and Battery at MOTOR CAR CORNER heavily shelled. Trench 124 received 60 shells. C.O. visited whole front.	
	12th		Work as usual, very quiet day. No 6/15488 Pte W. H. HARRIS wounded.	
	13th		Work as usual very quiet day	
	14th		Work as usual	
	15		Work as usual No 2 Platoon under 2/Lt H. SPEDE to MOATS FARM in relief of No 1 Platoon (5 Division) taking over [illegible] 2 Lt [illegible] 9th Seaforth Highlanders (Pioneers) 3 Pltn 24 hrs with Bttn during Trench [illegible]	

W1875—W.W593/826 [illegible] J.B.C. & A. A.D.S.S./Forms/C. 2118.

Instructions regarding War Diaries and Intelligence Summaries are contained in F. S. Regs., Part II. and the Staff Manual respectively. Title Pages will be prepared in manuscript.

WAR DIARY
or
INTELLIGENCE SUMMARY
(Erase heading not required.)

Army Form C. 2118

Place	Date	Hour	Summary of Events and Information	Remarks and references to Appendices
OOSTHOVE FARM	16		Wet as usual B Co to 74 area.	[illegible]
"	17		Wet as usual B Co to 74 area. 2 Officers of incoming Unit for the day to inspect area. C.O. to BAYICULLE for 2 Corps H.Q conference. ~~B Co returned to~~ [illegible].	[illegible]
"	18		Wet as usual. B Co returned to 75 Pt area.	
"	19.		Wet as usual No6/17429 Pte E. DAVIES wounded. Heavy bombardment of LE TOQUET Salient. 12.30-4.00 by our artillery, followed by at the latter hour, a Bombs & [illegible] attack and assault from [illegible] 92-101 by the R. I. Rifles. with the 13th Cheshires in support. Very heavy firing, Germans burning many flares, very lights, rockets etc. Our Trench Mortars very active.	[illegible]
"	20		Wet as usual, but sent B Co to Salient to assist repairing damage, which was considerable. G. S. Officer called up the C.O and stated the attack had been very successful in the opinion of Div [illegible] and Regt Commander	[illegible]
"	21		Wet as usual. after Division Coy returned to Billets to prepare for move to Divisional Rest Billets at ROUGE CROIX the 9th Seaforth Highlanders (Pioneers) 9th Division and ourselves exchanged billets.	[illegible]
ROUGE CROIX	22		Batt paraded 8 am moving off by Platoons at 5 minute intervals. March was via ROMARAIN, RABOT, LE CRECHE, BAILLEUL, MOOLENACHER, thus avoiding the Pavé and mass of transport on main road. Divisional after passing BAILLEUL. Arrived ROUGE CROIX 3.30 pm. distance marched 13 miles day fine early but wet mist came up at noon, weather cleared up at 2 pm. 13 men fell out on the road 4 of whom were admitted to Field Ambulance.	[illegible]

1875 Wt. W593/826 1,000,000 4/15 J.B.C. & A. A.D.S.S./Forms/C. 2118.

Instructions regarding War Diaries and Intelligence Summaries are contained in F. S. Regs., Part II. and the Staff Manual respectively. Title Pages will be prepared in manuscript.

WAR DIARY
or
INTELLIGENCE SUMMARY
(Erase heading not required.)

Army Form C. 2118

Place	Date	Hour	Summary of Events and Information	Remarks and references to Appendices
ROUGECROIX.	23		Settling down. Billets in farms scattered over a wide area of country. Very little work done to improve local conditions by former occupants.	[illegible]
–	24		Route March & Kit inspection. Working party of 50 men under 2nd Lieut. Rattenbury constructing sheds at MERRIS for Divisional Motor Cars.	[illegible]
–	25		Musketry & Route March. Classes in Machine gun & Bombing commenced. Football by all Coys started.	[illegible]
–	26		Musketry & Route March. 2 working parties of 25 men each under 2nd Lieuts RATTENBURY and MARSHALL for construction of bath huts at METEREN and OUTTERSTEENE.	[illegible]
–	27		Work as yesterday	[illegible]
–	28		Work as yesterday. Motor & Lewis gun drill in addition.	[illegible]
–	29		Work as yesterday, in addition A Co to OUTERSTEENE to repair huts of Divisional Bombing School	[illegible]
–	30		Church Parade 11.30	[illegible]
–	31		Musketry, Bayonet Fighting and Route March. Weather mild and foggy.	[illegible]

1875 Wt. W593/826 1,000,000 4/15 J.B.C. & A. A.D.S.S./Forms/C. 2118.

25th. DIVISION

6th. SOUTH WALES BORDERERS

(PIONEERS)

F E B R U A R Y   1 9 1 6.

6 Bn.

S. Wales Bordy

25 Div.

Vol. 6.

Feb 1916

G.S.
3 pp.

6th Battn South Wales Borderers (Pioneers)

WAR DIARY or INTELLIGENCE SUMMARY

(Erase heading not required.)

Army Form C. 2118

Instructions regarding War Diaries and Intelligence Summaries are contained in F. S. Regs., Part II. and the Staff Manual respectively. Title Pages will be prepared in manuscript.

Place	Date	Hour	Summary of Events and Information	Remarks and references to Appendices
ROULE CROIX	1916 1 Feb		Musketry, Platoon Drill & Route March. Class of Signalling commenced.	[illegible]
"	2.		As above, classes for Machine Gun and Bombing commenced.	[illegible]
"	3		As above in addition bayonet fighting	[illegible]
"	4		Concentration Route March by Coys. 9.15–1. Coy Commanders tried their march well. Case of meningitis in II Coy, the three Platoons isolated by order of A.D.M.S. these Platoons to carry on programme of Battn work by themselves.	[illegible]
"	5		Physical Training, musketry, route marching.	
"	6		Church Service 11.30. The two working parties of 25 men each, employed on constructing baths, from this date attached to 2 Inf Bde H.Q. and 2 South Lancashire respectively.	[illegible]
"	7		Marching order Parade and inspection of equipment, clothing, transport etc. Lieut. White R.A.M.C. transferred to Field Ambulance, Lieut. GIBBS RAMC reported for duty	[illegible]
"	8		Concentration march cancelled owing to rain. Musketry, bathing, signalling etc carried on during fine intervals.	[illegible]
"	9		Inspection by II Army Corps Commander 2nd Lieut W. G. EDWARDS reported for duty with Battn.	[illegible]
"	10		Captain EASTERBROOK, 2 Lieuts [illegible] and 125 men A Coy proceeded to BAILLEUL to the constant railway siding. Captain CHOINIER 2nd Lt Jones and 125 men B Coy proceeded to NIEPPE siding to the constant siding	[illegible]

1875 Wt. W593/826 1,000,000 4/15 J.B.C. & A. A.D.S.S./Forms/C. 2118.

Instructions regarding War Diaries and Intelligence Summaries are contained in F. S. Regs., Part II. and the Staff Manual respectively. Title Pages will be prepared in manuscript.

WAR DIARY
or
INTELLIGENCE SUMMARY
(Erase heading not required.)

Army Form C. 2118

Place	Date	Hour	Summary of Events and Information	Remarks and references to Appendices
ROUGE CROIX	11		Wet. Day & cold. Football match for Divisional Cup (Association Football) against 105 Co. R.E. a very close and keenly contested game. One goal each at end of time so 10 minutes each way was played. result again result one each so game has to be replayed.	[signature]
	12		Musketry, Bayonet fighting route march.	[signature]
	13		Wet & cold church parade cancelled. Football match (replayed) against 105 Co. R.E. hard fought game and certain bitterness at times. result 3–1 in favour of Batt. We gave R.E. Team [illegible] and tea afterwards. Lieut. BEESTON reported for Duty.	[signature]
	14		Work as usual	
	15		Work as usual.	
	16		Concentration March rendezvous near BAILLEUL (8 miles) secret orders issued at 9 am to all Coy. and H.Q. Cos, then to at NIEPPE Siding (distance 13 miles from ROUGE CROIX) reaching there about 8 am. At 12 noon all Batt had concentrated in full marching order with tools carts & ammunition. When orders were received by O.C. Cos many were route marching, others at musketry while the Classes in Bombing, M.G. and Signalling were going on.	[signature]
	17		Concentration March rendezvous MONT des CATS	[signature]
	18		Wet Day. Work as usual so far as possible. At midnight 17/18 a German aeroplane flew over ROUGE CROIX [illegible] [illegible] [illegible] HAZEBROUCK & some dropped on the Town. a brilliant moonlight night.	[signature]
	19		Work as usual.	

1875 Wt. W593/826 1,000,000 4/15 J.B.C. & A. A.D.S.S./Forms/C. 2118.

Instructions regarding War Diaries and Intelligence Summaries are contained in F. S. Regs., Part II. and the Staff Manual respectively. Title pages will be prepared in manuscript.

WAR DIARY
or
INTELLIGENCE SUMMARY.
(Erase heading not required.)

Army Form C. 2118.

Place	Date	Hour	Summary of Events and Information	Remarks and references to Appendices
BOULE CROIX	20		Church Parade 11.30 No 6/17066 Pte C. CLEMENTS killed in action. No 6/16326 Pte A. SMART wounded.	
"	21		Work as usual. 2nd Lieut W.F. RENWICK reported for duty with the Battn and was posted to D Co. Football. Battn versus 7th Field Ambulance victory for Battn score 5–4. Det working on METERENE Battn returned to H.Q. on completion of work.	
"	22		Concentration march underground VERTE RUE. 2nd Lieut S. EVANS and No 6/16961 Pte W. JONES wounded in bombing accident. Det. working on OUTTERSTEENE. Battn returned to H.Q. on completion of work.	
"	23		Work as usual. Orders received to move into 21 Div Area at ARMONTIERES. Pretty day.	
"	24		Detachments of A + B Cos at BAILLEUL and NIEPPE SIDING relieved by D + C. Cos. Conference at D.H.Q of all Div + Bde Staffs and C.O. units. Had great [illegible] a couple of inches of snow, bright [illegible]	
"	25		Refitting Detachments. Officers and 100 men attended exhibition of German Flammenwerfer at OUTTERSTEENE. Very hard frost.	
"	26		Refitting, Detachments and preparing for move.	
ARMENTIERES	27		Battn marched at 9 am via BAILLEUL dropping D Co for work on BAILLEUL siding (on Det.) halted one hour at midday and arrived ARMENTIERES 3 pm. Men marched well in spite of trying conditions due to sleet and snow and sodden roads. The transport had difficulties owing to ice underneath the slush. Took over billets in Ecole des FILLES, Rue des JESUITES and ECHOL MATERNEL RUE DE QUESNOY. A+B Cos in former C in latter billet. C.E. II Corps told the C.O. some proposed sites for work which commence the 28 and are to be marked.	
"	28.		C. Co vacated ECHOL MATERNAL and occupied billets at CHEZCOLOMBIER the former place being too exposed to shell fire. Orders received to be ready to move at 9 hours notice by rail.	
"	29.		Coys at work on Divisional defence line LA CHAPELLE D'ARMENTIERES to RIVER LYS. C.E. II Corps accompanied C.O. round work and expressed himself as highly pleased with work done by Battn. Bright sunny day. Aircraft of both sides very busy and some heavy shelling.	

DIARY.

6th (S) Battalion
S.W. Borderers,
(Pioneers)

By.

Lt. Col E.V.O.Hewett.

25th. DIVISION

6th. SOUTH WALES BORDERERS

(PIONEERS)

M A R C H 1 9 1 6.

6 SWB

Vol 7

March 1966

25 DW

Instructions regarding War Diaries and Intelligence Summaries are contained in F. S. Regs., Part II. and the Staff Manual respectively. Title pages will be prepared in manuscript.

WAR DIARY
6th South Wales Borderers (Pioneers)
INTELLIGENCE SUMMARY.

(Erase heading not required.)

Army Form C. 2118.

Place	Date	Hour	Summary of Events and Information	Remarks and references to Appendices
ARMENTIERES	March 1st		Work on wire. Coy joined up first detailed. Grant from Institute Funds of 1/- per effective (on the St David's Day) to be expended on extra messing. Officers dined at Restaurant in Town.	[initials]
"	2		Battn employed on wiring its area. "The Corps Commander this morning visited the line of entanglements being constructed by the Battn. He wishes to convey to all ranks his high appreciation of the good and rapid work carried out." 2nd Lieut. JENKINS and [illegible] from Detachment to [illegible] for 4 days	[initials]
"	3		Work as usual. Wet Day. Battn Football Team beaten 7–3 by the Machine Gun Company 7th Brigade. Lieut. Neale and 2nd Lt Rettenburg sent to Field Ambulance the former for rest the latter to have hammer toe removed. 2nd Lieut RENWICK taken over duties of Transport Officer.	[initials]
"	4		Work on wire as usual. Thawing but heavy snow falling. From 3.15 pm – 5.30 pm Germans shelled the Town, no casualties in Battn, but half a dozen badly [illegible] were carried into C. Coy Billets	[initials]
"	5		½ day work it being Sunday.	
"	6	9.30 am	Ordered to move H.Q. and 3 Coys at ARMENTIERES to RENINGHSELST, personnel by train, transport by Road. Transport brought in from NIEPPE transport lines and loaded at 1 pm, and moved off at 2.15 via BAILLEUL, LOCRE	[initials]
		9.30 pm	Battn entrained 9.30 at goods Station and were finally detrained at OUDERDON at 3.30 am the 7th. Very cold night, the men crowded in goods wagons. Company at work on the wiring line recalled at 12 noon, [illegible] 12.30. 2nd Lts RANDOLPH and JONES admitted to Field Ambulance suffering from influenza.	
DICKEBUSEH.	7	3.30	Detrained at OUDERDUN and marched to CANADA HUTS where the men were put into tents and the officers into the huts. Transport had had a most trying march the road after BAILLEUL being very heavy so only arrived at 2. am worn out. Got men breakfast as soon as possible.	[initials]
		11 am	Received orders to proceed to DICKEBUSEH as their billet. Men all settled down by dinner at 1 pm.	

2353 Wt. W2544/1454 700,000 5/15 D. D. & L. A.D.S.S./Forms/C. 2118.

Instructions regarding War Diaries and Intelligence Summaries are contained in F. S. Regs., Part II. and the Staff Manual respectively. Title pages will be prepared in manuscript.

WAR DIARY
or
INTELLIGENCE SUMMARY.
(Erase heading not required.)

Army Form C. 2118.

Place	Date	Hour	Summary of Events and Information	Remarks and references to Appendices
	March			
DICKEBUSCH	7	3 pm	Orders received for night work parties furnished by RE. Marched off 6.15 but in addition to ordinary traffic French relief was being carried out so congestion terrific. It was 5 hours before parties arrived at working site at THE BLUFF communicating and fire trenches. [illegible] blown to pieces and dead not as yet removed. After 2 hours work men returned arriving 4 am tired out by the bad going and unending checks on the road. Coys returned about 4 am	
"	8	5.45	Battn paraded for night work in conjunction with – A Co and Field Coy RE CHESHIRE Territorials on PEAR TREE WALK, B Co with 9? F Coy RE on HEDGE ROW and FIR LANE, C Co with 106 F. Coy RE on LOVERS LANE. Bright moonlight night – heavy frost. Mud in places very deep and 2 feet of water in trenches. The whole area terribly shattered by German bombardment, our parties employed in clearing and remaking trenches and evacuating the dead.	
"	9		Work as usual during night. 2 Lieuts JONES and RANDOLPH rejoined from Field Ambulance. No. 6/17262 L/Cpl GARRIN admitted to Field Ambulance from Cerebro Spinal Meningitis (all contact cases isolated) Very heavy work, 12 miles marching and digging in broken trenches full of mud and water (B Co alone recovered 30 bodies) the whole front strewn with rifles equipment and [illegible].	
"	10		Work as laid down. Continuous shelling.	
"	11		Work as usual. Ordered to discontinue work at midnight and return to billets as Battn was to proceed to new area on the 12th. No 6/16871, Pte J. PHILLIPS wounded. B. Co & 1 Platoon C (BAILLEUL) entrained at 3pm for new area to which 17 Corps [illegible] Division had already proceeded by road. Lieut AMOS rejoined Battn from Base Hospital.	

Instructions regarding War Diaries and Intelligence Summaries are contained in F. S. Regs., Part II. and the Staff Manual respectively. Title pages will be prepared in manuscript.

WAR DIARY
or
INTELLIGENCE SUMMARY.
(Erase heading not required.)

Army Form C. 2118.

Place	Date	Hour	Summary of Events and Information	Remarks and references to Appendices
DICKEBUSH	12		Day of rest. Fine sunny day, aircraft of both sides very active and some heavy shelling. Orders received to move tomorrow the 13th to new area.	[illegible]
HAUTE-AVESNES	13		Move as per orders attached. Batt (less D Co) arrived SYNLAND siding POPERINGHE at 1.30 am, men entrained in trucks (30 in each) removed equipment and then had dinners. Transport loading facilities very limited, also not sufficient flat trucks for waggons. Train left at 1 pm and arrived AUBIGNY at 6 pm, where it detrained and Companies marched to their billets, H.Q and B. Co to HAUTE-AVESNES, A Co to MONT ST ELOY, C. Co to ACQ and D Co to MARCOUIL – This Co had taken two days to complete journey having proceeded via CALAIS. No arrangements for billeting had been made and the French troops had not vacated villages. By 10 pm all were settled down thanks to the kindness of French Officers. The French troops and our men fraternised at once, the former giving our men, tinned meat, bread and wine. Draft of 5 men joined at AUBIGNY.	[illegible]
"	14		The French troops marched out at 8 am [illegible]. An enormous number of A.S.C. and Artillery flooded the village and billets were crowded. The whole area very congested. The C.O. visited all Detachments and found British troops crowded in. Water in all villages very bad and scarce.	[illegible]
"	15		A & D Cos engaged on construction and running light railways from BRAY to the gun positions on line SOUCHEZ – NEUVILLE. B & C Cos road making in triangle HARAREQ – VILLIERS-au-BOIS – St. CATHERINE. 2 Lieut MANNERS left Batt for duty on Intelligence Staff G.H.Q.	[illegible]

2353 Wt. W2544/1454 700,000 5/15 D. D. & L. A.D.S.S./Forms/C. 2118.

Instructions regarding War Diaries and Intelligence Summaries are contained in F. S. Regs., Part II. and the Staff Manual respectively. Title Pages will be prepared in manuscript.

WAR DIARY
or
INTELLIGENCE SUMMARY
(Erase heading not required.)

Army Form C. 2118

Place	Date	Hour	Summary of Events and Information	Remarks and references to Appendices
HAUTE-AVESNES	16		Work on scheme from mid day At 2 PM orders received to move H.Q and Company [illegible] to TILLEY les HERNAVILLE C.O. visited new village during the afternoon	
TILLEY les HERNAVILLE	17		Work on scheme by A. C & D Cos. H.Q & B moved during the morning to TILLEY les HERNAVILLE and there billeted. Transport has to go 2¼ miles to water. Men of B Co 6 miles from scene of work. Reported to [illegible] and Division that I propose seeking more suitable billets. Lieut NEALE rejoined from sick rest.	
"	18		Work on scheme	
"	19		Work on scheme.	
"	20		Work on scheme. D Co and Transport moved to AGNIERES, and the section attached to D Co rejoined its Company.	
"	21.		Work on scheme.	
"	22		Work on scheme.	
"	23		Work on scheme. B Co changed billets in AGNIERES. Lt CHARTER, 2nd Lieut D. EVANS, W.B.C. MORGAN and T.L. EVANS reported for duty.	
"	24		Work on scheme. Heavy snow storm during the night. Lieut H. DAVIES rejoined from sick leave.	

1875 Wt. W593/826 1,000,000 4/15 J.B.C. & A. A.D.S.S./Forms/C. 2118.

Instructions regarding War Diaries and Intelligence Summaries are contained in F. S. Regs., Part II. and the Staff Manual respectively. Title Pages will be prepared in manuscript.

WAR DIARY
or
INTELLIGENCE SUMMARY
(Erase heading not required.)

Army Form C. 2118

Place	Date	Hour	Summary of Events and Information	Remarks and references to Appendices
TILLEY les HERMAVILLE	25		Work as scheme.	
"	26		Work as scheme cold.	
"	27		Work as scheme hot & cold	
"	28		Work as scheme raw cold day	
"	29		Work as scheme. Bright sunny day but cold.	
"	30		Work as scheme fine sunny day but cold. 1 5.2 shell fell in area W. of BETHUNE road cutting long cable for a length of 500 yds.	
"	31		Work as scheme. Bright and warm.	
			During the passed fortnight the Batt has been employed on important work in connection with improving communication with the advanced positions of the 17 Corps area and have been frequently under fire when at work.	
			A & C Cos under Captain CHOINIER were responsible for upkeep of roads in area and construction of new road BRAYE St ELOY, BRAY-MAREUIL, ACQ-LE PENDU road, regulating supply of trucks of material at base stations.	
			A & D Cos working day and night have repaired and maintained the light-railways in the area and taken over the entire running control of trains from base stations to trenches and gun positions.	[signature]

1875 Wt. W593/826 1,000,000 4/15 J.B.C. & A. A.D.S.S./Forms/C. 2118.

25th. DIVISION

6th. SOUTH WALES BORDERERS

(PIONEERS)

APRIL 1916.

Army Form C. 2118

XXV

6. S. W Borders
Vol 8

WAR DIARY
or
INTELLIGENCE SUMMARY

Instructions regarding War Diaries and Intelligence Summaries are contained in F. S. Regs., Part II. and the Staff Manual respectively. Title Pages will be prepared in manuscript.

6th South Wales Borderers (Pioneers) (Erase heading not required.)

Place	Date	Hour	Summary of Events and Information	Remarks and references to Appendices
TILLEY les HERMVILLE	April 1st	1916	work as usual. half days work owing to Sunday.	
"	2nd		work as usual. Col: Hewitt went on leave. Major Saunders visited B. C & A. Coys. Obtained 8 motor lorries for carting material for road repairs.	
"	3rd		work as usual. visited C & A Coys.	
"	4th		work as usual. visited A. Coy.	
"	5th		work as usual. Except C. Coy. who bathed in the morning.	
"	6th		work as usual. Lieut BEETSON. admitted to hospital suffering from Synovites.	
"	7		work as usual.	
"	8		work as usual.	8 S 54

1875 Wt. W593/826 1,000,000 4/15 J.B.C. & A. A.D.S.S./Forms/C. 2118.

WAR DIARY
or
INTELLIGENCE SUMMARY
(Erase heading not required.)

Instructions regarding War Diaries and Intelligence Summaries are contained in F. S. Regs., Part II. and the Staff Manual respectively. Title Pages will be prepared in manuscript.

Army Form C. 2118

Place	Date	Hour	Summary of Events and Information	Remarks and references to Appendices
TILLEY les HERMAVILLE	9		Work as usual.	
"	10		Work as usual. Col HEWETT returned from leave.	
"	11		Work as usual. Conference at C.E. 17 Corps. Decision to form a Light Railway Company to consist of 2 Platoons (120 men + 3 officers) from each of the three Pioneer Battns in the Corps. Major MORLAN (6th S.W.B.) in Command for Administration & Discipline. Capt. EASTERBROOK 6th [illegible] Managing Director & Traffic Superintendent	[illegible]
"	12		Work as usual.	
"	13		Work as usual.	
"	14		Work as usual ~~No 6/17620 Pte JENNINGS. A.C. Killed in action~~	
"	15		Orders received for Battn to relieve MONMOUTHSHIRE Territorials in occupation of NEUVILLE ST. VAAS. C.O & Adjt spent the day inspecting village & defences. The village a "Strong Point" in line of defence, some part to German line 600. Here Crater B6 commands the whole village, which is but a mass of ruins, and under continuous fire from the German artillery.	
"	16		German dug outs cellars & dug outs mostly built by the Germans when in occupation last year. No 6/17846 Pte D.J. JAMES, A.C., Killed in action. Work as usual.	

1875 Wt. W593/826 1,000,000 4/15 J.B.C. & A. A.D.S.S./Forms/C. 2118.

Instructions regarding War Diaries and Intelligence Summaries are contained in F. S. Regs., Part II. and the Staff Manual respectively. Title Pages will be prepared in manuscript.

WAR DIARY
or
INTELLIGENCE SUMMARY

(Erase heading not required.)

Army Form C. 2118

Place	Date	Hour	Summary of Events and Information	Remarks and references to Appendices
TILLEY les HERMAVILLE	April 17		Work as usual. C.O. visited NEUVILLE St VAAS	
"	18		Work as usual.	
"	19		Work as usual	
"	20		Work as usual. C.O. visited NEUVILLE St VAAS	
"	21		Work as usual Captain JAMES as Town Major & Intelligence Officer, 2nd Lt JENKINS, 4 N.C.Os and 4 [illegible] Lewis Detachment, Lieut DAVIES, Signalling Sergt & 8 Signallers proceeded to NEUVILLE St VAAS to take over their various duties. Very wet day.	
NEUVILLE St VAAS	22		In accordance with orders the Battn vacated billets at TILLEY and proceeded to NEUVILLE St VAAS (after dark) and relieved the 1st MONMOUTH Regt (Territorials) at 8.30 relief completed by 10 pm, Transport arrived 11 pm and rations issued. Very wet day and cold, all ranks wet through. II. Co went into reserve road at ECRIVRES. C.O. assumed duties of Military Governor of Village. C.O. and chief G.S.O Division went over ground and finally arranged scheme of Defence upon which Battn will be employed upon.	
"	23		Morning spent in settling men down. C.O. took up Commanders round proposed scheme of Defence and allotted them their work. During the afternoon Germans put some 20 shells into Village and frequently traversed its streets with Machine gun fire. Village but a mass of ruins, Officers & men live in cellars and dug outs made by the Germans when in occupation. Battn on night work in 2 reliefs 6-12 & 12-6. The village being in full view of the German lines, H.Q. but some 600 yds away, the greatest care has to be exercised when moving about the village by day. Communication trenches only being used except by individuals. Village strewn with Enemy & accoutrements both German and French, numerous unexploded shells, several Torpedoes, bombs and many unburied bodies, while thousands of graves to be seen everywhere, bodies being built into the parapets of [illegible] trenches.	

1875 Wt. W593/826 1,000,000 4/15 J.B.C. & A. A.D.S.S./Forms/C. 2118.

Instructions regarding War Diaries and Intelligence Summaries are contained in F. S. Regs., Part II. and the Staff Manual respectively. Title Pages will be prepared in manuscript.

WAR DIARY
or
INTELLIGENCE SUMMARY
(Erase heading not required.)

Army Form C. 2118

Place	Date	Hour	Summary of Events and Information	Remarks and references to Appendices
NEUVILLE St-VAAS	April 24		Work on new retrenchment line to East of CHEPSTOW – CENTRAL ~~[illegible]~~ REDOUBT and CHATEAU F.P. men employed by day clearing ROY and COMBOW(?) Trenches. Machine gun fire at intervals on village during the night. Few shells into village during the day.	[initials]
"	25		Work as for 24th. The LEWIS Detachment making their own gun emplacements under 2nd Lt JENKINS. Night but stormy day. C.O. attended RE Conference at Div H.Q.	[initials]
"	26		Work as programme. C.R.E. went round line and approved of line selected and commented upon the good work done. About 20 HE shells fired into village, chiefly at CHURCH CORNER. Decided to retrench CHATEAU WORK besides; line to be extended.	[initials]
"	27		Work as for 26th. Village shelled 10 am and 12 noon about 150 shells chiefly HE No 9 fell in village. II Co arrived from ECRUVIRES(?) for night work ZOUAVE VALLEY. Lieut S. EVANS rejoined from leave and 2nd Lieut THOMAS reported for duty from the 10th Battn.	[initials]
"	28		Work as for 27th. Village being shelled from 6.45–7.20 pm about 100 shells falling chiefly in vicinity of LUNDI ISLAND and CEMETARY ROAD. II Co to LIVERPOOL Dump ZOUAVE VALLEY then to bivouac for three days for night-work retrenching craters.	[initials]
"	29		II. Co + ½ C retrenching craters position in 74 Bde area. ½ Co on village line known as the BRECAN LINE. B Co digging back to hay(?) Light Railway in ZOUAVE VALLEY. After dark the 74 Bde made a futile attempt to capture the crater, the noise of heavy HE & Trench Mortars [illegible] while the affair lasted.	[initials]

(875) W. W593/826 1,000,000 4/15 J.B.C. & A. A.D.S.S./Forms/C. 2118.

Instructions regarding War Diaries and Intelligence Summaries are contained in F. S. Regs., Part II. and the Staff Manual respectively. Title Pages will be prepared in manuscript.

WAR DIARY
or
INTELLIGENCE SUMMARY
(Erase heading not required.)

Army Form C. 2118

Place	Date	Hour	Summary of Events and Information	Remarks and references to Appendices
NEUVILLE St VAAS	April 30		D. Co after work last night came to NEUVILLE St VAAS there to be billeted.	
			Work as for last night, but only 1 Platoon to go to ZOUAVE VALLEY for work on the Railway.	[illegible]
			Two heavy bursts of fire on right and left of village after dark	
			Captain THOMAS returned from 3 week course at ARMY School.	

1875 Wt. W593/826 1,000,000 4/15 J.B.C. & A. A.D.S.S./Forms/C. 2118.

25th. DIVISION

6th. SOUTH WALES BORDERERS

(PIONEERS)

MAY 1916.

6 S W Bord

Vol 9

XXV

Army Form C. 2118

WAR DIARY or INTELLIGENCE SUMMARY

6th South Wales Borderers Pioneers

(Erase heading not required.)

Instructions regarding War Diaries and Intelligence Summaries are contained in F. S. Regs., Part II. and the Staff Manual respectively. Title Pages will be prepared in manuscript.

Place	Date	Hour	Summary of Events and Information	Remarks and references to Appendices
NEUVILLE St-VAAS	May 1	1916	Work as for 30th inst., in addition wiring and filling in shell holes and levelling mounds and walls in order to afford clear field of fire for the BRECON LINE. Some 60 shells fell in village. A week bright hot sunny weather.	
"	2		As for yesterday, a new M.G. Emplacement commenced on ruins of Church. Corps Commander visited village & the line held in rebuilding. He confirmed the name BRECON for the line of walls out of compliment to the Battn. About 50 shells fell in village a dozen in neighbourhood of Church ruins. No 6/19645 Pte STACEY A.C. died of heart failure due to shock.	
"	3		As for 2nd inst., 1 Co to Light Railway ZOUAVE VALLEY, 1½ Co returning Crater in 74th Bde area. Dugouts Say. Enemy mines went up. 10 shells into village chiefly on line of main street. Captain CHOINIER to Army School for 3 weeks.	
"	4		As for 3rd	
	5.		As for 4th. Heavy action on front of 7th & 74th Bde Area commencing 7.30 pm. About 100 shells fell in village, the BRECON LINE being hit in several places. Weather threatening rain and turned much cooler. Strong S.W. wind. No 6/17081 Pte NEWEY wounded in action.	
	6		As for 5th. Two complete Cos ordered to work in 74th Bde area thus leaving no further men for work on defences of Village. The T.P. Men employed repairing trenches and collecting wire and material	9 S

1875 Wt. W593/826 1,000,000 4/15 J.B.C. & A. A.D.S.S./Forms/C. 2118.

*Instructions regarding War Diaries and Intelligence Summaries are contained in F. S. Regs., Part II. and the Staff Manual respectively. Title Pages will be prepared in manuscript.

WAR DIARY
or
INTELLIGENCE SUMMARY
(Erase heading not required.)

Army Form C. 2118

Place	Date	Hour	Summary of Events and Information	Remarks and references to Appendices
NEUVILLE ST VAAST	May 7		As for 6th inst. but R Co moved from ZOUAVE VALLEY to CARIERIER to make bed for light railway. No 6/17202 Pte L. FALLEN killed in action, No 6/14476 Cpl R. CLARK wounded in action. About 20 shells fell in village. 2 6th M.E. Emplacement commenced in BRECON LINE.	[illegible]
"	8.		As for 7th	[illegible]
"	9		As for 8th. 10 shells into village. Wiring BRECON LINE and commenced two more M.G. Emplacements. Rain all night and at times during the day.	[illegible]
"	10		As for 9th. Commenced constructing a covered way to well from DENIS LEROQUE. 70 shells into village, many falling close to H.Q. 75 Btn. Heated a large gas alarm. 2nd Lt JOSS reported for duty from 9th Batt & posted to C. Co.	[illegible]
"	11		As for 10th. Some 80 shells into village 75 Btn HQ again receiving attention. Cloudy day. Submitted Defence Scheme for village. Notice received to be prepared to move in light order	[illegible]
"	12		As for 11th. Two more M.G. EMPLACEMENTS commenced and further wiring. A communication trench from DENIS LAROQUE to main well in village commenced About 20 shells into village mainly in vicinity of the PORTIQUE	[illegible]

1875 Wt. W593/826 1,000,000 4/15 J.B.C. & A. A.D.S.S./Forms/C. 2118.

Army Form C. 2118

WAR DIARY
or
INTELLIGENCE SUMMARY
(Erase heading not required.)

* Instructions regarding War Diaries and Intelligence Summaries are contained in F. S. Regs., Part II. and the Staff Manual respectively. Title Pages will be prepared in manuscript.

Place	Date	Hour	Summary of Events and Information	Remarks and references to Appendices
NEUVILLE ST VAAST	13		As for 12th. Wet day & chilly. Heavy action in front of 7th & 74 Bdes from 7.15 – 9. In consolidating the lip of a crater in 74 Bde area, the mine of which was discharged by the Germans at 7.15 pm and constructing a communication trench to same. C & D Coys came under heavy fire but all ranks behaved with distinguished gallantry. The following casualties occurred 2nd Lieut. EDWARDS severely wounded 2nd Lieuts MARSHALL and RENWICK wounded. Killed in action Ptes No 6/17221 C. COLLIER and No 6/16880 LESTER. Wounded in action Ptes ~~No 6/17518 FENNESSEY, No 6/17619 DAVIES,~~ No 6/17728 ROBERTS No 6/25616 JOYNES, No 6/16885 MORGAN, No 6/17088 CURTIS, No 6/17236 YATES No 6/16319 SWEENEY. Village rather heavily shelled during the evening.	[illegible]
"	14		Work as usual and rehearsal for operation to take place on night of 15th inst. The attached true copy of communication received from Commander 74 Bde. The following recommendations for Special Mention have been forwarded. 2nd Lieuts EDWARDS, MARSHALL and RENWICK, Sergts LLEWELYN and THOMAS Ptes No 6/17246 LEWIS, No 6/16889 GRIFFITHS, No 6/97236 YATES and No 6/1956 /EVANS. Wet day and village shelled as usual.	[illegible]
"	15		But little work during the during the day men resting for nights operation.	

1875 Wt. W593/826 1,000,000 4/15 J.B.C. & A. A.D.S.S./Forms/C. 2118.

Army Form C. 2118

WAR DIARY
or
INTELLIGENCE SUMMARY
(Erase heading not required.)

Instructions regarding War Diaries and Intelligence Summaries are contained in F. S. Regs., Part II. and the Staff Manual respectively. Title Pages will be prepared in manuscript.

Place	Date	Hour	Summary of Events and Information	Remarks and references to Appendices
NEUVILLE St VAAST	16		The operations against craters 89-90 in front of the 74 Bde area, were successfully carried out on the 15-16. Being captured and made good. Under very heavy fire and in the face of several counter attacks C & D Cos behaved in most gallant fashion winning the praise of all concerned.	
			The following casualties occurred. Killed 2nd Lieut G. W. JONES, No 6/17077 Sergt N. THOMAS, No 6/16121 Sergt C. LLEWELLYN, Pte No 6/16532 G. JAMES, No 6/19541 H. SMITH, No 6/17606 J. COX. Wounded Captain E. LLOYD, 2 Lieut E. AMOS and S. EVANS. ~~No 6/16...~~ No 3/14665 L/Cpl W. MORRIS, No 6/17462 L/Cpl T. EVANS, Pte No 6/17217 H. STEWART, 6/16222 T. MORGAN, 6/17452 E. MORGAN 6/17492 G. WILLIAMS, 6/17554 W. WILLIAMS. 6/17488 M. RYAN, 6/16780 F. PHILLIPS, 6/17162 E. LEWIS, 6/17059 Sergt J. JONES, Pte No 6/16404 H. JAMES, 6/16526 D. DALEY, 9/14434 M. NOLAN, 6/16830 G. EVANS, 6/16426 W. DOWNES, No 6/14382 Pte E. HUGHES missing	[initials]
			B. Coy to work during night on consolidating the craters.	
			The following telephone received from G.O.C. Corps and Division.	
	~~17~~		~~C. Co on work during day on craters~~	
			To O.C. 6 Bn. Corps Commander has wired congratulations to all ranks for last night's operations From G.O.C. 74 Bde.	
			To O.C. 6 Bn. G.O.C. 25 Division wishes to express his appreciation to all ranks 6th S.W.B engaged in the minor operations on the 15th May for the excellent work they did. Kindly inform all ranks accordingly. Considerable number of shells fell in village.	[initials]
	17		C. Co on work during the day on craters 74 Bde area. B & D on night work on craters 74 Bde area. No 6/16764 Sergt R. BERRY, No 6/17250 L/Cpl W. ELVIN & No 6/17464 Pte WILSON wounded in action. About 60 shells fell in village during the day.	

Instructions regarding War Diaries and Intelligence Summaries are contained in F. S. Regs., Part II. and the Staff Manual respectively. Title Pages will be prepared in manuscript.

WAR DIARY
or
INTELLIGENCE SUMMARY
(Erase heading not required.)

Army Form C. 2118

Place	Date	Hour	Summary of Events and Information	Remarks and references to Appendices
NEUVILLE VITASSE	18.		Weather as on 17th village shelled at intervals. No 6/14578. C.S.Major B.W. CLAYDON, 6/17471 Pte H. WRIGHT, 6/17244 Pte O. JONES 6/17405 Pte H.C. WALTERS, 6/14409 Pte T. WILLIAMS, wounded in action, No 6/17464 Pte F. GARDNER shell and No 6/17246 Pte J. RICHARDSON Killed in action.	
	19		Men resting during the day. Whole Battn on strengthening local defences during the night. Heavy bombardment with chiefly shrapnel from 9-10.30 pm 4 hitting vicinity to H.Q. PORTIQUE	
	20		Weather as on 19th.	
	21		Weather as for 20th Very heavy bombardment of P & Q Sector commencing at 4 pm. At least 300 shells fell in village & the BRECON LINE was hit in several places.	
	22		Weather as on 21. The ROY Trench cleared & cleaned and new duck boards laid. This trench is to be used for evacuating of wounded from Front Line. Heavy bombardment at intervals during the day of P & Q Sector	
	23		All Coys working by day on defences of village & revetting fire steps. B. Coy out for night work in addition the Battn being reported to assist retrench lost ground in P Sector Village heavily shelled with Tear shells & shrapnel. Tram line cut in 7 places.	
	24		B & D. Coys retrenching ground lost in P Sector. C working in ROY and revetting BRECON LINE. BRECON LINE shelled in several places.	

1875 Wt. W593/826 1,000,000 4/15 J.B.C. & A. A.D.S.S./Forms/C. 2118.

Instructions regarding War Diaries and Intelligence Summaries are contained in F. S. Regs., Part II. and the Staff Manual respectively. Title Pages will be prepared in manuscript.

WAR DIARY
or
INTELLIGENCE SUMMARY
(Erase heading not required.)

Army Form C. 2118

Place	Date	Hour	Summary of Events and Information	Remarks and references to Appendices
NEUVILLE ST-VAAST	25		Battn entrenching P sector each night. Trenches in shocking condition. Water to hips & many bodies about. Village shelled	[illegible]
"	26		As for 25th. State of water in trenches very bad. M.G. Detachment making a new emplacement & cutting.	[illegible]
"	27		As for 26th. No 6/17567 Pte A. THOMAS and No 6/17184 Pte H. JONES wounded in action	[illegible]
"	28		As for 27. Village shelled.	[illegible]
"	29		As for 28th. Village heavily shelled at intervals. VIII Corps Commander inspected defences	[illegible]
"	30		As for 29th	[illegible]
"	31		As for 30th. Battn retires to rest billets at ACQ.	[illegible]

1875 Wt. W593/826 1,000,000 4/15 J.B.C. & A. A.D.S.S./Forms/C. 2118.

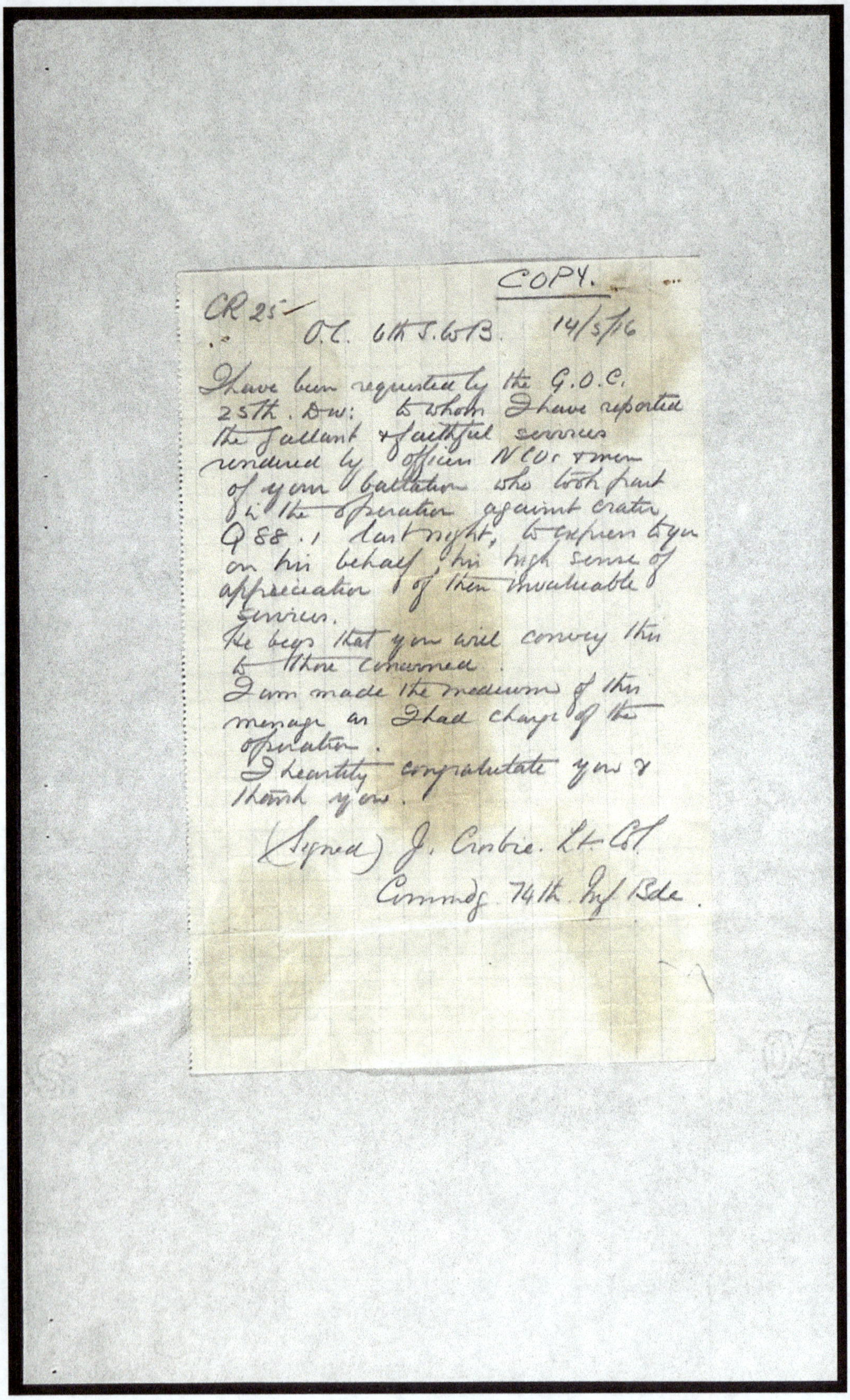

COPY.

CR 25

O.C. 6th S.W.B. 14/5/16

I have been requested by the G.O.C. 25th. Div: to whom I have reported the gallant & faithful services rendered by officers NCOs & men of your battalion who took part in the operation against crater Q88.1 last night, to express to you on his behalf, his high sense of appreciation of their invaluable services.
He begs that you will convey this to those concerned.
I am made the medium of this message as I had charge of the operation.
I heartily congratulate you & thank you.

(Signed) J. Crosbie. Lt Col
Commdg. 74th. Inf Bde.

6th. SOUTH WALES BORDERERS

(PIONEERS)

J U N E 1 9 1 6.

Instructions regarding War Diaries and Intelligence Summaries are contained in F. S. Regs., Part II. and the Staff Manual respectively. Title Pages will be prepared in manuscript.

XXV

WAR DIARY
or
~~INTELLIGENCE SUMMARY~~
(Erase heading not required.)

Army Form C. 2118

6TH. (S) BTN. S. WALES BORDERERS (PIONEERS)

VOL 10

Place	Date	Hour	Summary of Events and Information	Remarks and references to Appendices
	1. JUNE	1916		
Bois de Bray	1		Owing to no billets available at ACQ the Battn bivouaced for the night 31-1. Day spent in resting & cleaning up. Paraded 8 pm and marched to VILLERS CHATEL & then occupied billets arriving 10 pm.	[illegible]
VILLERS CHATEL	2		Battn paraded 9 am for farewell address by Major General H. Doran C.B. on his relinquishing command of the Division. Companies refitting.	[illegible]
			Lieuts C. MUMFORD and H.M. CARPENDALE and 2nd Lieuts N. GRIFFITHS and W.H. BELCHER joined the Battn on appointment.	[illegible]
"	3		Route march & bathing at SAVEY.	[illegible]
"	4		Musketry, Bayonet fighting, 3 hours route march, Knotting & lashing. Commenced inoculating Battn for fever. Lt Col E.V.O. HEWETT awarded the C.M.G	[illegible]
"	5		Work on 4th Rifle range continued and firing commenced at 100 & 600 yds (6 targets)	[illegible]
"	6		Work on 5th [illegible] great delay in obtaining sufficient supplies for refitting, Battn.	[illegible]
"	7		Inspection by new Divisional Commander Major Gen Bainbridge C.B. Lecture to Officers	[illegible]
"	8		Musketry, bayonet fighting, rapid wiring & Co Drill	[illegible] 10 S 5th

Instructions regarding War Diaries and Intelligence Summaries are contained in F. S. Regs., Part II. and the Staff Manual respectively. Title Pages will be prepared in manuscript.

WAR DIARY
or
INTELLIGENCE SUMMARY
(Erase heading not required.)

Army Form C. 2118

Place	Date	Hour	Summary of Events and Information	Remarks and references to Appendices
VILLERS CHATEL	9		Work as for 8th + route march	
–	10		As for 9th. B. Co HQ & 120 men with 1 officer & 60 men of C. Co to TINQUES for work with RE.	
–	11		Church Parade 11 remainder of day rest.	
"	12		M.G. Detachments range practice. B. Co (Batt) working with RE, remainder of Batt M. Order Parade, route march & Co Drill. A. Co returned from duty with Light Railway Company.	
"	[illegible]		At 4 pm orders were received to entrain at TINQUE station at 8 pm. Batt paraded 6 pm and marched to TINQUE arriving 7.30 pm. Train not arrived, raining and cold. Commenced entraining at 8.30, that one [illegible] [illegible] for loading wagons etc. All loaded by 12.45. Batt proceeded to [illegible]. Raining all night.	
BOUZINCOURT	13		Train arrived at LONGUEAU 6 am. Batt detrained & breakfasted. No information about Batt, but at 10.30 a S.S.O. arrived from the 32 Division & stated that we were to be attached to it & had been sent to [illegible] station. He reported that the Batt had a 20 mile march before it. 32 Div is in X Corps. Marched off at 11.30 am in pouring rain, but it cleared at noon. Arrived BOUZINCOURT at 8.30 pm where we found billets told off to us. 45 men fell out on the road & were brought in in ambulances. March a very creditable one considering men had been working & carried in cattle trucks all previous night and had recently come from 6 months in the trenches.	

1875 Wt. W593/826 1,000,000 4/15 J.B.C. & A. A.D.S.S./Forms/C. 2118.

Instructions regarding War Diaries and Intelligence Summaries are contained in F. S. Regs., Part II. and the Staff Manual respectively. Title Pages will be prepared in manuscript.

WAR DIARY
or
INTELLIGENCE SUMMARY
(Erase heading not required.)

Army Form C. 2118

Place	Date	Hour	Summary of Events and Information	Remarks and references to Appendices
BOUZINCOURT	14		Day of rest & cleaning up. At 6pm 100 men of A. Co were sent to the trenches	
"	15		Detail of work Men 100 excavating trench HARLEY Street by day " 200 " " " by night " 10 BLIGHTY Valley road, dugouts by day " 100 making assembly trenches AUTHUILLE by night " 50 Battle Centre & German Prisoners enclosure by day enclosure to hold 1000 men " 100 CORPS Artillery emplacements by day " 50 RE Store AUTHUILLE by day	
"	16		As for 15. C.O. reported to G.O.C. 32 Division (General RYECROFT) Day cold & dull	
"	17		Work as for 16 cold & dull.	
"	18		Work as for 17 bright warm day.	
"	19		Battle Centre & enclosure completed otherwise work as for 18th	
"	20		Work as for 19th but 300 men by night on HARLEY Street night very cold. 1106/41714 Pte R. ANDREWS wounded in action	

Instructions regarding War Diaries and Intelligence Summaries are contained in F. S. Regs., Part II. and the Staff Manual respectively. Title Pages will be prepared in manuscript.

WAR DIARY
or
INTELLIGENCE SUMMARY
(Erase heading not required.)

Army Form C. 2118

Place	Date	Hour	Summary of Events and Information	Remarks and references to Appendices
BOUZINCOURT	21		As for 20th	
"	22		Work on HARLEY Street 100 men, remainder of Batt on INVERARY Street, THIEPVAL AVENUE, GEMMILL and BISSET Trenches. all by night. No 6/17075 Pte DAVIES. J. wounded in action. Very hot sunny day.	
"	23		Work on HARLEY Street continued, revetting HAMILTON, GREENOCK, OBAN and BURY AVENUES. Deepening ORKNEY Street all work by night.	
		2.30pm	Very heavy thunder storm during which one of our observation balloons broke from its moorings & vanished	
"	24	2.40pm	By order of X Corps B Co moved ½ Co to LEALVILLERS ½ Co to SENLIS and D Co to FORCEVILLE. The 12" guns fired several rounds for the first time. Several heavy thunder squalls. Major Parsons struck off strength of Batt owing to illness.	
PIERREGOT	25	noon 12.10	Received orders for HQ & Batt less 2 Cos on detached to proceed at once to PIERREGOT and there go into billets. Passed 2 pm & marched via SENLIS - CONTAY. On arrival found village full of RAMC & Div Train but secured billets. Fine sunny day but thunder about.	
"	26		Route march & inspection by Co.	
"	27		C.O.'s parade & route march. 2 Lieut Clark reported for duty with Batt & posted to C. Coy. Some heavy thunder showers	
"	28		2 hours route march. Batt ordered to concentrate at SENLIS, moving at 9.15. Kit Inspection	
		2pm	Orders received to stand fast.	

1875 Wt. W593/826 1,000,000 4/15 J.B.C. & A. A.D.S.S./Forms/C. 2118.

Instructions regarding War Diaries and Intelligence Summaries are contained in F. S. Regs., Part II. and the Staff Manual respectively. Title Pages will be prepared in manuscript.

WAR DIARY
or
INTELLIGENCE SUMMARY
(Erase heading not required.)

Army Form C. 2118

Place	Date	Hour	Summary of Events and Information	Remarks and references to Appendices
PIERREGOT	29		3 Hours route march, M.G. & Signallers exercised. Issue of boots & clothing, & general overhaul of equipment	[illegible]
	30		Orders to move to SENLIS are detailed for the 2 Bn.	
			2 Hours route march M.G. & Signallers exercised.	[illegible]
		9 pm	Paraded & marched to SENLIS where the Battn went into billets — march held up by traffic one man only fell out	[illegible]

1875 Wt. W593/826 1,000,000 4/15 J.B.C. & A. A.D.S.S./Forms/C. 2118.

Pioneers.
25th Div.

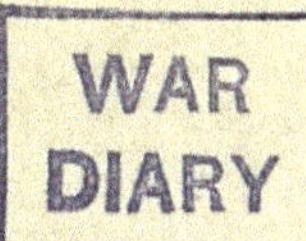

6th BATTN. THE SOUTH WALES BORDERERS.

J U L Y

1 9 1 6

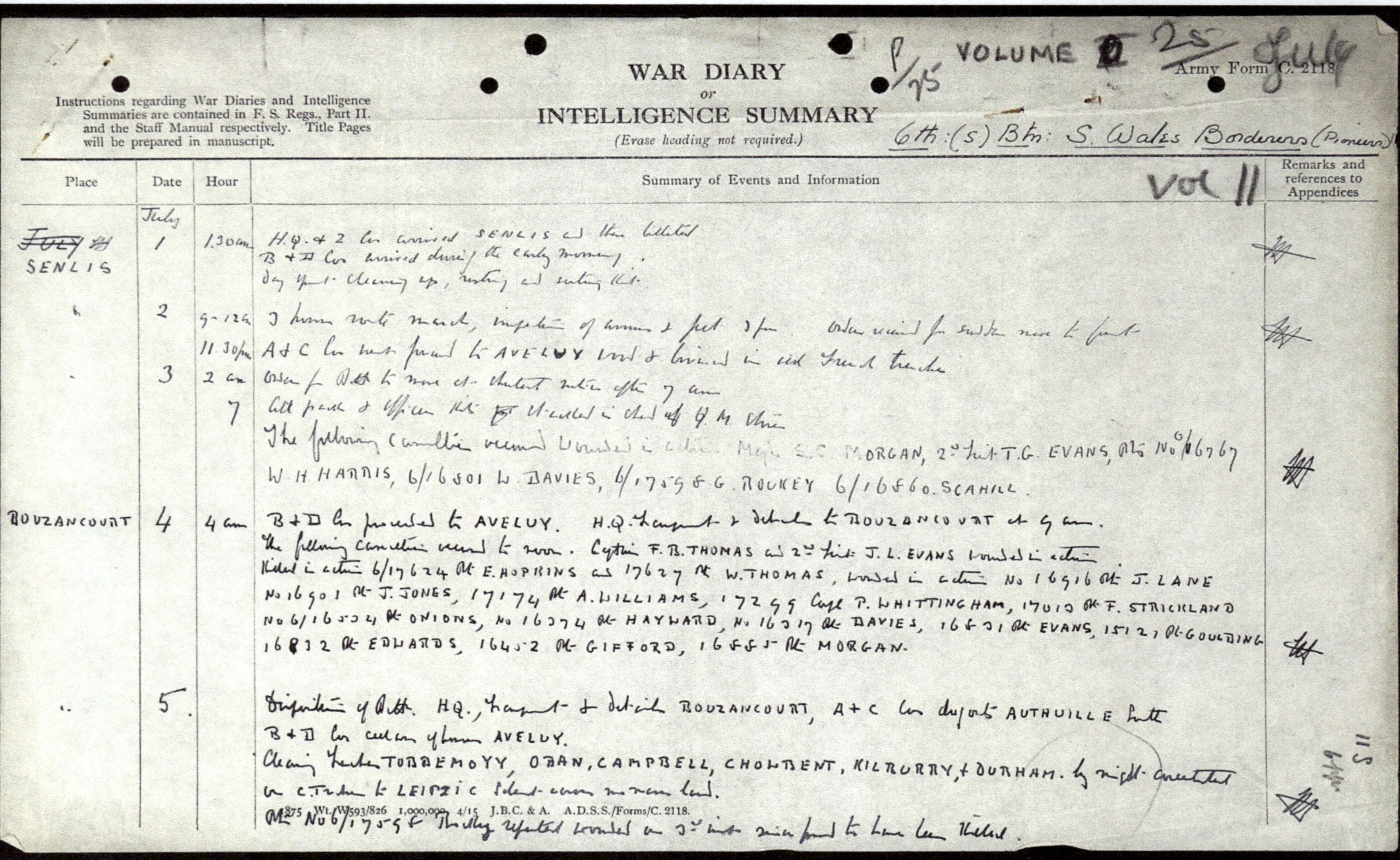

Instructions regarding War Diaries and Intelligence Summaries are contained in F. S. Regs., Part II. and the Staff Manual respectively. Title Pages will be prepared in manuscript.

P/75 VOLUME II 25 July

WAR DIARY
or
INTELLIGENCE SUMMARY
(Erase heading not required.)

Army Form C. 2118.

6th (S) Btn: S. Wales Borderers (Pioneers)

Vol II

Place	Date	Hour	Summary of Events and Information	Remarks and references to Appendices
SENLIS	July 1	1.30am	H.Q. & 2 Cos arrived SENLIS and then billeted. B & D Cos arrived during the early morning. Day spent cleaning up, resting and sorting kit.	
"	2	9-12a	3 hours route march, inspection of arms & feet 3pm. Orders received for sudden move to front	
		11.30pm	A & C Cos went forward to AVELUY Wood & bivouacked in old French trenches	
"	3	2 am	Orders for Batt. to move at short notice after 7 am	
		7	All packs & officers kits [illegible] stacked in charge of Q.M. Stores	
			The following casualties occurred Wounded in action Major E.C. MORGAN, 2nd Lieut T.G. EVANS, Ptes No 6/16767 W.H. HARRIS, 6/16501 W. DAVIES, 6/17559 G. ROOKEY 6/16560 SCAHILL.	
BOUZANCOURT	4	4 am	B & D Cos proceeded to AVELUY. H.Q. Transport & details to BOUZANCOURT at 9 am. The following casualties occurred to noon. Captain F.B. THOMAS and 2nd Lieut J.L. EVANS wounded in action. Killed in action 6/17624 Pte E. HOPKINS and 17627 Pte W. THOMAS, wounded in action No 16916 Pte J. LANE No 16901 Pte J. JONES, 17174 Pte A. WILLIAMS, 17299 Corpl P. WHITTINGHAM, 17010 Pte F. STRICKLAND No 6/16524 Pte ONIONS, No 16374 Pte HAYWARD, No 16317 Pte DAVIES, 16831 Pte EVANS, 15127 Pte GOULDING 16832 Pte EDWARDS, 16452 Pte GIFFORD, 16885 Pte MORGAN.	
"	5.		Disposition of Batt. H.Q., Transport & details BOUZANCOURT, A + C Cos dugouts AUTHUILLE Wood. B & D Cos cellars of houses AVELUY. Clearing trenches TOBERMORY, OBAN, CAMPBELL, CHOWBENT, KILBURNY, & DURHAM. By night connected up C Trench to LEIPZIG Salient across no man's land. Pte No 6/17558 Thomas reported wounded on 3rd inst since found to have been killed.	

W875 Wt. W593/826 1,000,000 4/15 J.B.C. & A. A.D.S.S./Forms/C. 2118.

Instructions regarding War Diaries and Intelligence Summaries are contained in F. S. Regs., Part II. and the Staff Manual respectively. Title Pages will be prepared in manuscript.

WAR DIARY
or
INTELLIGENCE SUMMARY
(Erase heading not required.)

Army Form C. 2118

Place	Date	Hour	Summary of Events and Information	Remarks and references to Appendices
BOUZAINCOURT	6		Work concentrated on, CHOWBENT, KERARA, TYNDRUM and SANDA leading to LEIPZIG Salient. By midnight 6-7th all with the exception of TYNDRUM down to depth of 6 ft throughout. TYNDRUM [illegible]. Men worked 14 hours under very trying conditions.	
			No 6/19969 Pte COLES. J, No 6/19652 Pte CRANE. G, No 6/17620 Pte HENNING, No 9/25675 Pte WALL, No 6/14409 Pte WILLIAMS. T, No 6/16462 Pte MANSFIELD, No 6/16525 Pte LLOYD. S, No 6/17360 Sergt ALLISON. D, No 6/14424 Pte MORGAN. T, No 6/17151 Pte PRITCHARD. J, No 3/20550 Pte MAKEPEACE wounded in action.	
"	7		Intense bombardment of enemy positions 6-9 am covering attack, all working parties withdrawn to cover before 7 am. Orders to move tomorrow. Orders issued to Coy to rendezvous AVELUY Wood 9.30 am, [illegible] the German shelled village.	
AVELUY Wood	8		Batt. assembled AVELUY Wood and stood by all day for orders. At 10 pm occupied dug outs vacated by 17 R.I.R.. Wood shelled during the night. Wounded in action Nos 1726[?] Sergt WEST, 17195 Pte DAVIES, 14378 Pte HARRIS, 17003 Pte SHEA.	
ALBERT	9	8 am	At 8 am orders to proceed at once to ALBERT at which town the Batt arrived 10 am. Remained all day expecting instructions and [illegible] ordered to take over billets vacated by 1st S.W.B. (Pioneers) which was done at 9 pm.	
			Wounded in action Nos 17275 Pte RICHARDS, 16755 Pte SUSH, 14470 Pte DONEGAN, 17051 Pte HODGES. C.O. reconnoitred line from 6.30 - 10 pm.	
		10.30 pm	One Company to C.T.s La BOISSELLE.	
"	10		Batt employed in making good C.T.s in La BOISSELLE. B Co had the running of light tramway (base NORTH CHIMNEY) [illegible] 2 Officers (Lt COOK & RUMSEY) and 60 men. Wounded in action 2nd Lt RENWICK, Nos 17403 Pte SILLOX, 17145 Pte WATERS, 17052 L/Cpl PALMER. C.O. reconnoitred La BOISSELLE [illegible] Batt [illegible].	

1875 Wt. W593/826 1,000,000 4/15 J.B.C. & A. A.D.S.S./Forms/C. 2118.

Instructions regarding War Diaries and Intelligence Summaries are contained in F. S. Regs., Part II. and the Staff Manual respectively. Title Pages will be prepared in manuscript.

WAR DIARY
or
INTELLIGENCE SUMMARY
(Erase heading not required.)

Army Form C. 2118

Place	Date	Hour	Summary of Events and Information	Remarks and references to Appendices
ALBERT	11		Work on consolidating LA BOISSELLE all day (14 hours)	
			Killed in action 2nd Lieut GRIFFITHS.M, Nos 16344 Sgt. TURNER.C, 16975 Cpl LAMB.F, 17058 2nd Cpl THEOBALD.E, Pte 16421 DAVIES.R, 19968 BEACHEL.N, 17207 EDDLESTONE.P, 16951 LLOYD.T, 14008 DAVIES.G, Wounded in action 16424 Pte DOWNES.W, 17246 LEWIS.L, 17026 EVANS.D, 19552 O'CONNELL.S, 25520 WALTERS.W, 16560 GOULD.J, 17168 MILLARD.A, 16946 PRICE.E, 16979 CALLAGHAN.D, 17546 FRANCES.R, 17322 DAVIES.A.	
–	12		Consolidating LA BOISSELLE all day	
			Wounded in action Lieut ESKELL.R, Nos 16759 Pte BERRY.C, 16766 BROWN.W, 17031 PROTHEROE.D, 17630 PEARCE.J, 17154 L/Cpl ELSDON.J.	
			On the night of the 11-12 inst. Lieut M.C.EDE showed great courage and presence of mind when under shell fire he got on the parapet and walked down the line encouraging the men and getting them to return to their work. Company Sgt Major O'NEIL under shell fire, and wounded himself, bound up the wounds of the men of the X CHESHIRE Regt and assisted them to the Dressing Post.	
–		11.pm	Ordered to send ½ Co (C Co. [illegible]) to assist 7th Bord consolidate. Party out all night although only returned from working all day at 6 pm.	
–	13		Consolidating LA BOISSELLE.	
			Killed in action 6/16258 Sgt. HICKEY. Wounded in action Nos 17684 Pte JENKINS.L, 17094 Pte ROWLANDS, 17527 C.S. Major O'NEIL.J, Shell shock 17045 Pte EVANS.D.T, 16951 Pte FRANCIS J.	
			Major RENWICK 14th Northumberland Fusiliers attached for duty as second in command.	
–	14		Consolidating LA BOISSELLE	
			Wounded in action 17622 Pte JENNINS.J + 16786 Pte MERIDITH.W. Day wet & cold	

1875 Wt. W593/826 1,000,000 4/15 J.B.C. & A. A.D.S.S./Forms/C. 2118.

Instructions regarding War Diaries and Intelligence Summaries are contained in F. S. Regs., Part II. and the Staff Manual respectively. Title Pages will be prepared in manuscript.

WAR DIARY
or
INTELLIGENCE SUMMARY
(Erase heading not required.)

Army Form C. 2118

Place	Date	Hour	Summary of Events and Information	Remarks and references to Appendices
ALBERT	15		Consolidating LA BOISSELLE. Fire trenches completed and front wired. 4 M.G. Emplacements commenced. 1 Co repairing road LA BOISSELLE towards POZIERES by night to carry lorries of 5-Ton weight.	[initials]
	16		Consolidating LA BOISSELLE. M.G. Emplacements completed and rear face of village fire trenched. Wet chilly day. 1 Co by night constructing new road past big crater entrance to LA BOISSELLE. 25 Division withdrawn to rest but, 105 & 106 Cos RE and the Battn transferred for work to the 48 Division, remaining in the line.	[initials]
	17		Work as for 16 but road work by day.	
		8 pm	A Co on CT X.5 – X 5.0 by night but owing to check [illegible] general [illegible] of Field [illegible] which had been allowed to become very dirty [illegible]	[initials]
	18		Work as on 17th. As many men as possible bathed.	
	19		Work on LA BOISSELLE discontinued, OVILLERS having been captured. Battn were employed on making & repairing the OVILLERS and POZIERES Roads ½ Bn mostly by night and ½ by day. 1 Platoon C. Co unloading stores from trucks at BRICKFIELDS night 19-20. Killed in action 6/16458 Pte HALL. J, No 6/16986 Pte JAMES. H. Wounded in action No 6/17065 Pte JONES. D.	[initials]
	20		D. Co completing road cover into LA BOISSELLE. Took over [illegible] and commenced [illegible] the [illegible].	
		3 pm	at 3 pm received orders to stand by for a move.	

1875 Wt. W593/826 1,000,000 4/15 J.B.C. & A. A.D.S.S./Forms/C. 2118.

Instructions regarding War Diaries and Intelligence Summaries are contained in F. S. Regs., Part II. and the Staff Manual respectively. Title Pages will be prepared in manuscript.

WAR DIARY
or
INTELLIGENCE SUMMARY
(Erase heading not required.)

Army Form C. 2118

Place	Date	Hour	Summary of Events and Information	Remarks and references to Appendices
AVELUY Wood	21		Battn moved to AVELUY Wood and there bivouaced. Orders & counter orders during afternoon & evening. finally orders received to move to BUS les ARTOIS.	[illegible]
BUS les ARTOIS	22		Paraded 9 am & marched to BUS les ARTOIS where it arrived 12 noon and took over huts. C. Co & detach who had been working all night 21-22 were conveyed in lorries after Dinner	[illegible]
"	23		Church Parade and cleaning billets. Received orders to move to MAILLY Wood tomorrow. C.O. & Co Commanders reconnoitred new front line.	[illegible]
"	24		Battn paraded 9 am and proceeded to MAILLY WOOD where it took over huts vacated by the 2nd MONMOUTHS. C. Co on night work on [illegible] communicating trenches. Wounded in action No 6/16822 Pte THOMAS. E. No 8/16240 Pte LEWIS. D. No 6/14379 Pte JONES. D. No 9/13644 Pte MERIDITH. C.	[illegible]
BEAUSSART	25		Battn moved to BEAUSSART during the morning and there took over billets from 1st NORTHANTS	[illegible]
"	26		Battn working on whole front constructing deep dug outs. and during night C. Co on C.T. to [illegible]	
"	27		B Co took over the running, upkeep and supply of trench [illegible] in Div area. Remainder of Battn as on 26th. A & C Cos moved to dug outs near there [illegible] A to SEAFORTH [illegible] C to KNIGHTSBRIDGE. Work in 6 hour reliefs continuously day and night. Draft of 11 men arrived. B Co Bathed & clean clothes.	[illegible]
"	28		Work as for 27th. Battn less A & D Co bathed & clean clothes. No 6/14515 Pte JAMES wounded in action.	[illegible]

1875 Wt. W593/826 1,000,000 4/15 J.B.C. & A. A.D.S.S./Forms/C. 2118.

Instructions regarding War Diaries and Intelligence Summaries are contained in F. S. Regs., Part II. and the Staff Manual respectively. Title Pages will be prepared in manuscript.

WAR DIARY
or
INTELLIGENCE SUMMARY
(Erase heading not required.)

Army Form C. 2118

Place	Date	Hour	Summary of Events and Information	Remarks and references to Appendices
BEAUSART	29		1 Coy on deep dug outs on divisional front. One L(B) running & repairing tram line. M.G. Det completed 3 ammunition dug outs at MAILLY. 25 men with Tn Coy burying cable	[initials]
"	30		Work as for 29th. Bright, hot sunny day – temperature 85° by day 55° by night. Wounded in action No 6/17622 Pte WILLIAMS. H.	
			" " " No 11/22150 Pte HIGGINS. T (11th S. Lancs attached)	[initials]
"	30		Work as for 30th but B Coy on completion of work on tram line has commenced work on CT's in 5th Div area. Hot, sunny day.	[initials]

1875 Wt. W593/826 1,000,000 4/15 J.B.C. & A. A.D.S.S./Forms/C. 2118.

PIONEERS 25 DIVN

125
64

6. S.W.B
Vol 12

REF:
WAR DIARY

To. H.Q. "A"
25th. Division

Herewith please find War Diary for this Battn: for month of AUGUST.

[signature] Lt. Col.
Commdg. 6th. S.W.B
(Pioneers)

Instructions regarding War Diaries and Intelligence Summaries are contained in F. S. Regs., Part II. and the Staff Manual respectively. Title Pages will be prepared in manuscript.

WAR DIARY
or
INTELLIGENCE SUMMARY
(Erase heading not required.)

Army Form C. 2118

6th Service Battn South Wales Borderers (Pioneers)

Place	Date	Hour	Summary of Events and Information	Remarks and references to Appendices
BEAUSSART	Aug 1.		3 Cos continuing deep dug outs on Divisional front. B Co having completed work on tramway were employed on CT's in 5th Bde Area. L.G. det. strengthening cellars in AUCONVILLERS. Hot sunny day. Cooler towards 5 o'clock, 6.30 to night. Wounded in action No 6/16480 Pte PRICE. J. Battn Sgt Major Casey detailed to take over charge of R.E. Dump at MAILLY. The following Officers joined Battn 2 Lieuts SEDEN, RIGG, STICKLER, & COX from 14th Welsh Regt. 2nd Lieuts HURLEY, MARCH & PEARCE from 3rd S.L.B.	[initials] [initials]
"	2		As for 1st. Weather hot.	
"	3		As for 2nd Wounded in Action No 6/17454 L/Cpl WHITEHEAD. R and No 6/17073 Pte BRINKWORTH. C	[initials]
"	4		As for 3rd Division taking over 61st Bde area to North.	
"	5		As for 4th. D Co moved to COLINCAMPS & billets. Hot day	[initials]
"	6		As for 5th. C Co moved from MESNIL to COLINCAMPS & billets - bright hot day.	[initials]
"	7		As for 6th Commenced a Div Communication dug near BERTRANCOURT with 30 men of C. Co. Transport lines shelled 9.30 to 10.30 pm 2 men wounded 8 horses hit two died. Captain REID KELLETT (8 Batt N. Staffords Pioneers) joined Battn for duty. Wounded in Action No 6/14806 Pte WESTON. T, No 6/17020 Pte WATERS. H, & No 6/17507 Pte PARKER	
"	8		Work as for 7. Orders received to be relieved by 4th COLDSTREAM Guards Pioneers on 9 & 10th and Battn to proceed to LEALVILLERS	[initials]

1875 Wt. W593/826 1,000,000 4/15 J.B.C. & A. A.D.S.S./Forms/C. 2118.

Army Form C. 2118

Instructions regarding War Diaries and Intelligence Summaries are contained in F. S. Regs., Part II. and the Staff Manual respectively. Title Pages will be prepared in manuscript.

WAR DIARY
or
INTELLIGENCE SUMMARY
(Erase heading not required.)

Place	Date	Hour	Summary of Events and Information	Remarks and references to Appendices
BEAUSSART	9		A + B Cos relieved by corresponding Cos of 4th Coldstream Guards and proceeded to LEALVILLERS. At 7 pm orders received for Battn to proceed to AUTHIE on 10th. 2nd Lieut. BELCHER attached to Divisional Signal Company for duty.	
AUTHIE	10		H.Q. & Cos paraded 9 am at respective billets and proceeded to AUTHIE where Battn was assembled and settled in billets by 11.30 am. Cloudy day with some showers. C & D. Cos & H. Quarters relieved by the Guards at 9 am & all were handed over.	
AUTHIE.	11		Programme of work while at rest. 7-8 Physical drill & Bayonet fighting. 9-12.30 pm 2 hours route march and 1 hours close order drill & handling arms. ½ hour lecture daily. Arrangements being made for Battn Sports and an item carrying Fusiliers & boxing competition. Day hot & muggy.	
"	12		H.M. The King inspected the Division in its different billeted areas. Battn formed 1 Co [illegible] and lined the road its VAUCHELLES, 18th Battalion & S. S. Lancs prolonging the line at 11 am. H.M arrived by motor, and descending the O.C. Offrs & Units were introduced to His Majesty. He held a short conversation with each enquiring the work & casualties suffered by their units. Lt Col. when introducing the C.O made some flattering remarks upon the good work done by the Battn. The King then drove along the line of troops amidst loud cheers. Very hot day.	
"	13	11	Church Parade, cloudy & some showers, cooler.	
"	14		Training as per Table of Parade. B Co on completion of Bombing & Trench Mortar Battery training there near LEALVILLERS. On completion of Tank [illegible] this Co proceeded to LEALVILLERS & there billeted.	

1875 Wt. W593/826 1,000,000 4/15 J.B.C. & A. A.D.S.S./Forms/C. 2118.

WAR DIARY
or
INTELLIGENCE SUMMARY

(Erase heading not required.)

Army Form C. 2118

Instructions regarding War Diaries and Intelligence Summaries are contained in F. S. Regs., Part II. and the Staff Manual respectively. Title Pages will be prepared in manuscript.

Place	Date	Hour	Summary of Events and Information	Remarks and references to Appendices
LEALVILLERS	15		Batt paraded 12 noon & marched to LEALVILLERS and then billeted. 2 5th Division transferred to II Army. C.O. proceeded on short leave to England.	
	16.		Training as per scale of parades laid down. Boxing & football competitions in evening.	
	17		do do do do do do do	
			Lt. Neale proceeded on leave.	
MARTINSART WOOD	18		Btn. paraded at 8 A.M & proceeded to MARTINSART WOOD & there went into huts. Transport at HEDAUVILLE. C.O. & 2 coy commanders carried out reconnaissance of communication trenches in left sector. Baths for L.S. Section & 80 men of ? Coy.	
	19		Coys. worked in new area in afternoon & evening. Enemy shelled MARTINSART at 10 P.M. & the wood at mid-night. Following casualties resulted from shell fire. 6/17050 Pte. JEFFRY 6/17069 Pte. GEORGE, 6/14516 Pte. HURST 6/17014 Pte. JARMAN, 6/17367 PTE. RICHARDS. 6/16796 L/CPL. MORGAN 9/25294 Pte. JONES 22224 Pte. BROWN (S. LANCS)	
	20.		Coys. working as usual. 2/Lt. Renwick rejoined for duty.	
	21.		Work as per programme. MARTINSART Wood shelled at 10 & 12.30 pm. Wounded in action Captain E.C. CHOINIER. No 6/17451 Pte J. HOPKINS	

1875 Wt. W593/826 1,000,000 4/15 J.B.C. & A. A.D.S.S./Forms/C. 2118.

Army Form C. 2118

Instructions regarding War Diaries and Intelligence Summaries are contained in F. S. Regs., Part II. and the Staff Manual respectively. Title Pages will be prepared in manuscript.

WAR DIARY
or
INTELLIGENCE SUMMARY
(Erase heading not required.)

Place	Date	Hour	Summary of Events and Information	Remarks and references to Appendices
MARTINSART Wood	22		Work as per programme. MARTINSART Wood again shelled at 9.30 & 12.30 pm rapid fire from 5.9". Batt H Q's shelled with H E & shrapnel, fortunately all officers had time to take cover in [illegible] in rear of camp before [illegible] shells started. 1 Horse (white) killed 1 wounded and three missing having bolted away from farm. All officers [illegible] of 105th Co RE wounded at same time.	
"	23		Work as per programme. dug out being built for Batt H.Q.'s in Sunken road. All men available of A.B.&C. Cos ordered out for emergency work at 7.30 to WOOD MILL	
"	24		Consolidating LIPSIC Salient captured this day (2 lines). All available men of Batt working all night. No 2/15459 Lcpl DAVIES. J, No 6/16461 Pte DONOVAN. E Killed in action No 9/17420 Pte SULLIVAN. J ~~No 6/16500 Pte SUTTON. J, No 6/16549 Pte LAWRENCE. A, 6/17599 Pte TOM~~ Wounded in action 2 Lieut JONES. R, 6/16500 Pte SUTTON. J, 6/16549 Pte LAWRENCE. A, 6/17599 Pte TOMMEY. A, 6/17189 WALTERS. G, 6/17181 Lcpl RUDALL. J, 6/17158 Lcpl SMITH. G, 6/17485 Pte RYAN. M, 6/17114 Pte COOMBES. J, 6/18129 Pte BENNETT (13 [illegible]) 6/16847 Lcpl HEMUS. C, 6/17042 Pte MAZZIE. A, Missing 3/9621 Lcpl DRISCOLL. J 6/16783 Pte WALTERS. D	
"	25		Work as for 24th 2nd Lieut MARCH. G. J admitted to Hospital Severe Shell shock	
"	26		Work as for 25. Wounded in action No 17628 Pte GINGELL No 6/17053 Pte JONES.	
"	27		A & C Cos working by day in LIPSIC Salient. Heavy rain during the night & showers by day. Some bombardment of Salient by Germans. Orders received to proceed to AVELUY tomorrow	

1875 Wt. W593/826 1,000,000 4/15 J.B.C. & A. A.D.S.S./Forms/C. 2118.

Instructions regarding War Diaries and Intelligence Summaries are contained in F. S. Regs., Part II. and the Staff Manual respectively. Title Pages will be prepared in manuscript.

WAR DIARY
or
INTELLIGENCE SUMMARY
(Erase heading not required.)

Army Form C. 2118

Place	Date	Hour	Summary of Events and Information	Remarks and references to Appendices
AVELUY	28		Work continued in LEIPSIC Salient. B Coy proceeding intervals of work to AVELUY and then billeted ½A + ½D under Lieut. Carpenter detailed for consolidation of captured portion by S. LANCS. Wounded in action No 6/17226 Pte TREASURE. J, No 6/16295 Pte WILLIAMS. W. Shell shock 2 Lieut. SEDEN. R.M.	[illegible]
"	29		Work A & C. Cos. C.T.s in LIPSIC Salient, D on approaches to MOUQUET Farm, B on light railways Wounded in action Lieut. M.C. EDE, No 6/17323 Pte FOOTE. J, No 3/19944 Pte WARD. J Heavy thunderstorm and much rain.	[illegible]
–	30		Work as for 29th. 2 Cos A & C detailed for consolidation after attack by 7th Div. operation postponed on account of weather. Very wet day and cold.	[illegible]
–	31		Work as per programme. Fine sunny day. Captain C. MUMFORD. wounded in action	[illegible]

1875 Wt. W593/826 1,000,000 4/15 J.B.C. & A. A.D.S.S./Forms/C. 2118.

25th. DIVISION

TROOPS

6th. SOUTH WALES BORDERERS
(PIONEERS)

S E P T E M B E R

1 9 1 6.

Instructions regarding War Diaries and Intelligence Summaries are contained in F. S. Regs., Part II. and the Staff Manual respectively. Title Pages will be prepared in manuscript.

Army Form C. 2118.

Vol 13

WAR DIARY
or
INTELLIGENCE SUMMARY

(Erase heading not required.)

6th (S) Btn: S. Wales Borderers (Pioneers)

Place	Date	Hour	Summary of Events and Information	Remarks and references to Appendices
AVELUY	SEPT. 1.		A & C Coy working in 75th Bde area LEIPSIC Salient. B Co on light tram line, D on 4th Avenue and BRIMSTONE Trench right behind MOUQUET FARM. Killed in action 1356/17159 Pte WALTERS. T. Wounded in action No 8/16580 L/Cpl HORTON. J. 6th Bttn East Yorks (Pioneers) 11 Division attached to 25 Division and affiliated with the Bttn for work.	
"	2.		A & C working in 75th Bde area, pushed forward for consolidation, position during operation night 2-3. D. Co night work BRIMSTONE Trench. Wounded in action 11/22111 Pte GUTHRIE (S. Lancs attached.	
"	3		Work as per programme. Killed in action C.S. Major WATKINS. J, 11/22106 Pte PLOMPTON (S Lancs attached) Wounded in action 11/21957 Pte HAYES. M (S Lancs attached) 11/21957 Pte HAYES. M. (S. Lancs attd.) 11/22221 Pte VOSE. J. (S Lancs attached) 11/22048 Pte SMART. J. (S. Lancs attd) 3/15259 Pte PADDOCK. J.	
"	4		Work as per programme. B Co (light tramway) replacing timber rails with steel in BLIGHTY Valley. The line very much cut up during the night.	
"	5		Work as per programme. Wounded in action 6/13769 Pte PRICE, 11/22061 Pte CAREY (S Lancs attached) 6/17566 Pte WHITE. W	

133
5pp

1875 Wt. W593/826 1,000,000 4/15 J.B.C. & A. A.D.S.S./Forms/C. 2118.

Instructions regarding War Diaries and Intelligence Summaries are contained in F. S. Regs., Part II. and the Staff Manual respectively. Title Pages will be prepared in manuscript.

WAR DIARY
or
INTELLIGENCE SUMMARY
(Erase heading not required.)

Army Form C. 2118

Place	Date Sept	Hour	Summary of Events and Information	Remarks and references to Appendices
AVELUY	6		Work as per programme. BLIGHTY Valley tramline completed with steel rails. Orders received that the Battn would be relieved by the 6/EAST YORKSHIRE Regt (Pioneers) representatives of this unit taken round and shown all work in hand by Battn.	[illegible]
ACHEUX	7	9AM.	Battn paraded and moved to ACHEUX Wood and there occupied huts and tents. Wounded in action No 3/15121 Pte GOLDING. W. 2 Lieut RUMSEY detailed by Division H.Q. to take over duties of Div Salvage Officer.	[illegible]
"	8		Day devoted to cleaning up and 1 hour rifle drill C.O. inspected clothing and arms of Battn	[illegible]
"	9	9-12	Physical training, Bayonet Fighting and Platoon Drill Divisional Band played in Battn Lines Orders received that men of the 13th GLOUCESTERS and 11th S. LANCS attached had been transferred to S.W.B. from 6th inst.	[illegible]
AMPLIER	10	9am	4 Cos proceeded by Motor Buses A to CREMONT, B to DOMQUER, C to FRANSU, D to COULONVILLERS to construct Bombing Trenches for Div and each of the Brigades.	
		6.40am	H.Q by march to AMPLIER arriving 11.40 and billeted. Captain MUMFORD and 2 Lieut MARSH rejoined from Hospital	[illegible]
FEINVILLERS	11		Cos as for 10th H.Q to FEINVILLERS by route march arriving 4 pm and billeted	[illegible]
		5.30pm	Draft of 100 men transferred from 2nd MONMOUTHS arrived and were taken on strength of Battn	

1875 Wt. W593/826 1,000,000 4/15 J.B.C. & A. A.D.S.S./Forms/C. 2118.

Instructions regarding War Diaries and Intelligence Summaries are contained in F. S. Regs., Part II. and the Staff Manual respectively. Title Pages will be prepared in manuscript.

WAR DIARY
or
INTELLIGENCE SUMMARY
(Erase heading not required.)

Army Form C. 2118

Place	Date	Hour	Summary of Events and Information	Remarks and references to Appendices
	Sept		Con. as for 11th	
LONGVILLERS	12	9am	H.Q. to LONGVILLERS arriving 12 noon and billeted C.O. visited all Coys at work.	#
"	13	–	Coys. all worked on bombing grounds.	WWD
"	14	–	do. do.	WWD
"	15	–	Coys: all came into LONGVILLERS & then billetted. Day spent cleaning up & settling down. C.O. went on leave to England.	WWD.
"	16	.	A & B Coys. inspected by C.O. Training carried out all day as per programme. Boxing competition in evening.	WWD.
"	17		Bn. paraded for divine service in morning.	WWD.
"	18		Heavy rain all day. Training carried on under cover.	WWD
"	19		do. do. do. do.	WWD.
"	20.		Heavy rain in morning. Bn. played & beat R.E.'s in afternoon.	WWD.
"	21.		Heavy rain all day. Training carried out as well as possible under cover.	WWD.
–	22		Fine Day Training as per programme. Bn played & beat Div A.S.C	#

1875 Wt. W593/826 1,000,000 4/15 J.B.C. & A. A.D.S.S./Forms/C. 2118.

Instructions regarding War Diaries and Intelligence Summaries are contained in F. S. Regs., Part II. and the Staff Manual respectively. Title Pages will be prepared in manuscript.

WAR DIARY
or
INTELLIGENCE SUMMARY
(Erase heading not required.)

Army Form C. 2118

Place	Date	Hour	Summary of Events and Information	Remarks and references to Appendices
LONGVILLERS	23		Holiday. Batt Sports successfully carried out. Fine day	
"	24		Batt paraded for Divine Service. Orders received to move on the 25th	
AMPLIER	25	7.10	Batt paraded 7.10 am (attached to 75th Bde) and marched to AMPLIER and there went into huts – distance marched 16 miles.	
ACHEUX Wood	26	11.20	Batt paraded and marched to ACHEUX Wood and occupied huts. Fine warm day. News received of the capture of THIEPVAL, MORVAL and COMBLES.	
		3 pm.	Ordered to be ready to proceed at 2 hours notice.	
"	27		Company training. Trench digging competition.	
"	28		Company training	
		4 pm	B & D Cos under Major RENNICK to AVELUY Wood by motor buses for work on the Railway.	
			Lt Colonel E.V.O. HEWETT awarded the D.S.O.	
"	29		Company training.	
			The 2 Cos at AVELUY Wood moved into billets in AVELUY	
AVELUY	30	11.30	H.Q. A & C Cos proceeded to AVELUY and there billeted	
			C.O. and C.R.E. inspected new line and arranged work	

1875 Wt. W593/826 1,000,000 4/15 J.B.C. & A. A.D.S.S./Forms/C. 2118.

25th. DIVISION

6th. SOUTH WALES BORDERERS

(PIONEERS)

O C T O B E R 1 9 1 6.

To.

Headquarters 25th: Div: "A."

REF:

WAR DIARY

Herewith please find war diary for the month of OCTOBER 1916 for the Btn: under my command.

[signature]

Major.

Commdg. 6th.(S) Btn: S.W.B. (Pioneers)

Vol 14

Instructions regarding War Diaries and Intelligence Summaries are contained in F. S. Regs., Part II. and the Staff Manual respectively. Title Pages will be prepared in manuscript.

WAR DIARY 6th South Wales Borderers (Pioneers) INTELLIGENCE SUMMARY

(Erase heading not required.)

Army Form C. 2118

Place	Date	Hour	Summary of Events and Information	Remarks and references to Appendices
AVELUY	Octr 1.		A. D + C Cos on communication trenches from MOUQUET FARM area forward to STUFF Trench and Redoubt. B. Co repairing new road CRUCIFIX CORNER to THIEPVAL – MOUQUET FARM Road. Killed in action No 6/16550 Pte HEAD. J, 6/39234 Pte LAYCOCK, W, wounded in action 6/39252 Pte RIMMER 6/42304 Pte HOLT. J, 6/42301 Pte VOSE. J, 3/19934 Pte JAMES. W, 6/42309 Pte GRADY. J. Weather fine & sunny.	[illegible]
"	2		Work as for 1st also Headquarters Coy employed in erecting huts at CRUCIFIX CORNER. Wounded in action 3/15152 Pte SEALEY, 6/39256 Pte RICHARDS. Wet cold day.	[illegible]
"	3		Work as for 2nd Wounded 6/19702 Pte ADDISON. E, Injured on duty 6/39235 Pte DAVIES. R Misty wet day.	[illegible]
"	4		Work as for 3rd but B Co taken over construction of tramway from AVEULEY to THIEPVAL – MOUQUET FARM Road. Killed in action No 6/17250 Pte DAVIES. W. J. 6/17622 Cpl DAVIES. G. Wounded in action 6/39246 Pte DAVIES. T. J. 6/16939 Pte WILLIAMS. R, 6/16954 Pte HUGHES. O, 6/42235 Pte CLOTHIER. J, 6/39236 Pte HOLMSHAW. H, ~~6/39247 Pte CHARLES. J~~. Injured while walking in the trenches 3/19764 Pte EDWARDS. J. Misty wet day.	[illegible]
"	5.		Work as per programme for 4th. Wounded in action No 39259 Pte COLES. R, 6/16319 Pte HOLLAND. W, 39232 Pte THOMAS. F, 39267 Pte BRYARD. G. Shell shock 32150 Pte HIGGINS. T (11th [illegible] attached)	
"	6.		Work as per programme for 4th Fine day & wind mild. C & D Cos moved to huts & dug outs CRUCIFIX CORNER.	[illegible]

1875 Wt. W593/826 1,000,000 4/15 J.B.C. & A. A.D.S.S./Forms/C. 2118.

Instructions regarding War Diaries and Intelligence Summaries are contained in F. S. Regs., Part II. and the Staff Manual respectively. Title Pages will be prepared in manuscript.

WAR DIARY
or
INTELLIGENCE SUMMARY
(Erase heading not required.)

Army Form C. 2118

Place	Date	Hour	Summary of Events and Information	Remarks and references to Appendices
AVELUY	Oct 7		A + B Cos on Tramline. A communicating new line from POZIERS down to Battn H.Q. MAPLE ROAD. C & D on No II. C.T.	
		6.30pm	C. Co to construction of No IV C.T. Wounded in action 6/14354 Pte PLEWETT.T, 6/17207 Pte NEAL.J, No 39267 Pte BYARD.G. Shell shock 5/18962 Pte DRAPER.W.J. Fine day. Wounded in action 2nd Lieut COX.W, No 39270 Pte ELLIS.E, ~~[illegible]~~	
"	8.		Work as for 7th Day wet and thick wind S.W. 100 shells fired into village during night. Capt EVANS admitted to Hospital suffering from neurasthenia. Wounded in action No 6/46952 Pte JAMES.T.	
"	9		A + B Cos on Tramways. C + D Cos standing by for night work on communicating – they proceeded to site but were sent back conditions being unfavourable. Village again heavily shelled. A + B Cos on Tramline from POZIERS down MAPLE ROAD.	
"	10	5.30pm	C & D Cos paraded to join working party for construction of fire trench connecting HESSIAN Trench + STUFF Redoubt. party consisted of the above Cos 105 Bn RE and detachment of XI Cheshire and N and S Lancs Total 820 all ranks. Half the trench was dug but party had to retire owing to the heavy artillery barrage, casualties and M.G. fire. Total casualties 8 Officers and some 80 men. Cos returned at 5 am the 11th. Killed in action No 3/15121 Pte GOULDING.W, 3/15209 Pte PADDOCK, 6/17608 Pte JENNER Wounded in action 2nd Lieut RENWICK, No 6/17555 L/Cpl JONES.A, 6/19112 L/Cpl PHILLIPS. 6/42257 L/Cpl WAKELEY, 6/42259 Pte ~~GREEN~~ GRIFFIN, 6/42262 Pte HOCK 6/42246 Pte LESTER, 6/42260 Pte TUCKER, 6/17246 Pte LEWIS. Shell shock 6/16861 Pte SCHOLES.	

1875 Wt. W593/826 1,000,000 4/15 J.B.C. & A. A.D.S.S./Forms/C. 2118.

Instructions regarding War Diaries and Intelligence Summaries are contained in F. S. Regs., Part II. and the Staff Manual respectively. Title Pages will be prepared in manuscript.

WAR DIARY
or
INTELLIGENCE SUMMARY
(Erase heading not required.)

Army Form C. 2118

Place	Date	Hour	Summary of Events and Information	Remarks and references to Appendices
AVELUY	11.		A + B Cos on fatigues as for 10th. C. Co resting ~~Deepening & widening REGENT STREET~~	
		9. pm	D Co paraded for work on trenches commenced last night.	
"	12.		A + B Cos on fatigues as for 11th, C. Co Deepening and widening REGENT STREET	
		5.30 am	D Company returned having accomplished their task in most brilliant manner in spite of heavy M.G. fire. Captn MUMFORD by the skillful manner in which he conducted his Co to its task, and afterwards carried it out, did so without the loss of a man. Lieut. Colonel EV.O. HEWETT slightly wounded at duty but carried on his work. Wounded in action 6/17950 Pte HARGREVES.	
"	13		Work as for 12th but D Co only worked one platoon during night 12-13 in extending right flank of trench they were working on, remainder of Co during day revetted fire step and deepened C.T.	
"	14		A + B Cos on fatigues, C & D Cos commencing deep dug outs in HESSIAN Trench. Wounded in action No 6/17236 Corpl YATES. G, ~~Missing [illegible] night 12/13~~ Wounded [illegible] No 6/19694 Pte LEECH	
"	15		A + B Cos on fatigues C & D Cos deep dug outs in HESSIAN TRENCH very heavy bombardment throughout evening and night.	
"	16		A + D Cos on C.Ts. Part of STUFF REDOUBT, B fatigues, C. deep dug out. Lt. Col. Hewitt admitted to hospital.	

1875 Wt. W593/826 1,000,000 4/15 J.B.C. & A. A.D.S.S./Forms/C. 2118.

Instructions regarding War Diaries and Intelligence Summaries are contained in F. S. Regs., Part II. and the Staff Manual respectively. Title Pages will be prepared in manuscript.

WAR DIARY
or
INTELLIGENCE SUMMARY
(Erase heading not required.)

Army Form C. 2118

Place	Date	Hour	Summary of Events and Information	Remarks and references to Appendices
AVELUY.	17th:	6.30 A.M.	Enemy aeroplane dropped a bomb on our transport lines. Following casualties resulted. 6/42266 Pte West killed; 6/14525 Pte. Evans, 5/15066 Pte. Weston 6/17073 Pte Thomas 6/42284 Pte Brotherstone 6/16842 Pte Hayes 3/35016 Pte Stokes, 6/42246 Pte. Ash 6/16810 Pte Smith 6/16333 Pte Bird, 6/17256 Pte. Boast all wounded – 6 officers chargers killed & 7 wounded. Two eventually were shot. 2 mules wounded.	
			Coys: working as usual. 39277. Pte. Crump wounded in action. Lt Col. Hewitt evacuated from 29 C.C.S to Base.	H.W.D.
do.	18th.		Work as usual. A Coy: on C.T. B Coy: tramways. C Coy. C.T. D Coy C.T. (A Coy by night) Wet night. AVELUY VILLAGE shelled off & on all night	H.W.D.
do.	19th.		Coys: did not work with the exception of Tramway Coy: Very wet day.	H.W.D.
do.	20th:		Coys: worked by day. Heavy traffic on tramways. 6/14491 Sgt. Thomas killed. 6/17027 Pte. Williams 6/13644 Pte: Meredith. 6/42279 Pte Hicks wounded.	H.W.D.
do.	21st.		Div: attack. Coys (A. C & D) went up at night to dig C.T's to new captured line (REGINA TR:) A Coy: with 106th Co. R.E. & C & D Coys with 130th Co. R.E. Tasks successfully accomplished. "A" Coy: sustained following casualties 6/17279 Pte. Mahoney missing 6/19673 Pte Totten. Wounded 6/14337 C.S.M. O'Neil. 6/17106 L/Cpl. Fellows 6/42252 Pte. Russell 6/35679 Pte. Wall. 6/16466 Pte. Berry. 39220 Pte Southgate. 6/17360 Sgt. Allison.	H.W.D.
do.	22nd.		Relieved by 5th: S.W.B & proceeded to W.27.A. (ALBERT BRICKFIELDS) & bivouaced.	H.W.D.
CONTAY.	23rd.		Proceeded to CONTAY & billetted. G.O.C. Div: addressed Btn: & thanked them for good work done.	H.W.D.
CANDAS	24th		Proceeded to CANDAS & billetted.	H.W.D.

1875 Wt. W593/826 1,000,000 4/15 J.B.C. & A. A.D.S.S./Forms/C. 2118.

Instructions regarding War Diaries and Intelligence Summaries are contained in F. S. Regs., Part II. and the Staff Manual respectively. Title Pages will be prepared in manuscript.

WAR DIARY
or
INTELLIGENCE SUMMARY
(Erase heading not required.)

Army Form C. 2118

Place	Date	Hour	Summary of Events and Information	Remarks and references to Appendices
CANDAS.	25.		Coys: cleaning up generally & resting. Wet day	LLWD
"	26.		Coys. cleaning up. Owing to wet weather no outdoor work was possible.	LLWD
"	27.		Coys: under O's.C. Coys. Very wet day	LLWD.
	28.		Btn: paraded 10 A.M. C.O inspected all coys.	LLWD.
"	29		Sunday. Day was observed as a general holiday. Capt. Mumford awarded Military Cross.	LLWD.
EECKE	30		Btn: entrained at CANDAS-FIENVILLERS at 10 A.M & proceeded by rail to CAESTRE. Detrained at CAESTRE at 7 p.m. & marched to billets at EECKE	LLWD
"	31.		Coys. paraded under coy: commanders. till noon. Orders received for Btn. to move on 1st. Nov:	LLWD

1875 Wt. W593/826 1,000,000 4/15 J.B.C. & A. A.D.S.S./Forms/C. 2118.

25th. DIVISION

6th. SOUTH WALES BORDERERS

(PIONEERS)

NOVEMBER 1916.

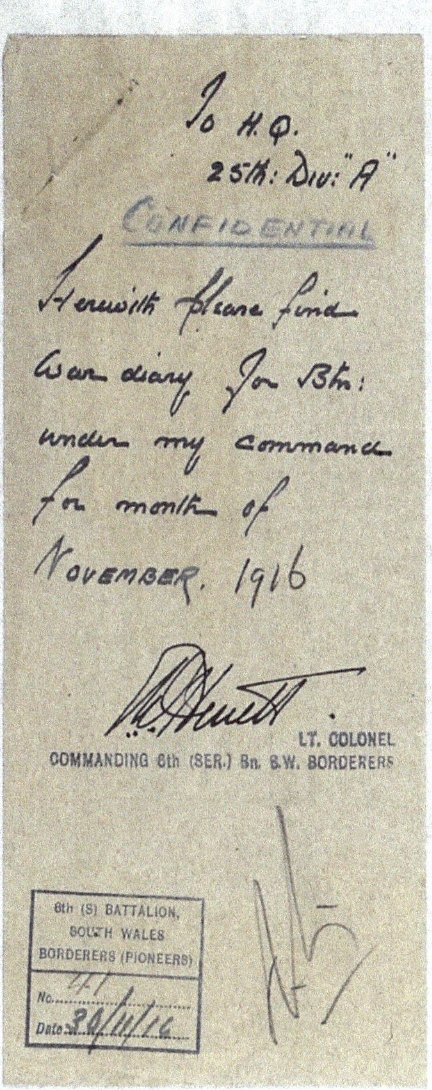

To H.Q.
25th: Div: "A"

CONFIDENTIAL

Herewith please find War diary for Btn: under my command for month of NOVEMBER. 1916

W. Hewett
LT. COLONEL
COMMANDING 6th (SER.) Bn. S.W. BORDERERS

6th (S) BATTALION, SOUTH WALES BORDERERS (PIONEERS)
No. 41
Date 30/11/16

Instructions regarding War Diaries and Intelligence Summaries are contained in F. S. Regs., Part II. and the Staff Manual respectively. Title Pages will be prepared in manuscript.

WAR DIARY
or
INTELLIGENCE SUMMARY
(Erase heading not required.)

Army Form C. 2118

6th (S) BATTALION, SOUTH WALES BORDERERS (PIONEERS)

Vol 15

Place	Date	Hour	Summary of Events and Information	Remarks and references to Appendices
MONT DE CATS.	Nov: 1.		Btn: paraded at 10 a.m. on EECKE Square & marched to METEREN area & billetted on Southern slopes of MONT DE CATS.	LLWD.
"	2.		Very wet weather. Coys: carried on with possible training under cover. C.O. visited new area with C.R.E.	LLWD.
OOSTHOVE FARM.	3.		Btn: paraded at 8.30 a.m. at MT. DE CATS & marched to OOSTHOVE FARM via BAILLEUL – NIEPPE – PONT DE NIEPPE. distance 12 miles. Billetted at OOSTHOVE FARM & surrounding huts.	LLWD.
"	4.		Day was spent settling down into billets & improving same.	LLWD.
"	5.		"A" Coy: commenced work in right sector with 130th: Co. R.E. Remaining coys. patching up the huts & draining etc: Wet day.	LLWD.
"	6		"A" Coy: worked in right sector. Remaining coys cleaning up the camps & improving existing huts. "D" Coy: worked in afternoon on drainage of fulces at B. 12. Very wet day.	LLWD.
"	7.		Coys: working as usual. 2/LTS. Richards & Hanna & draft of 79 other ranks reported for duty.	LLWD.

1875 Wt. W593/826 1,000,000 4/15 J.B.C. & A. A.D.S.S./Forms/C. 2118.

15.S
5 pp

Instructions regarding War Diaries and Intelligence Summaries are contained in F. S. Regs., Part II. and the Staff Manual respectively. Title Pages will be prepared in manuscript.

WAR DIARY
or
INTELLIGENCE SUMMARY
(Erase heading not required.)

Army Form C. 2118

Place	Date	Hour	Summary of Events and Information	Remarks and references to Appendices
OOSTHOVE FARM.	Nov. 8		2nd Lieut W. H. Kent reported for duty & posted to A Coy	D.J.
	9		A fine day. A, B & C Coys at work in the trenches. D Coy improving huts ~~&~~	D.J.
	10		A fine day. A. B & C Coys at work as yesterday. D Coy at work in the back area. One platoon proceeded on detachment to TROIS ARBRES to build huts.	D.J.
	11.		Another fine day. A. B & C Coys working as yesterday. D Coy at work in the back area. A start made with new transport lines under supervision of 2nd Lieut W.A. COX. Pioneers and ~~etc~~ details from Coys still busy with improvements to billets.	D.J.
	12		Coys working as yesterday. One platoon of D Coy proceeded on detachment to work at the Divisional Bombing School, METEREN. 31 other ranks reported for duty from no 5, I.B.D.	D.J.
	13		Coys working as usual. 2nd Lieuts Brook + Kelly reported for duty.	D.J.
	14.		Distinguished Conduct Medal awarded to: C.S.M. Shermer } for gallantry displayed on the night of Oct. 10/11th in C.S.M. Brooke } the vicinity of STUFF + SCHWABEN REDOUBTS. C.S.M. O'Niel for gallantry displayed on the night of Oct. 21/22nd in digging a new communication trench to REGINA TRENCH.	D.J.

1875 Wt. W593/826 1,000,000 4/15 J.B.C. & A. A.D.S.S./Forms/C. 2118.

WAR DIARY
or
INTELLIGENCE SUMMARY
(Erase heading not required.)

Army Form C. 2118

Instructions regarding War Diaries and Intelligence Summaries are contained in F. S. Regs., Part II. and the Staff Manual respectively. Title Pages will be prepared in manuscript.

Place	Date	Hour	Summary of Events and Information	Remarks and references to Appendices
OOSTHOVE FARM	15.		Coys working as usual. Military medals awarded to the following: 6/17159 Sgt Whitehouse J, 6/16401 Sgt W.H. Goodman, 6/19233 Sgt Ranson J, 6/16925 Cpl W. Davies 6/16329 Sgt A. Williams, 6/11305 Sgt Gibbin J, 6/16327 L. Cpl Lihon G, 6/16971 Pte J. Pearce 6/17188 Pte F. Moore, 6/16884 Pte W. Griffiths, 6/17154 Cpl J. Elsdon, 6/16917 Pte D. Keohane, 6/17437 L. Cpl A.J. Quinlon, 6/17285 Sgt A.T. Jones, 6/17074 L. Cpl W. Jutkins, 6/16567 ~~Pte~~ L. Cpl H. Thomas, 6/17433 Pte H. Corbett, 6/16946 Pte E. Price, 6/16409 Pte F. Perrins, 6/17432 Pte G. Kew, 6/16769 Pte Berry A.	D.J.
"	16		Coys working as usual. Fine weather continues.	D.J.
"	17		Capt. E.C. Choinier rejoined the Battalion after sick leave	D.J.
"	18		2nd Lieut A.D. Roberts reported for duty + posted to C. Coy. 'A' Coy at work in right sector. 'B,' 'C' + 'D' bathing. Cold rain after a spell of fine weather.	D.J.
"	19		Lt Colonel Hewett rejoined from sick leave and took over command of Battn. Coys working as usual. C.O inspected all billets of Battn and visited Coys working in 4th Bde area.	H.H.
"	20		Coys working as usual. 2nd Lieuts H.L. THOMAS and W.T. DAVIES and 15 other ranks reported for duty and as reinforcements. C.O. visited Coys at work in 74 + 7th Bde areas.	H.H.
"	21		Coys working as usual. Lieut BEESTON transferred from Town Major AVUELY to O i/c [illegible] at RABOT	H.H.

1875 Wt. W593/826 1,000,000 4/15 J.B.C. & A. A.D.S.S./Forms/C. 2118.

Instructions regarding War Diaries and Intelligence Summaries are contained in F. S. Regs., Part II. and the Staff Manual respectively. Title Pages will be prepared in manuscript.

WAR DIARY
or
INTELLIGENCE SUMMARY
(Erase heading not required.)

Army Form C. 2118

Place	Date	Hour	Summary of Events and Information	Remarks and references to Appendices
OOSTHOVE FARM	22		Corps working as usual.	[illegible]
"	23		Corps working as per scheme. 2 Lectures (1 N.C.O. & 4 men strength of lecture) German Prisoners working under II. [illegible] until further orders.	[illegible]
"	24		Corps working as per scheme.	[illegible]
"	25		Work as per programme	[illegible]
"	26		Work as per programme	[illegible]
"	27		Work as per programme	[illegible]
"	28		Work as per programme.	[illegible]
"	29		Work as per programme	[illegible]
"	30		Work as per programme	[illegible]

1875 Wt. W593/826 1,000,000 4/15 J.B.C. & A. A.D.S.S./Forms/C. 2118.

6th. SOUTH WALES BORDERERS

(PIONEERS)

D E C E M B E R 1 9 1 6.

Headquarters, "A",

25th. Division.

Herewith War Diary for the Battalion under my Command for month of December 1916.

January 1st. 1917.

[signature] Lieut. Colonel,

Commdg. 6th. (S). Bn. S. W. Borderers (Pioneers).

6th (S) BATTALION,
SOUTH WALES
BORDERERS (PIONEERS)
No. 416
1/1/17

Instructions regarding War Diaries and Intelligence Summaries are contained in F. S. Regs., Part II. and the Staff Manual respectively. Title Pages will be prepared in manuscript.

WAR DIARY
or
INTELLIGENCE SUMMARY
6th South Wales Borderers (Pioneers)

(Erase heading not required.)

Army Form C. 2118

6th (S) BATTALION, SOUTH WALES BORDERERS (PIONEERS)

Vol 16

Place	Date	Hour	Summary of Events and Information	Remarks and references to Appendices
OOSTHOVE FARM	Dec 1		Work in hand. A Co TOUQUET Salient, B Co Subsidiary line N of GAS Trench. C. Co Revetting & repairing the C.P.R., D Constructing Huts Reserve area. L.G.S & H.Q. Co Stables & Bath huts	
"	2		As above.	
"	3		As per programme. Gas alarm 10 pm	
"	4		As per programme. Weather foggy and cold, some rain	
"	5		As per programme. Gas alarms at 6.30 and 11.30 pm	
"	6		As per programme. Weather foggy & cold	
"	7		As per programme " " "	
"	8.		As per programme. 2 Platoons B Co making T saps by night. Weather mild & foggy	
–	9		As per 2nd Lieut R.L. ESKELL invalided out of the Service gazette today's date	
–	10		As per programme	
–	11		As per programme	
–	12		Service to B.C. & D. Co. a Week of National Mission, Baths, drills etc in afternoon. 2 platoons D Co per work on hutting reserve area to 75 A[illegible]. Area front line, weather heavy rain, some snow strong wind S.W.	
–	13		As per programme Machine gunners opening up track from HARNIMAN Avenue to WATLING St by night	

1875 Wt. W593/826 1,000,000 4/15 J.B.C. & A. A.D.S.S./Forms/C. 2118.

16 S
5 M

Instructions regarding War Diaries and Intelligence Summaries are contained in F. S. Regs., Part II. and the Staff Manual respectively. Title Pages will be prepared in manuscript.

WAR DIARY
or
INTELLIGENCE SUMMARY
(Erase heading not required.)

Army Form C. 2118

Place	Date	Hour	Summary of Events and Information	Remarks and references to Appendices
OOSTHOVE FARM	14		As per programme.	[illegible]
–	15		As per programme. Ordered today to take over running and working control of Divisional Tram Line. 1 Platoon to METERINE to construct Div Rifle Range. 4th Army Commander to visit.	[illegible]
"	16		As per programme. C.O visited Detachment at METEREN. Weather mild & foggy. Wounded in action. No 40131 Pte JAMES.C.H, 6/19035 Pte JONES, 6/25970 Pte WALTERS.	[illegible]
–	17		As per programme. Work being carried out. A Co constructing, to firing line NAPOO Trench, maintaining & extending the G.N.R.T.T. Construction, KENT and MACAULAY. CTs to firing line. B Co mending Trench boards for CHESHIRE Trench, draining ECKLES Avenue in PLOEGSTEERT Wood and improving C.T. 107. C Co working on C.P.R., D Co constructing TT for Heavy T. Mortar in front of HUNTERS Avenue. Hutting at REGINA Camp, 1 Platoon constructing range at METEREN. Weather mild and foggy. Greater part of C.T. work has to be done by night.	[illegible]
–	18		As per programme.	[illegible]
–	19		As per programme.	[illegible]
–	20		As per programme (fine sunny day)	[illegible]

1875 Wt. W593/826 1,000,000 4/15 J.B.C. & A. A.D.S.S./Forms/C. 2118.

Instructions regarding War Diaries and Intelligence Summaries are contained in F. S. Regs., Part II. and the Staff Manual respectively. Title Pages will be prepared in manuscript.

WAR DIARY
or
INTELLIGENCE SUMMARY
(Erase heading not required.)

Army Form C. 2118

Place	Date	Hour	Summary of Events and Information	Remarks and references to Appendices
OOSTHOVE FARM	21		As per programme — C.O. visited Det at Meteren	[illegible]
"	22		As per programme (wet & foggy day)	[illegible]
"	23		As per programme. (mild hazy [illegible])	[illegible]
			2nd Lt BROOK. D.C. took over duties of Instructor at Divisional Training School. C.O. visited Det at Meteren.	[illegible]
"	24		As per programme. Killed in action No 6/17347 Cpl COLLINS. J.	
"	25		Xmas Day divine service made of day a holiday. Dinner good Sergts serving the men.	[illegible]
"	26		Baths, interior economy, drills. Sergts held their Xmas Dinner	[illegible]
"	27		As per programme. very mild day with sunshine	[illegible]
			2nd Lieut JACOB reported for duty on being posted to the Battn.	
"	28		As per programme	[illegible]

1875 Wt. W593/826 1,000,000 4/15 J.B.C. & A. A.D.S.S./Forms/C. 2118.

Instructions regarding War Diaries and Intelligence Summaries are contained in F. S. Regs., Part II. and the Staff Manual respectively. Title Pages will be prepared in manuscript.

WAR DIARY
or
INTELLIGENCE SUMMARY
(Erase heading not required.)

Army Form C. 2118

Place	Date	Hour	Summary of Events and Information	Remarks and references to Appendices
OOSTHOVE FARM	29		A. Co 3 Platoons working in right sector 1 Platoon building huts Regina Camp. B Co LOUNDES Avenue (Le GHEER) C. Co front line trenches, D Co 3 Platoons front line trenches 1 Platoon making rifle range METERIN. Mild day, some rain.	[illegible]
"	30		Work as per programme. Wounded in action 2nd Lieut JOSS, No 6/17515 Pte FENESSEY. E, 6/17625 Pte GINGALL. C, 6/17541 Pte DAVIE. E, 6/39647 Pte PARR. P, 39617 Pte PASTEUR. G, 6/17506 Pte WHITE. J.	[illegible]
"	31		Work as per programme. Fine day, mild.	[illegible]

1875 Wt. W593/826 1,000,000 4/15 J.B.C. & A. A.D.S.S./Forms/C. 2118.

51-7496/Forms/A3091/9/44

Army Forms A3091 (Foolscap)

Cover for Documents

Nature of Enclosures.

War Diary
of
6th Bn. S. Wales Bdrs.
Jany to Decbr. 1917.

Notes, or Letters written.

To:-

H.Q. 25th: Div: 'A'

Herewith please find War Diary for month of JANUARY. 1917 for the Btn: under my command.

W. Hewett LT. COLONEL
COMMANDING 6th (SER.) Bn. S.W. BORDERERS

6th (S) BATTALION,
SOUTH WALES
BORDERERS (PIONEERS)
No. 792
Date 1/2/17

Instructions regarding War Diaries and Intelligence Summaries are contained in F. S. Regs., Part II. and the Staff Manual respectively. Title Pages will be prepared in manuscript.

WAR DIARY
or
~~INTELLIGENCE SUMMARY~~
(Erase heading not required.)

Army Form C. 2118

6th: (S) BTN: SOUTH WALES BORDERERS (PIONEERS)

Vol 17

Place	Date 1917	Hour	Summary of Events and Information	Remarks and references to Appendices
OOSTHOVE FARM.	JAN. 1		Work as per programme.	
"	2		Work as per programme weather very mild	
"	3		Work as per programme. His Majesty the King has been graciously pleased [illegible] M.C. to Captain E.C. CHOINIER, Lieuts L.C.W. DEANE and S.E. RUMSEY. Authority London Gazette 1 Jan 1917	
"	4		Work as per programme.	
"	5		Work as per programme	
"	6		Work – A Co. 3 Platoons on MACAULAY Trench, HARNIAN + LONG AVENUES and WATLING Street. 1 Platoon Hutting ([illegible] Camp) B Co. LOUNDRES AVENUE & Convent, C Co. 3 Platoons assisting No. 3 CANADIAN Tunnelling Company at St IVES. 1 Platoon on C.P.R. TTS, D Co. 2 Platoons H.T. Motor line TTS. 1 Platoon [illegible], [illegible] METEREN and 1 Platoon erecting screens in front line. C.O. visited METEREN [illegible]	
	7		As for 6th	
"	8		As for 6th The following Officers & N.C.O's were mentioned in despatches (Gazette 3rd Jan) for distinguished and gallant services and devotion to duty. Lt-Col HEWETT, Lieut. COX. R.M., Lieut. NEALE. T.T., Regt. Sergt. Major CASEY and Company Sergt. Major O'NIEL	17/S 5 [illegible]

1875 Wt. W593/826 1,000,000 4/15 J.B.C. & A. A.D.S.S./Forms/C. 2118.

Army Form C. 2118

Instructions regarding War Diaries and Intelligence Summaries are contained in F. S. Regs., Part II. and the Staff Manual respectively. Title Pages will be prepared in manuscript.

WAR DIARY
or
INTELLIGENCE SUMMARY
(Erase heading not required.)

Place	Date	Hour	Summary of Events and Information	Remarks and references to Appendices
OOSTHOVE FARM.	Jan 9		Work as per programme	[illegible]
"	10		Work as per programme. 10 men returned from METEREN Det.	[illegible]
"	11		Work as per programme. (snowing at times)	[illegible]
"	12		Work as per programme. The following were wounded in action:— No 6/16940 1st Cpl NORRIS. J, 6/42319 Pte CUNLIFFE. J, 6/42315 Pte WALSH. W. Heavy firing from 10 to 12 pm. (wet & snowing)	[illegible]
"	13		Many trenches damaged by fire last night. A Co working on LONG AVENUE, MACAULAY and WATLING Streets. clearing the REBECQUE from front line to G Tree Redoubt, B Co at CONVENT, LOUNDES AVENUE and C.T's 119, 116 + 109. C Co Tunnelling, 1 Platoon T.T's. D Co 2 Platoons T.T's. 1 Sniping 1 Rifle Ranges. Party under 2nd Lieut. DAVIES returned from METERINE on completion of work, G.O.C. complimented the party upon the good work they had done. (Wet and stormy wind N.W. some snow) Wounded in action No 29189 Pte ROLLISON. J.	[illegible]
	14		Work as per programme.	[illegible]
	15		Work as per programme. cold some snow, wind NE.	[illegible]

1875 Wt. W593/826 1,000,000 4/15 J.B.C. & A. A.D.S.S./Forms/C. 2118.

Instructions regarding War Diaries and Intelligence Summaries are contained in F. S. Regs., Part II. and the Staff Manual respectively. Title Pages will be prepared in manuscript.

WAR DIARY
or
INTELLIGENCE SUMMARY
(Erase heading not required.)

Army Form C. 2118

Place	Date	Hour	Summary of Events and Information	Remarks and references to Appendices
OOSTHOVE FARM	16		Work as per programme. Cold, some snow wind N E.	[illegible]
"	17		Work as per programme. Cold morning strong N wind. 2nd Lieut. T. G. P. LUCAS reported for duty and posted to A Co.	[illegible]
"	18		Work as per programme. Cold	[illegible]
"	19		Work. A Co. 2 Platoons WATLING St & LONG AVENUE, 2. Hutting. B.Co LOWNDES AVENUE, C.T. 117 and TORONTO avenue. C Co 3 Platoons Tunnelling 1 in T.T.s. D Co 3 Platoons T.T.S. 1 Scouring. (Snow & cold)	[illegible]
"	20		Work as for 19th (Cold snow with frost.)	[illegible]
"	21		As for 20th but one platoon B to WESTMINSTER AVENUE. (hard frost)	[illegible]
"	22		Work as for 21st but 2 Platoons B Co working on WESTMINITER AVENUE. (hard frost. Sunny) Very heavy artillery action 1.30 – 9 pm German raid at La CHEER repulsed.	[illegible]
"	23		Work as per programme. Killed in action No 5/16126 Pte GRANT. C. hard frost. Light snow	[illegible]
"	24		Work - A Co 2 Platoons support line 96 – 97, 2 Platoons hutting. B Co 2 Platoons LOWNDES AVENUE 1 in TORONTO and 1 HARNIANS AVENUES, C Co 3 Platoon Tunnelling 1.T.T's. D Co 3 Platoons St. IVES front line 1 Scouring. (very cold, light snow)	[illegible]

1875 Wt. W593/826 1,000,000 4/15 J.B.C. & A. A.D.S.S./Forms/C. 2118.

Army Form C. 2118.

Instructions regarding War Diaries and Intelligence Summaries are contained in F. S. Regs., Part II. and the Staff Manual respectively. Title pages will be prepared in manuscript.

WAR DIARY
or
INTELLIGENCE SUMMARY.

(Erase heading not required.)

Place	Date	Hour	Summary of Events and Information	Remarks and references to Appendices
OOSTHOVE FARM	25		Work as for 24th (cold bright time)	[illegible]
"	26		Work as per programme. "	[illegible]
"	27		Work as per programme " 21 degrees frost by day 15 by night.	[illegible]
"	28		Work as per programme " "	[illegible]
			Major A.H.J. ELLIS reported for duty.	
"	29		Work as per programme. " "	[illegible]
			Wounded in Action No 6/17403 Pte PRICE. A, 6/17002 Pte GREEN. A.	[illegible]
"	30		Work as per programme. Wounded in action No 6/16519 Pte MULLINS. L.	[illegible]
"	31		Platoon baths and rest-day (Interior Economy) day cold with bright sun	[illegible]

2353 Wt. W2544/1454 700,000 5/15 D. D. & L. A.D.S.S./Forms/C. 2118.

Instructions regarding War Diaries and Intelligence Summaries are contained in F. S. Regs., Part II. and the Staff Manual respectively. Title pages will be prepared in manuscript.

WAR DIARY
or
~~INTELLIGENCE SUMMARY.~~
(Erase heading not required.)

Army Form C. 2118.

6th: S. WALES BORDERERS (PIONEERS)

Vol 18

Place	Date	Hour	Summary of Events and Information	Remarks and references to Appendices
	February 1917			
OOSTHOVE FARM	1st		Work as per programme, 8.20pm – by heavy bombardment of Div Front (cold bright day)	[illegible]
"	2		Work as per programme. (cold bright day)	[illegible]
"	3		" " " " (cold bright day Zero at night)	[illegible]
"	4		" " " " (cold bright day Zero at night)	[illegible]
"	5		" " " " B & C Coys changed over work, also platoon of A changed. C.O. proceeded on leave to England.	
"	6th:		Work as per programme. Hard frost.	[illegible]
"	7th:		Work as per programme. Draft of 12 arrived – 6 were original members of the Btn:	[illegible]
"	8th:		All Coys: bathed at PONT-DE-NIEPPE. Hard frost.	[illegible]
"	9th		Coys worked as per programme. Hard frost.	[illegible]
"	10th.		Coys worked as per programme. A Coy had 2 Casualties. 6/42295 PTE: HIGGINS killed in action, 40119 L/cpl: PRICE wounded, remained at duty.	[illegible]
	11th.		Coys: worked as per programme. Hard frost.	[illegible]

2353 Wt. W2544/1454 700,000 5/15 D. D. & L. A.D.S.S./Forms/C. 2118.

Instructions regarding War Diaries and Intelligence Summaries are contained in F. S. Regs., Part II. and the Staff Manual respectively. Title pages will be prepared in manuscript.

WAR DIARY
or
INTELLIGENCE SUMMARY.
(Erase heading not required.)

Army Form C. 2118.

Place	Date	Hour	Summary of Events and Information	Remarks and references to Appendices
OOSTHOVE FARM	Feb: 12th.		Coys: worked as per programme. 39565 Pte: DAVIES wounded remained at duty.	LWOD.
"	13th.		Coys: worked as per programme. Lieut. E.O. HILL reported for duty. 39257 PTE: WOODWARD killed in action. 39195 Pte: ROY wounded	LWOD.
"	14th.		Coys: worked as per programme. One platoon of A Coy: under 2/LT STICKLER proceeded in lorries on detachment to STEENVOORDE. A Coy: did not go to work.	LWOD.
"	15th.		Coys: worked as per programme except A Coy: A Coy: less 2/LT Stickler's platoon proceeded on detachment to CAESTRE. Hutting party at TROIS ARBRES relieved by platoon of B Coy: under 2/LT Brook.	LWOD.
	16th.		B. C. & D Coys: worked as usual. 6/17114 Pte COOMBES wounded in action.	LWOD.
"	17th.		B. C. & D Coys: worked as usual. A Coy: on detachment.	LWOD.
"	18th.		B. C. & D Coys: worked as usual. A Coy: on detachment.	LWOD.

2353 Wt. W2544/1454 700,000 5/15 D. D. & L. A.D.S.S./Forms/C. 2118.

Instructions regarding War Diaries and Intelligence Summaries are contained in F. S. Regs., Part II. and the Staff Manual respectively. Title pages will be prepared in manuscript.

WAR DIARY
or
INTELLIGENCE SUMMARY.
(*Erase heading not required.*)

Army Form C. 2118.

Place	Date	Hour	Summary of Events and Information	Remarks and references to Appendices
OOSTHOVE FARM.	19th:		Coys: bathing. D Coy: N.Z. Pioneers arrived & billetted in huts vacated by A Coy:	LWD.
"	20th.		B.C. & D Coys: & D Coy: N.Z. Pioneers worked as per programme. 2/LT.S. J.H. DAVIES, W.F. WILLIAMS, & E.W.S. KITE reported for duty.	LWD
"	21st.		B & D Coys: & D Coy: N.Z. Pioneers worked as per programme.	LWD.
"	22nd.		Coys: worked as per programme. C Coy: proceeded to THIEUSHOUK & there billetted. C Coy: New Zealand Pioneers arrived at OOSTHOVE & occupied huts vacated by C Coy.	LWD.
"	23		Coys: worked as per programme.	
"	24.		Day spent preparing for move. French tramway detachment rejoined.	LWD.
"	25.		Bn: (less A & C Coys) proceeded by march route to CAESTRE - THIEUSHOUK area & there billetted. N.Z. Pioneers relieved the Bn.	LWD.

2353 Wt. W2544/1454 700,000 5/15 D. D. & L. A.D.S.S./Forms/C. 2118.

Instructions regarding War Diaries and Intelligence Summaries are contained in F. S. Regs., Part II. and the Staff Manual respectively. Title pages will be prepared in manuscript.

WAR DIARY
or
INTELLIGENCE SUMMARY.
(Erase heading not required.)

Army Form C. 2118.

Place	Date	Hour	Summary of Events and Information	Remarks and references to Appendices
THIEUSHOUK	26		Day spent cleaning up & settling down in billets. Working parties of A & C Coys working with R.E. on stables etc.	[illegible]
"	27.		Coys: trained under O's. C. Coys. Working parties of A & C Coys: working with R.E. on stables etc:	[illegible]
"	28		4 Officers + 100 men. B. [illegible] by motor lorry to SETQUES for work on R.F.A. [illegible] Lt Col Hewett returned from leave and took over command of Battn	[illegible]
	March			
"	1		St David's Day. observed as a holiday by permission of G.O.C. C.O. inspected billets, horse lines and [illegible]	[illegible]

2353 Wt. W2544/1454 700,000 5/15 D. D. & L. A.D.S.S./Forms/C. 2118.

CONFIDENTIAL.

To,

Headquarters, "A".

25th. Division.

Herewith War Diary for the Month of March 1917 for the Battalion under my Command.

1/4/17.

L W Deane Capt. Adjt.

for Lieut. Colonel,

Commdg:6th.(S).Bn.South Wales Borderers(Pnrs:).

Instructions regarding War Diaries and Intelligence Summaries are contained in F. S. Regs., Part II. and the Staff Manual respectively. Title Pages will be prepared in manuscript.

WAR DIARY
or
INTELLIGENCE SUMMARY
(Erase heading not required.)

Army Form C. 2118

6/S.W.B

Vol 19

Place	Date	Hour	Summary of Events and Information	Remarks and references to Appendices
THIEUSHOUK	March 2.		Btn: Route marched in morning. Football etc: in afternoon.	L.C.W.D.
"	3.		Coys: carried out training as per programme.	L.C.W.D.
"	4.		Coys. paraded for Divine Service. C.O. proceeded to 2nd. Army H.Q. on Course.	L.C.W.D.
"	5.		Coys. carried out training as per programme. 2/Lt. W. T. Davies & 25 other ranks D Coy: proceed to SETQUES by lorry for work at LUMBRES	L.C.W.D.
"	6.		Coys: carried out training as per programme. Football in afternoon.	L.C.W.D.
"	7.		Coys: route marched & trained as per programme. do do	L.C.W.D.
"	8.		Coys. trained as per programme. Heavy snow.	L.C.W.D.
"	9.		Coys. trained as per programme. C Coy: working with 106th Co. R.E.	L.C.W.D.
"	10		Lt & Adj. L C W Deane proceeded to England to report at the India Office. C.O returned from Course at 2nd Army H.Q. Coys trained as per programme in the morning. Football match Probables v. Possibles in the afternoon.	D.J.

195 5-M

1875 Wt. W593/826 1,000,000 4/15 J.B.C. & A. A.D.S.S./Forms/C. 2118.

Instructions regarding War Diaries and Intelligence Summaries are contained in F. S. Regs., Part II. and the Staff Manual respectively. Title Pages will be prepared in manuscript.

WAR DIARY
or
INTELLIGENCE SUMMARY
(Erase heading not required.)

Army Form C. 2118

Place	Date	Hour	Summary of Events and Information	Remarks and references to Appendices
THIEDSHOUK	11		Work as per programme.	
"	12		Work as per programme	
le NIEPPE	13		Batt^n proceeded by route march to le NIEPPE, parading 10 am arrived at billets 3 pm. distance marched 15 miles, Day fine & cool.	
			2nd Lieut Cox and 20 men proceeded to STEENVOORD for wood cutting	
"	14		Work as per programme.	
			2 Lieuts R. A. JORY and H. DAVIES reported for duty and were posted to D Co.	
"	15		Training as per programme.	
			B Co returned from building horse lines at LUMBRES, D. Co. HQ and 67 men relieved them this day	
"	16		Training as per programme	
"	17		Training as per programme. Night very dry & warm.	
			Batt^n practised the formation for moving in threes instead of fours.	
"	18		Church Parade	
"	19		Route March	

1875 Wt. W593/826 1,000,000 4/15 J.B.C. & A. A.D.S.S./Forms/C. 2118.

Instructions regarding War Diaries and Intelligence Summaries are contained in F. S. Regs., Part II. and the Staff Manual respectively. Title Pages will be prepared in manuscript.

Army Form C. 2118

WAR DIARY
or
INTELLIGENCE SUMMARY
(Erase heading not required.)

Place	Date	Hour	Summary of Events and Information	Remarks and references to Appendices
SWARTHENBROCK Area	20	10 am	Battn proceeded by route march to SWARTHENBROCK Area and there billeted (relieving the 5th Battn S.W.B. 25 Div). Billets very scattered. The last three hours of march in heavy rain & snow. Men marched well and showed great improvement due to their period of rest & training.	[illegible]
"	21		Cleaning up & training. Epidemic of Diphtheria in area so all estaminets out of bounds and every precaution taken against use of milk & butter obtained locally.	[illegible]
"	22		Training as per programme. Heavy snow squalls at intervals throughout the day.	[illegible]
NEUVE EGLISE	23	9 am	Battn marched to NEUVE EGLISE arriving 12 noon and were billeted in Convent, School and huts. Battn attached to the II ANZAC Div for work. Cloudy and cold.	[illegible]
"	24		Morning spent in cleaning billets, taken over in a most dirty condition, Work commenced at 2 pm. Bright sunny day but cold N.E. wind.	[illegible]
"	25		2 Cos widening the NEUVE EGLISE – WOLVERGHEM Road A + B. 1 Co (D) + 1 Platoon C. Support trenches R.E. Farm Southwards. 3 Platoons C.Co Transhipping road metal to A+B Cos by night.	[illegible]
"	26		As for 25th.	[illegible]

1875 Wt. W593/826 1,000,000 4/15 J.B.C. & A. A.D.S.S./Forms/C. 2118.

Instructions regarding War Diaries and Intelligence Summaries are contained in F. S. Regs., Part II. and the Staff Manual respectively. Title Pages will be prepared in manuscript.

WAR DIARY
or
INTELLIGENCE SUMMARY
(Erase heading not required.)

Army Form C. 2118

Place	Date	Hour	Summary of Events and Information	Remarks and references to Appendices
NEUVE EGLISE	27		A Co work on NEUVE EGLISE - WOLVERGHEM Road. C. Co 3 platoons loading road metal & dumping same for A Co by night. B Co ½ excavating trench for water main DE SOUTE Road ½ on support line with D Co. D Co digging support trenches from RE FARM to southward. (cold & foggy)	[illegible]
"	28		As for 27th but ½ B Co on trench south of WESTHOF Farm. (bright sunny day wind N. E)	[illegible]
"	29		Work as for 28th. 2nd Lt. JENKINS joined Batt and posted to A Co. (cold wet & foggy)	[illegible]
"	30		" " " 29th Captain REID-KELLET rejoined from III Army Training S[illegible] Wounded in Action No 6/42230 Pte SOMMERHAYES. A.	[illegible]
"	31		Work A Co Tunnelling with 171 T. Co RE. Support trenches in drain " B Co Pipe line for II Army. " C. Co Trenches support line. " D " Trenches support line. (Fine sunny day & warmer.)	[illegible]

1875 Wt. W593/826 1,000,000 4/15 J.B.C. & A. A.D.S.S./Forms/C. 2118.

Instructions regarding War Diaries and Intelligence Summaries are contained in F. S. Regs., Part II. and the Staff Manual respectively. Title Pages will be prepared in manuscript.

WAR DIARY
or
INTELLIGENCE SUMMARY
(Erase heading not required.)

Army Form C. 2118

6 SWB

Vol 20

Place	Date	Hour	Summary of Events and Information	Remarks and references to Appendices
NEUVE EGLISE	April 1st	1917	Work. A. Co Tunnelling. B " Draining, water pipe laying and building Ammunition Dump C. – Support Trenches Battn played 2 Bde 2 Div H.Q. New Zealanders at Rugby Football D – Support Trenches. Lost 5–0 in favour of New Zealanders. Good sporting game played very well	
"	2		As for 1st. Cold and strong W. wind. At 4.30 heavy snowstorm which continued into the night. 2nd Lieut SALTER joined the Battn and was posted to C. Co.	
"	3		Work as for 2nd. Cold, snow & rain. Weather cleared up during the afternoon	
"	4		Work as for 3rd. Milder, but cloudy with showers	
"	5		Work as for 4th. At 12 noon H.Q. and C & D Cos ordered to vacate NEUVE EGLISE. By 4 pm the Cos were encamped 1 mile N.W of Village and H.Q. established in Transport Lines 2 miles from village. II New Zealand Bde vacated area which was taken over by 75 Bde 25 Div British.	
"	6		Work as for 5th. Cold & wet day.	
"	7		Work as for 6th. Camp T.13 vacated and the 2 Cos billeted in WEITHOF Farm.	
"	8		Sunday. Fine bright day	
"	9		Work A Co Tunnelling (S.6) remainder doing [illegible] of night, B Trenching, C Roads. D Trenching Strong N.W wind. Showers of rain & sleet.	

1875 Wt. W593/826 1,000,000 4/15 J.B.C. & A. A.D.S.S./Forms/C. 2118.

205
3pp

Instructions regarding War Diaries and Intelligence Summaries are contained in F. S. Regs., Part II. and the Staff Manual respectively. Title Pages will be prepared in manuscript.

WAR DIARY
or
INTELLIGENCE SUMMARY
(Erase heading not required.)

Army Form C. 2118

Place	Date	Hour	Summary of Events and Information	Remarks and references to Appendices
NEUVE-EGLISE district ~~10~~	10		Work as for 9th. Heavy snow storm, strong N.W. gale	[illegible]
11.	11		A Co tunnelling and loading stores for road by night, B Co 2 platoons trenching, 1 platoon tunnelling, D trenching C roads	[illegible]
"	12		As for 11th. Strong N.W. gale with snow, intervals of sunshine Lieut. HOLYOAKE and 2nd Lieut LLOYD reported for duty with the Battn and are posted to A + B Cos respectively.	[illegible]
"	13		Work on trenches discontinued, B Co now working on [illegible] trench + C.T. from N. MIDLAND Farm. C Co on support trenches. 2 Lieuts KERLEY and PETTS reported for duty and are posted to C + D Coys respectively. Strong N W wind, sunny but cold.	[illegible]
"	14		Work as for 13th	[illegible]
"	15		As for 14th but B Co on new C.T. from N. MIDLAND Farm.	[illegible]
"	16		Work A Co all tunnelling, B. C.T. C trenches, D trenching.	[illegible]
"	17		As for 16th Strong N.W. gale and heavy rain C.R.E. called for an officer to assist 106 Co R.E. Lt STICKLER detailed for this duty C. Co moved from WEITHOF Farm to billets in NEUVE EGLISE.	
"	18		As for 17th cold & wet	[illegible]
"	19		As for 18. milder	[illegible]

1875 Wt. W593/826 1,000,000 4/15 J.B.C. & A. A.D.S.S./Forms/C. 2118.

Instructions regarding War Diaries and Intelligence Summaries are contained in F. S. Regs., Part II. and the Staff Manual respectively. Title Pages will be prepared in manuscript.

WAR DIARY
or
INTELLIGENCE SUMMARY
(Erase heading not required.)

Army Form C. 2118

Place	Date	Hour	Summary of Events and Information	Remarks and references to Appendices
NEUVE EGLISE Area.	20		Work as for 19th.	
"	21		Work as for 20th	
"	22		As for 21st. D. Co moved from WESTHOF Farm to ~~billets in NEUVE EGLISE~~ camp T. 12. d. 1. 7	
"	23		Baths, Interior economy and Infantry training. Fine sunny day with cold N. wind.	
"	24		Work as for 22nd. Fine sunny day warm.	
"	25		Work as for 24th but 1. N.C.O. & 10 men B Co revetting TEAL AVENUE	
"	26		Work as for 25th but 40 men B Co now working with A Co on Tunnelling (cloudy wind N.W.)	
"	27		Work as for 26th. cloudy, strong N.W wind.	
"	28		Work as for 27th. cloudy, bright intervals, N.W. wind milder. Lieut. H.M. CARPENDALE proceeded to join the 1st Battn. S.W.B. and 2nd Lieut. C. HOLYOAKE to the II Battn S.W.B.	
"	29		Work as for 28th. Hot sunny day. At 4 pm notice was received that the Battn and Division would move the following day. At 6 pm March Orders were received and all working parties recalled.	
SWARTENBRUCK	30	9 am	Battn paraded and marched to SWARTENBRUCK where it billeted. Hot day with bright sun.	

1875 Wt. W593/826 1,000,000 4/15 J.B.C. & A. A.D.S.S./Forms/C. 2118.

CONFIDENTIAL.

To,
Headquarters,
25th. Division "A".

Herewith War Diary of the Battalion under my Command for the Month of May 1917.

1/6/17.

[signature] Lieut.Colonel,
Commdg:6th.(S).Bn.S.W.Borderers (Pioneers).

Instructions regarding War Diaries and Intelligence Summaries are contained in F. S. Regs., Part II. and the Staff Manual respectively. Title Pages will be prepared in manuscript.

6/S.W.B.

WAR DIARY
or
INTELLIGENCE SUMMARY
(Erase heading not required.)

6 S W B
Vol 21

Army Form C. 2118

Place	Date	Hour	Summary of Events and Information	Remarks and references to Appendices
	May			
SWARTENBRUCK	1st		Platoon Drill, Fire control, Handling Arms, Formation for Wood fighting. Lecture (Hot bright day)	[illegible]
"	2nd		Fire Control, Handling Arms, Wood fighting. Lecture (")	[illegible]
"	3rd		As for 2nd (")	[illegible]
"	4th		As for 3rd. 2 Platoons B Co making Bombing Trench at Div School LE MOTTE (")	[illegible]
"	5		Wood fighting formation, bayonet fighting, Platoon Drill, fire control, (")	[illegible]
"	6.		Church Parade Non conformists 10 am C of E 11 am 195 M.G. Co attended (")	[illegible]
"	7		As for 5th C. Co Improvised bridging of Canal. (")	[illegible]
"	8.		As for 7th (hot day wind NE) (")	[illegible]
"	9.		A + C Cos Bridging, B Co Outpost Scheme, D. Div Bombing School. bright hot day.	[illegible]
"	10	9.30	Batt marched to NEUVE EGLISE Area, HQ returned to WATERLOO LINES, 4 Cos to hutments T.13 central. first march of 11 miles – no men fell out. cool breeze & fine.	[illegible]
"	11		Work. A Co ½ WOLVERGHAM Road ½ Bridge Trench, C ½ Nicholson Road ½ Bridge Trench B + D Cos on Trench Tramway	[illegible]
"	12		As for 11th (very hot muggy day)	[illegible]
"	13		A. ½ Trench Tramway, ½ Bridge Avenue, B + D Cos Trench Tramway, C. 1 Platoon Wiring, 1 Platoon unloading barges of [illegible] at ARMENTIERES, ½ C Nicholson Road. Lt STICKLER to assist 106 Field Co RE. (hot & thunder showers)	[illegible]
"	14		A Co Bridge Trench by night. B + D Trench Tramway, C Resting, all Batt Baths, (hot muggy day some showers)	[illegible]

21 S
4 [illegible]

1875 Wt. W593/826 1,000,000 4/15 J.B.C. & A. A.D.S.S./Forms/C. 2118.

Instructions regarding War Diaries and Intelligence Summaries are contained in F. S. Regs., Part II. and the Staff Manual respectively. Title Pages will be prepared in manuscript.

WAR DIARY
or
INTELLIGENCE SUMMARY
(Erase heading not required.)

Army Form C. 2118

Place	Date	Hour	Summary of Events and Information	Remarks and references to Appendices
NEUVE EGLISE Area	15		B & D Cos Front Line, A Co SNIPE Trench, C Co NICHOLSON Road Draft of 22 men joined Battn.	[initials]
"	16		Weather as for 15th (Cold wet day.	[initials]
"	17		Weather as for 16th Wounded in action No 6/17139 Pte HERN. D.J. Battn Capt. Major E. CASEY proceeded to 12 Battn Royal Fusiliers to take up appointment as Quartermaster	[initials]
"	18		B & D Cos Front Line, A Co ½ Snipe ½ Petit Pont Trench Line, C ½ Co Nicholson Road ½ [illegible] of Neuve Eglise [illegible]	[initials]
"	19		B & D Cos Front Line, ½ A Co T.T.s ½ NORTHUMBERLAND and DURHAM C.T.s by night C ½ NICHOLSON Road and ½ NEUVE EGLISE	[initials]
"	20		As for 19th (Hot & muggy day) Draft of 100 men arrived from 83 T.R.B.	[initials]
"	21		As for 20th (")	
"	22		As for 21st (Cool with rain at intervals N wind)	[initials]
"	23		As for 22nd but ½ Co A from T.T.s to building dugouts for Div H.Q. Bridge for Tanks over River DOUVRE (steel girders) and crossings over T.T.s commenced by parties of 10 men from A & C Cos (bright hot day)	[initials]
"	24		As for 23rd A. Co 1 Platoon on night work clearing the MESSINES Road. Draft of 27 men joined Battn. Bridge & crossings completed. (bright hot day)	[initials]

Instructions regarding War Diaries and Intelligence Summaries are contained in F. S. Regs., Part II. and the Staff Manual respectively. Title Pages will be prepared in manuscript.

Army Form C. 2118

WAR DIARY
or
INTELLIGENCE SUMMARY
(Erase heading not required.)

Place	Date	Hour	Summary of Events and Information	Remarks and references to Appendices
NEUVE EGLISE Area	25		As for 24th. Party of men (30) making Nissen huts completed 100 in 8 days (Bright hot day)	[illegible]
"	26		B & D Coys, A Coy 2 Platoons Div H.Q. Dugouts, 1 Platoon DURHAM AVENUE, 1. MESSINES Road, C. Coy 1 MESSINES Road, 3 Platoons DURHAM AVENUE Wounded in action No. 29240 Pte WATTS (Hot day)	[illegible]
"	27		B & D Coys, A Coy 1 Platoon MESSINES Road, 2 on H.Q Dugouts, 1 Platoon on road S.18.b.1, C Coy 2 Platoons T.T.s forward from FORT PINKIE, 1 on MEDECINE HAT TRAIL, 1 on MESSINES Road. Killed in action No 6/17042 Pte MAZZIE. A, Wounded in action Nos 6/17910 Pte MORLAND, 40090 Pte FORREST. A, (Very hot day)	[illegible]
"	28		As for 27th (")	
"	29.		A Coy. H.Q dugouts, B Coy T.T.s, C Coy ½ MESSINES Road by night (clearing the same) 1 Platoon new defensive road S.18.b.3.1. 1 Platoon T.T.s Batt moved into bivouacs at T.S.d. Wounded in action Nos 42283 Pte WRIGHT, 6/41260 Pte ALDERS, 30213 Pte HOWARTH, 40171 Pte JONES 201345 Pte ROBINSON, 40928 Pte STRANACH, 40929 Pte SKELTON. 41052 Pte ELLIOT, Casualties caused by explosion of ammunition dump which blew up as the ½ Coy was returning from work, Capt. OWEN and 2nd Lieut SALTER blown [illegible]	[illegible]
"	30		Work as for 29th but ½ Coy (C) were by my orders switched off to repair crater caused by explosion, the T.T. line is running across by 1 pm. This ½ Coy did excellent work in rapidly filling crater (some 50 yds long) and relaying the line of T.T. No 6/41260 Pte ALDERS died of wounds received on the 29th.	[illegible]
"	31		Work as for 29th.	[illegible]

1875 Wt. W593/826 1,000,000 4/15 J.B.C. & A. A.D.S.S./Forms/C. 2118.

CONFIDENTIAL

To H.Q.
25th: Div: A.

Herewith war diary for this Btn: for month of June 1917.

L.W. [illegible] Capt.
Adjt:
for O.C. 6th S.W.B.
(Pioneers)

30/6/17

*Instructions regarding War Diaries and Intelligence Summaries are contained in F. S. Regs., Part II. and the Staff Manual respectively. Title Pages will be prepared in manuscript.

WAR DIARY
or
INTELLIGENCE SUMMARY

(Erase heading not required.)

Army Form C. 2118

Vol 22

6th: S.W.B. (Pioneers)

Place	Date JUNE	Hour	Summary of Events and Information	Remarks and references to Appendices
NEUVE EGLISE Area	1.		A Co. Div H.Q. dugouts, B & D Field Train, C Co. DURHAM, AVENUE, NICHOLSONS Road and new Infantry road. S. 18. b.	[illegible]
"	2		A Co. on SNIPE, TEAL and SPRING AVENUES CT's, C. Co. on NORTHUMBERLAND & DURHAM CT's, B & D Field Train, at 2.45 pm Div barrage of German line. Party of C. Co. clearing MESSINES ROAD and placing artillery bridges by night. Wounded in action Nos 39548 Pte JONES, 6/17001 Pte CURTIS.	[illegible]
"	3		As for 2nd. C. Co. a platoon on NICHOLSON Road. Heavy bombardment of German front at 11 am and 3 pm. A considerable amount of damage done to our C.T's especially SNIPE.	[illegible]
"	4		B & D Train A Co. SNIPE-TOAD C.T's indeed Snipe heavily shelled & damaged. C. DURHAM, FROG & NORTHUMBERLAND C.T's. Wounded in action 40115 Pte LAYMAN, 29141 Pte JONES, 42277 Pte HAWKETTS, 20134 Pte ROBINSON 40935 Pte THYNNE, 39267 Pte BYARD, Intermittent shelling of roads by billets, usual bombardment of German lines	[illegible]
"	5		Work as for 4th Wounded in action 40913 Pte PAGE, 17619 Sgt PARKER, 39152 Pte PARTINGTON 39150 Pte DUNTHORN, 16519 Pte MULLINS, 39312 Pte RENNET. Bombardment of German line by Army. Billets shelled several times during the 24 hours. Wounded in action Captain KELLETT.	[illegible]

22.5
7¼

1875 Wt. W593/826 1,000,000 4/15 J.B.C. & A. A.D.S.S./Forms/C. 2118.

* Instructions regarding War Diaries and Intelligence Summaries are contained in F. S. Regs., Part II. and the Staff Manual respectively. Title Pages will be prepared in manuscript.

WAR DIARY
or
INTELLIGENCE SUMMARY
(Erase heading not required.)

Army Form C. 2118

Place	Date	Hour	Summary of Events and Information	Remarks and references to Appendices
NEUVE EGLISE AREA	6		A & C resting B & D ½ Coy in Line. Killed in action No 40096 Pte FIELD, 42322 Pte GALLAGHER, 39474 Pte COX, Died of Wounds 41044 L/Cpl FOSTER, 19850 Pte DAVIES. Wounded in action 42298 Pte CRAVEN, 36457 Pte KELLY, 40178 Pte OWEN, 41061 Pte POTTER 40852 L/Cpl SMITH, 17115 L/Cpl PIERSON, 42393 Pte EGERTON; 17488 Pte RYAN. 20159 Pte EVANS, 17284, Sgt LEWIS, 28999 Pte DAVIES, 26050 Pte WILDE, 39199 Pte RYDER, 40893 Pte HAYKIN, 39206 Pte HARBURN, 40103 Pte HEWITT 40860 Pte CLARK. Divisions shelled at intervals, Army bombardment of German lines.	[initials]
"	7		II Army Advance, successful capture of portion of the MESSINES - WYTSCHAETE Ridge allotted to 25 Division. Batt took up advance position in the WOLVERGHEM Switch by 1 am and at 1 hour and 1½ hours respectively after Zero (3.10 am) were in position to commence work, A & C Coy clearing MESSINES Road B & D Coy extending TT into German line. C Coy specially distinguished itself by carrying on work under very trying conditions. Awarded M.C. Birthday Honours gazette 3rd June Captain OWEN. Wounded in Action 2 Lieuts KITE and ROBERTS. No 29517 Pte FRANKLIN, 16908 Sgt KING, 16588 Pte REES, 17241 Pte HEYES, 40934, Pte TODD, 16385 Pte CORCORAN, 29105 Pte MORRISON, 1758 Sgt WILKINSON, 40152 Pte JONES. Captain CALDWELL reported for duty with B Coy 5/6/17 and is posted to A Coy	[initials]
"	8		A & C Coy clearing MESSINES Road, heavily shelled at times, B + D pushing forward T.T. line to MESSINES Ridge. Good head made to STEENBECKE River by 5 pm. Died of Wounds No 39199 Pte RIDER, 40109 Pte JONES.	[initials]

1875 Wt. W593/826 1,000,000 4/15 J.B.C. & A. A.D.S.S./Forms/C. 2118.

Instructions regarding War Diaries and Intelligence Summaries are contained in F. S. Regs., Part II. and the Staff Manual respectively. Title Pages will be prepared in manuscript.

WAR DIARY
or
INTELLIGENCE SUMMARY
(Erase heading not required.)

Army Form C. 2118

Place	Date	Hour	Summary of Events and Information	Remarks and references to Appendices
NEUVE EGLISE Area	8		Wounded in action No 16401 Sergt. GOODMAN, 17107 Sergt WILLIAMS, 17062 Pte DAVIES, 11796 Pte DREWITT, 17097 Pte HENRY, 17067 Pte RICHARDS, 23449 Pte COX 17455 Corpl JONES, 29280 Pte ROTHWELL, 42263 Pte KNIGHT, 40856 Pte ANDERSON 40864 Pte CHIPMAN, 16406 Pte REAL, 41052 Pte ELLIOTT, 42241 Pte WELLS Cooler day, slight rain during the night. 2nd Lieut JACOBS to Field Ambulance with [illegible].	[illegible]
"	9		The whole Battn concentrated on finishing [illegible] work of the TT to the MESSINES-WYTSCHAETE Road. By 5pm road open to traffic as far as the STEENBEEK River. Wounded in action 2nd Lieuts HANNA and HILL, No 17007 Pte DAVIES, 200917 Pte WILLIAMS, 200106 Pte WEAVER, 201682 Pte SAUNDERS, 40085 Pte BROOKES, 17369 Pte WILLIAMS, 42297 Pte LUTON. Died of wounds 40864 Pte CHIPMAN, 36457 Pte KELLY	[illegible]
"	10		Whole Battn on T.T. to MESSINES-WYTSCHAETE Road which should be completed by tomorrow evening. Heavily shelled all day while at work. Killed in action No 6/16790 L/Corpl WHITE, Wounded in action 2nd Lieut PIERCE, No 40947 Pte YOUNG, 17195 Pte DAVIES, 29281 Pte HUGHES, 29254 Pte DUNN, 16970 Pte CARTER. 40948 Pte GUNN (Shock) Died of wounds 200917 Pte WILLIAMS.	[illegible]
"	11		Work on TT, quiet day & cooler, some showers ½ Battn resting, the other half completing TT. Killed in action No 19049 Pte GUY, 40093 Pte EDWARDS,	[illegible]
"	12		Wounded in action 40878 Pte FREEMAN, 42258 Pte WALKER, 42057 Pte HILL, 42267 Pte HARPER Cool day & some rain – heavy thunder storm during the afternoon.	[illegible]

Instructions regarding War Diaries and Intelligence Summaries are contained in F. S. Regs., Part II. and the Staff Manual respectively. Title Pages will be prepared in manuscript.

WAR DIARY
or
INTELLIGENCE SUMMARY
(Erase heading not required.)

Army Form C. 2118

Place	Date June	Hour	Summary of Events and Information	Remarks and references to Appendices
NEUVE EGLISE Area	13		All Batt on T. Trench.	[initials]
	14		Night of 14-15. 3 Cos on forward C.T.s, 1 Co on T. Trench	[initials]
"	15		2 Cos on T. Trench, 2 constructing forward C.Ts.	
"			Killed in action, No 16346 Pte FLETCHER, 40137 Pte DANCEY, 17281 Pte LINDSAY,	
			Wounded in action Major G.A. RENWICK, No 16955 Sgt FOULKES, 16400 Sgt GOODMAN,	
			42234 L/Cpl LIDDINGTON, 41043 L/Cpl SMITH, 39267 Pte BYARD, 29376 Pte BAINES,	
			39264, Pte CRIMMINGS, 39246 Pte DAVIES, 16435 Pte BEAL, 40896 Pte KENNEDY,	
			40159 Pte GIDMAN, 40116 Pte MORGAN, 40142 Pte SOUTHERN, 40913 Pte PACE	[initials]
			(very hot day)	
"	16		2 Cos on C.T.s night 15-16, 2 Cos Front Trench.	
"	17		One Co (C) from T.T. to duty on C.Ts with A & B for night 17-18.	
			Wounded in action 2nd Lieut L. PETTS. (Stifling hot day, thunder clouds.	[initials]
"	18		Work as for 17th.	
			Killed in action Nos 17143 Pte HADLEY, 35169 Pte LUTTRELL.	
			Wounded in action Nos 42305 Pte ASPINALL, 40108 Pte JOHNSON, 17169 Sgt WHITEHOUSE	
			16291 Pte FRENCH, 41051 Pte ILLIDGE. (Hot day thunder storm during afternoon)	[initials]

1875 Wt. W593/826 1,000,000 4/15 J.B.C. & A. A.D.S.S./Forms/C. 2118.

Instructions regarding War Diaries and Intelligence Summaries are contained in F. S. Regs., Part II. and the Staff Manual respectively. Title Pages will be prepared in manuscript.

WAR DIARY
or
INTELLIGENCE SUMMARY
(Erase heading not required.)

Army Form C. 2118

Place	Date	Hour	Summary of Events and Information	Remarks and references to Appendices
NEUVE EGLISE Area	19		Weather as for 15th. Thunder squalls during the day	[illegible]
			Killed in action Sgt AINSWORTH, Wounded in action 6/17153 Pte WILLIAMS 6/16386 Pte GRIFFITHS.	
"	20		Weather as for 19th	[illegible]
"	21		Weather as for 20th Showers during the day.	[illegible]
"	22.		Coys: did not work. French tramway personnel was relieved & rejoined the Btn: C.O. proceeded on leave to England. Capt: Kellett took over temporary command of the Btn:	LWO
"	23.		Coys. resting	LWO
"	24		Coy. resting.	LWO
WIPPENHOEK	25		Btn: paraded at 9 A.M. & proceeded to WIPPENHOEK area for work with C.E.	
			II NO. Coys. Quartered in huts & under canvas	LWO
"	26		Coys resting.	LWO
"	27		Coys. resting.	LWO
OUDERDOM	28		Btn: proceeded to DOWNSHIRE CAMP, OUDERDOM. A coy: on detachment 1½ miles N. of DICKEBUSCH	LWO

1875 Wt. W593/826 1,000,000 4/15 J.B.C. & A. A.D.S.S./Forms/C. 2118.

Instructions regarding War Diaries and Intelligence Summaries are contained in F. S. Regs., Part II. and the Staff Manual respectively. Title Pages will be prepared in manuscript.

WAR DIARY
or
INTELLIGENCE SUMMARY
(Erase heading not required.)

Army Form C. 2118

Place	Date	Hour	Summary of Events and Information	Remarks and references to Appendices
OUDERDOM	29		Coy: commenced work on corduroy roads, running from KRUISTRAAT – N of ZILLEBEKE LAKE.	LWD
"	30.		Coy: working on above roads.	LWD.

1875 Wt. W593/826 1,000,000 4/15 J.B.C. & A. A.D.S.S./Forms/C. 2118.

Instructions regarding War Diaries and Intelligence Summaries are contained in F. S. Regs., Part II. and the Staff Manual respectively. Title Pages will be prepared in manuscript.

Div Troops 25 Div

WAR DIARY
or
INTELLIGENCE SUMMARY
(Erase heading not required.)

6 SWB
Vol 23

Army Form C. 2118

Place	Date	Hour	Summary of Events and Information	Remarks and references to Appendices
	JULY.	1917		
OUDERDOM.	1		Coys: all worked on KRUISTRAAT — ZILLEBEKE corduroy roads. Wounded in action 201747 Pte: GRAY, 40159 Pte: MORRIS 6/42273 Pte HOLDER. Capt: R.M. Cox awarded Military Cross.	L.G.W.S.
"	2.		Coys. continued work on KRUISTRAAT — ZILLEBERE roads. Wounded in action 6/42286 Pte: NEATE, 40883 PTE. HALL, 40157 Pte. MATTHEWS, 25279 PTE. WALL, 29506 PTE. JANES Vicinity of camp was shelled at intervals throughout the day.	L.G.W.S.
"	3		Work as for 2nd Wounded in action No 16470 Sgt CHATTINGTON, 29006 Pte WILLIAMS, 25570 Pte WALTERS, 39197 Pte FOSTER.	[illegible]
"	4		Work as for 3rd. Killed in action, Nos 40854 Pte ARMSTRONG, 29702 Pte BANWELL, 16852 Pte DART 40914 Pte PAULIN, 39219 Pte RING, 39217 Pte VINEY. Died of Wounds 40876 Pte FARTHING, 25679 Pte WALL. Wounded in action C.S.M. BROOKE, 400094 Pte FRY, 29061 Pte SMITH, 29246 Pte CHESWORTH, 10822 Cpl CRANE, 40876 Pte FARTHING, 17208 Pte NEAL, 39243 Pte MOORCROFT, 39252 Pte RIMMER, 40922 Pte STOREY, 39244 Pte YOULD.	[illegible]
	5		Work as for 4th. ~~[illegible]~~ Captain MUMFORD reported for duty, and draft of 51 other ranks	[illegible]

23S
5/[illegible]

1875 Wt. W593/826 1,000,000 4/15 J.B.C. & A. A.D.S.S./Forms/C. 2118.

Instructions regarding War Diaries and Intelligence Summaries are contained in F. S. Regs., Part II. and the Staff Manual respectively. Title Pages will be prepared in manuscript.

WAR DIARY
or
INTELLIGENCE SUMMARY
(Erase heading not required.)

Army Form C. 2118

Place	Date	Hour	Summary of Events and Information	Remarks and references to Appendices
OUDERDOM	6		Work as for 5th Killed in action 40903 Pte MURPHY, Wounded in action 42236 Pte RICHES 42301 Pte VOSE, 39203 Pte WHIPP. Draft of 47 other ranks reported for duty.	[illegible]
"	7		Work as for 6th, but concentrated on WARRINGTON & DERBY Roads (Corduroy) the whole work & getting up of material being handed over to the Bde.	[illegible]
"	8		Work as for 7th cool day with rain	[illegible]
"	9		Work as for 8th cool with rain. Camp shelled at 9 am	[illegible]
"	10		Work as for 9th Fine & cool.	[illegible]
"	11		Work as for 10th an exceptionally good nights work, 1974 bundles of timber got up & laid, and for first night work was undisturbed by shell fire. Draft of 39 other ranks arrived.	[illegible]
"	12		Work as for 11th Camp shelled & transport lines bombed by aeroplane during night. 7 other ranks reported for duty, Wounded in action No 16961 Pte PRICE, 42293 Pte GREEN, 201599 Pte EVANS, 29210 Pte BRIDGES, 17101 Pte NICHOL, 201586 Pte DAVIS, 44140 Pte GRIFFITHS, One horse killed one wounded.	[illegible]

1875 Wt. W593/826 1,000,000 4/15 J.B.C. & A. A.D.S.S./Forms/C. 2118.

Instructions regarding War Diaries and Intelligence Summaries are contained in F. S. Regs., Part II. and the Staff Manual respectively. Title Pages will be prepared in manuscript.

WAR DIARY
or
INTELLIGENCE SUMMARY
(Erase heading not required.)

Army Form C. 2118

Place	Date	Hour	Summary of Events and Information	Remarks and references to Appendices
OUDERDOM	13		Weather as for 12th. Wounded in action Nos 39222 Pte CONNETT, 40713 Pte SHAW, 40931 Pte THOMPSON, 17317 Pte WALTERS. Wounded gas shell Nos 13450 Pte ARCHER, 39196 Pte CRAWFORD, 40866 Pte CLARK, 40949 Pte CLARK, 40141 Pte DAVIES, 16911 Pte FRANCIS, 40055 Pte GREEN, 40887 Pte HARDING, 40854 Pte HOLMES, 19681 Pte McGOWAN, 29404 Pte O'BRIEN, 29634 Pte REES, 19233 Pte TAYLOR, 39262 Pte THOMAS, 40939 Pte WHITMORE, 39209 Pte WARNER. Weather cool with showers. A Co moved to PROVEN Area for instruction in Light Railway Construction.	[initials]
"	14		Weather as for 13th. Wounded accidentally No 40721 Pte VOWLES. Thunder Storm and rain, very close & hot — Camp shelled.	[initials]
"	15		Weather as for 14th. PIONEER DUMP (Ammunition) blew up 2.30 am, Roads very congested with transport all of which stampeded so little material was got up to working parties. Heavy Thunderstorms and rain during the night. Day cool & cloudy. Killed in action No 19683 Pte DARK, Wounded in action 2nd Lieut. J.H. DAVIES. Nos 10919 Pte RAYNER, 29553 Pte EVANS, 40908 Pte MENDALL, 42215 Pte WALSH, Wounded gas shell Nos 19202 Pte BINNS, 29463 Pte EVANS, 40163 Pte MATHER, 40911 Pte NIXON, 29199 Pte OWEN.	[initials]

1875 Wt. W593/826 1,000,000 4/15 J.B.C. & A. A.D.S.S./Forms/C. 2118.

Instructions regarding War Diaries and Intelligence Summaries are contained in F. S. Regs., Part II. and the Staff Manual respectively. Title Pages will be prepared in manuscript.

WAR DIARY
or
INTELLIGENCE SUMMARY
(Erase heading not required.)

Army Form C. 2118

Place	Date	Hour	Summary of Events and Information	Remarks and references to Appendices
OUDERDOM	16		Work as for 15th. Working parties heavily shelled & WARRINGTON Road much damaged	[illegible]
"	17		Work as for 16th. Hot day Thunder storm	[illegible]
"	18		Work as for 17th. All baths completed. 1 Section C. Coy under 2/Lt HANNA cleared REGENT Street Rest C.T. Wet day.	[illegible]
"	19		Work extension of WARRINGTON ROAD and repair of same and DERBY Road. Camp shelled during the night, Working Party heavily shelled. Killed in action Nos 40875 Pte ELLIS, 26375 Pte PUDNER, 227535 Pte JONES. Wounded in action Nos 14539 C.S.M. DORAN, 39565 Pte DAVIES, 40884 Pte HADDON, 40896 Pte HUDSON, 40836 Pte HORTON, 17053 Pte JONES, 39185 Pte WILCOX, 229462 Pte WARMAN, 227447 Pte PHILLIPS.	
"	20		Work as for 19th. First quiet night from shell fire.	[illegible]
STEENVOORDE Area	[illegible]	12.30 am	Batt paraded and marched via RENINGHEIST – ABEELE – STEENVOORDE to 3 miles on OUDERZEELE Road where it camped in a field N of Road.	[illegible]
"	21		Batt rested. Kit inspection. Light hazy day.	[illegible]
"	22		Batt rested washing & cleaning kit	[illegible]
"	23		Batt rested Lewis respiration Drill	[illegible]

1875 Wt. W593/826 1,000,000 4/15 J.B.C. & A. A.D.S.S./Forms/C. 2118.

Army Form C. 2118

WAR DIARY
or
INTELLIGENCE SUMMARY
(Erase heading not required.)

Instructions regarding War Diaries and Intelligence Summaries are contained in F. S. Regs., Part II. and the Staff Manual respectively. Title Pages will be prepared in manuscript.

Place	Date	Hour	Summary of Events and Information	Remarks and references to Appendices
STEENVOORDE [illegible]	24		Batt resting, cleaning equipment and Platoon & Company Drill, Lewis gun [illegible]	[illegible]
"	25		Batt resting, Route March [illegible] Day.	[illegible]
"	26		Batt resting Route March, Platoon & Company Drill [illegible] drill	
"	27		do. do. do.	[illegible]
"	28		do. do. do.	[illegible]
OUDERDOM	29		Btn: proceeded by march to HALIFAX CAMP, OUDERDOM	[illegible]
"	30		Btn. moved to H.24. central to await orders for work as soon as possible after zero on 31st.	[illegible]
BELGIAN CHATEAU	31.		Commenced work at 11 A.M & delivered road material on HOOGE Road. Casualties:- 2/Lt. Jury wounded. O.R's wounded:- 3/11932 Sgt. Hallury 6/16948 L/cpl: Coyle. 2/9693 Pte. Burton. 3/29422 Pte. Jones. 6/17620 Pte. Jennings 6/17593 Pte. Roberts 6/17030 Pte. Jeffry. 39232 Pte Thomas. 4/17171 Pte Tyrrell 3/19949 Pte. Ward 6/42241 Pte Wells 6/17530 Pte. Richards 41042 L/cpl: Hale	[illegible]

1875 Wt. W593/826 1,000,000 4/15 J.B.C. & A. A.D.S.S./Forms/C. 2118.

CONFIDENTIAL

25th: Div: A

Herewith War Diary for this Bn. for month of August 1917

L.A.W. Deane Capt.
Adjt:
f LT. COLONEL
COMMANDING 6th (SER.) Bn. S.W. BORDERERS

6th (S) BATTALION,
SOUTH WALES
BORDERERS (PIONEERS)
No. 148
Date 31:8:17

Instructions regarding War Diaries and Intelligence Summaries are contained in F. S. Regs., Part II. and the Staff Manual respectively. Title Pages will be prepared in manuscript.

WAR DIARY
or
INTELLIGENCE SUMMARY
(Erase heading not required.)

6th (S) BATTALION, SOUTH WALES BORDERERS (PIONEERS)
No. ....
Date ....

Vol 24

Army Form C. 2118

Place	Date	Hour	Summary of Events and Information	Remarks and references to Appendices
BELGIAN CHATEAU	August 1.		Shifted Camp from H. 24 central to site 200 S of BELGIAN CHATEAU.	
"	2		Night 1st-2nd Coy worked on SUPPORT line for 7th Bde and a C T for 75th Bde. Heavy rain and enemy fire harassing. Killed in action No 3/16419 Pte ANDREWS, wounded in action Nos 228993 Pte TREW, 29083 Pte SEARY	
"	3		Night 2nd-3rd Work as for 1st-2nd, weather conditions terrible, heavy rain and mud thigh deep, and the old German trenches serious obstacles to movement. Working parties held up by barrage, ~~within~~ for 2 hours three attempts were made to get through but without success. 2nd Lieut S.N. HILLIER reported for duty with the Battn. C. Co worked by day on IGUANA C.T. for 75th Bde and cleared 300 yds of same. Killed in action No 41045 Pte DELVES, wounded in action Nos 16803 Cpl TAYLOR, 42330 Pte WARBURTON, 19057 Pte ROGERS, 40874 Pte CROSS, 227344 Pte CLEEVELY, 39666 Pte PARRY, 40079 Pte BIRCHENOUGH, 40731 Pte WILLIAMS, 40653 Pte JONES, 201693 Pte EVANS, 17250 Sgt ELVIN, 18364 Pte DOWLING.	
"	4		Work as for night 2-3 but carried out by day. No interference by enemy who confined his fire to back area. Our medium artillery were firing short their shell bursting behind our front line – this continued in spite of signals from the front line. At noon five German planes flew up & down our line of trench, the lower but a few hundred feet high which fired his M.G. at the working parties. In response to signals from these planes a heavy barrage was opened on our line and the trench back and the Coy had to be withdrawn.	

24S.
644

1875 Wt. W593/826 1,000,000 4/15 J.B.C. & A. A.D.S.S./Forms/C. 2118.

Instructions regarding War Diaries and Intelligence Summaries are contained in F. S. Regs., Part II. and the Staff Manual respectively. Title Pages will be prepared in manuscript.

WAR DIARY or INTELLIGENCE SUMMARY

(Erase heading not required.)

Army Form C. 2118

Place	Date	Hour	Summary of Events and Information	Remarks and references to Appendices
BELGIAN Chateau	4		Killed in action 2nd Lieut KENT, No 16329 Sergt WILLIAMS, 45254 Pte COLES, 29699 Pte HOLLWORTH. Wounded in action No 16491 Pte LAWSON, 200947 Pte GIBBON, 40708 Pte SOUTHWELL, 39674 Pte PARR, 39273 Pte STAFFORD, 40885 Pte HEPPLE, 40881 Pte GANNON, 39261 Pte DRINKWATER. 2nd Lieut PETTS with 2 Lewis guns to neighbourhood of ZILLEBEKE LAKE on detachment. Major REID-KELLETT awarded the M.C.	[initials]
"	5		Work. B Co constructing gun pits and shelters by ZILLEBEKE LAKE, C Co on trench at BIRR cross roads, D Co on plank road at GORDON HOUSE. Thick fog early morning clearing to bright hot day. Heavy bombardment by our guns commenced 9.45 pm & continued all night.	[initials]
"	6		Work as for 5th. Wounded in action No 17359 Cpl WALKER, 200907 Pte EDWARDS, 29679 Pte BUCKLEY. Foggy day with rain.	[initials]
"	7		Work as for 6th. Wounded in action No 17415 Pte JONES, 16384 Pte MAIN. Lieut JENKINS awarded the M.C.	
"	8		Work as for 7th. Wounded in action 2nd Lieut HANNA, Nos 40159 Pte ROBERTS, 45285 Pte CROFT, 42276 Pte WOLLER, 40889 Pte HUGHES. Killed in action No 42251 Pte VIMPANY. Foggy & wet, fine intervals. Heavy thunderstorm at 8.30 pm	[initials]
"	9		Work. Forward trenches, gun shelters and Brigade Control Post cover. Died of wounds on 6th No 29679 Pte BUCKLEY. Wounded in action No 42214 Pte MYERS, 8371 Cpl STEVENS, 42118 Pte CARTER, 41082 Pte NEAT, 42333 Pte EDGERTON, Self inflicted wound 41054 Pte TOWNLEY.	Fine day camp shelled [initials]

1875 Wt. W593/826 1,000,000 4/15 J.B.C. & A. A.D.S.S./Forms/C. 2118.

Instructions regarding War Diaries and Intelligence Summaries are contained in F. S. Regs., Part II. and the Staff Manual respectively. Title Pages will be prepared in manuscript.

WAR DIARY
or
INTELLIGENCE SUMMARY
(Erase heading not required.)

Army Form C. 2118

6th (S) BATTALION, SOUTH WALES BORDERERS (PIONEERS)
No.......... Date..........

Place	Date	Hour	Summary of Events and Information	Remarks and references to Appendices
BELGIAN CHATEAU	10th		Work, B Co continuing C.T. South of WESTHOEK on capture of same at 5 am, The work was completed under heavy fire the Company losing its C.O. and 17 men.	
			C. Co continuing shelters for Road Control Posts (3) and at 2 pm went forward to extend C.T. dug by B Co.	
			D Co Tile road GORDON HOUSE to MENIN Road. for some time 10.15 – 11 heavy shelling, delayed supply & bringing tiles but road was completed by 11.15 am.	
			Wounded in action Major H. CRAWFORD, No 25921 Pt LIPYARD, 41085 Pt OWEN, 41054 Pt POOL, 41091 Pt ROBERTS, 41092 Pt ROBERTS, 41090 Pt ROBERTS, 16661 Pt WHITCOMBE, 17100 Pt THOMAS, 29241 Pt HARRIS, 17476 Pt FRAYNE, 41071 Pt JONES, 14531 Pt RICHARDS, 19138 Cpl SANKEY, 29240 Pt WATT, 17443 Pt PARRY, 40909 Pt McCLUSKY, 39161 Pt MORGAN, 40123 Pt ROBERTS, 20165 Pt HUGH, 20066 Pt SHEAN. 41095 Pt WORTHINGTON, 40114 Pt LEE.	
"	11		Coy detailed for extending CT held up by barrage and were unable to reach their Task.	
			Major CRAWFORD died of wounds 10th inst. Killed in action 16505 Cpl. FOULKES, 17258 Pt COOMBES	
			Wounded in action 29566 Pt CHARLES, 40118 Pt OLIVER, 42323 Pt REID, 42043 Pt CUNNINGHAM, 40155 Pt HALES. (Foggy and rain)	
"	12		Work. EGG Road repaired throughout and three Road Control Posts built.	
			Wounded in action 40135 Pt MORRIS. Fine day but thunderstorm at 6 pm.	
			Wounded in action No 40582 Pt HEAD	
DEVONSHIRE Camp	13		Batt withdrawn for rest. Paraded 10 am and marched to DEVONSHIRE Camp (OUDERDOM area)	
			Camp in most dirty condition especially the Cook House. Thunderstorm + rain after noon	
"	14		Men resting. Cleaning up camp. Kit inspection. Rain all night.	
	15		Batt bathing	
			Cold + wet day	

1875 Wt. W593/826 1,000,000 4/15 J.B.C. & A. A.D.S.S./Forms/C. 2118.

Instructions regarding War Diaries and Intelligence Summaries are contained in F. S. Regs., Part II. and the Staff Manual respectively. Title Pages will be prepared in manuscript.

WAR DIARY
or
INTELLIGENCE SUMMARY
(Erase heading not required.)

[illegible] BATTALION, SOUTH WALES BORDERERS (PIONEERS)
No.
Date

Army Form C. 2118

Place	Date	Hour	Summary of Events and Information	Remarks and references to Appendices
DEVONSHIRE Camp	16		Work 1½ hrs on road II.H.Q. to REMINGHURST, 1½ hrs Drill & Handling Arms. Died of wounds No 6/17117 Pte WIGMORE.	[illegible]
EECKE Area	17	7am	Battn marched to EECKE Area and went into standing Camp. Fine cool day	[illegible]
"	18		Cleaning up.	[illegible]
"	19		Church Parade. Dismissed. Band played to Battn from 3-6 pm	[illegible]
OUDEZEELE	20	8am	Battn marched to OUDEZEELE and then H.Q. & C Coy billeted, B & D Coy half billeted ½ tents. Battn scattered over an area a mile in length. Fine light day.	[illegible]
"	21		Company & Platoon Drill, handling arms. Wounded in action No 16916 Pte LANE	[illegible]
BELGIAN CHATEAU Area	22	5.45	Battn marched to STEENVOORDE and then embussed for BELGIAN CHATEAU Area where it bivouaced & officers in huts. Transport moved independently.	[illegible]
PIONEER Camp	23		Work – new road (timber) running East from CAMBRIDGE ROAD from a point 100 yds South of RAILWAY WOOD. Found a mass of old shell holes and trenches. Work in full view of enemy from his line POLYGONEVELD – ANZAC. intermittent shelling.	[illegible]
"	24		Work on new road, now named the BELLEWAARDE Road – very heavy work owing to nature of soil. Some showers	[illegible]
"	25		Work as for 24th. At 8 am fairly heavy shelling of work for 20 minutes, advanced work in view of enemy [illegible] parties of 2 or 3 at little intervals. (Cold. Some showers) Distinguished Conduct Medal awarded 6/17476 Pte FRAYNE, Bar to Military Medal 6/17427 L/Cpl QUINTON.	[illegible]

1875 Wt. W593/826 1,000,000 4/15 J.B.C. & A. A.D.S.S./Forms/C. 2118.

WAR DIARY
or
[I]NTELLIGENCE SUMMARY
(Erase heading not required.)

Army Form C. 2118

Summary of Events and Information	Remarks and references to Appendices
AADE Road, good progress made in spite of continuous shelling. (Dry cool rain by evening)	
42279 Pte HICKS, 225479 Pte BREAKEY, Wounded in action 16546 L/Cpl BROWN,	
[illegible], 40550 Cpl RANDALL, 19697 Sgt ASHMAN, 42251 Pte PERKINS,	
[illegible]ON, 40691 Pte JONES, 40692 Pte JONES, 29780 Pte ROBERTS, 40560 Pte BREMS,	
Several transport animals killed & wounded bringing up timber	[initials]
(Cold with heavy rain)	[initials]
(Cold wet & stormy)	[initials]
Heavily shelled at times, wounded in action No 42289 Pte REACHES,	
[illegible]N, 201559 Pte EVANS, 29007 Pte CERIEZ, 40862 Pte BECKETT	
[illegible], (Cold & wet)	[initials]
[illegible] concentrated their shelling on road, which practically checked work being carried out.	
[illegible] me to discontinue work on the road, and instead to concentrate on CAMBRIDGE ROAD	
[w]ounded in action No 200947 Pte GIBBON, 39919 Pte JONES, 40734 Pte ROBERTS.	[initials]
[RO]AD successfully carried out, good progress being made there being but little shell fire this day	
[illegible] Pte McCLOSKEY (Fine but warmer some showers)	[initials]

D.S.S./Forms/C. 2118.

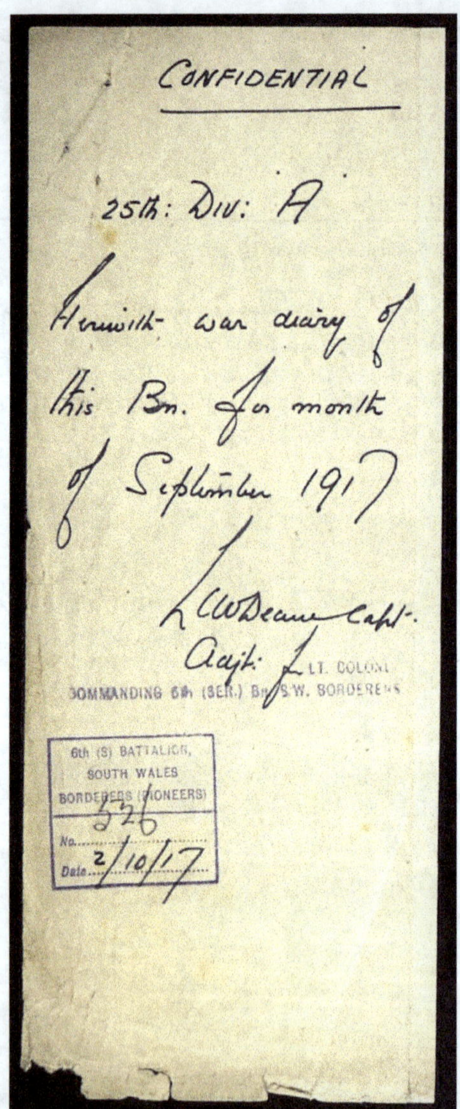

CONFIDENTIAL

25th: Div: A

Herewith war diary of this Bn. for month of September 1917

L W Deane Capt.
Adjt. for LT. COLONL
COMMANDING 6th (SER.) Bn. S.W. BORDERERS

6th (S) BATTALION,
SOUTH WALES
BORDERERS (PIONEERS)
No. 526
Date 2/10/17

Instructions regarding War Diaries and Intelligence Summaries are contained in F. S. Regs., Part II. and the Staff Manual respectively. Title Pages will be prepared in manuscript.

WAR DIARY
or
INTELLIGENCE SUMMARY
(Erase heading not required.)

Army Form C. 2118

8th (S) BATTALION, SOUTH WALES

Vol 25

Place	Date	Hour	Summary of Events and Information	Remarks and references to Appendices
PIONEER CAMP	September 1.		Work night 31-1 on BELLEVAARD Road junction level ½ R. L. remainder of Batt on CAMBRIDGE Road repairing and making junction level through RAILWAY WOOD trenches in extension of road to YPRES-ROULERS Railway	
"	2		Relieved from work for II Corps and rejoined the Division. Day of rest	
"	3		Work continued night tramline for BURR X roads forward for 2000 yds. Fine day and became very warm towards evening. Wounded in action No 6/17066 L/Cpl CAPEWELL, 3/13004 Pte TURBERVILLE. Major A. REID-KELLETT.	
"	4		Work on new tramline 600 yds junction level. Heavy shelling. Wounded in action No 40726 Pte TAYLOR.	
"	5		Work on new tramline Heavy shelling. Wounded in action No 39005 Pte FLOOD Died of wounds No 13004 Cpl TURBERVILLE on 4th	
"	6		Work on tramline 1000 yds now under construction very heavy shelling all morning working parties fortunately several hundred yards of tramway line.	
"	7		Work as for 6th quiet day and good progress made with work. Orders received that the Batt return to hold line on the 10th. Heavy fog during the early hours.	
"	8		Work as for 7th quiet day and good progress made with work. Heavy fog until noon.	

1875 Wt. W593/826 1,000,000 4/15 J.B.C. & A. A.D.S.S./Forms/C. 2118.

25.S

Instructions regarding War Diaries and Intelligence Summaries are contained in F. S. Regs., Part II. and the Staff Manual respectively. Title Pages will be prepared in manuscript.

WAR DIARY
or
INTELLIGENCE SUMMARY
(Erase heading not required.)

Army Form C. 2118

Place	Date	Hour	Summary of Events and Information	Remarks and references to Appendices
PIONEER CAMP	9		Work as for 8th. Wounded in action No 17433 Pte CORRETT. Transport lines bombed & shelled	[initials]
HALIFAX CAMP	10	4pm	Battn, less A Co, moved to HALIFAX CAMP. Camp shelled. Work during morning as for 9th. Killed in action 2nd Lieut R.F. HERLEY.	[initials]
"	11		Cleaning up. Camp shelled during the night.	[initials]
CAESTRE Area	12	2.30pm	Battn embussed for CAESTRE Area & billeted for the night. Draft of 71 O.R. joined Battn. B Team rejoined Battn	[initials]
LITTES	13	7am	Battn proceeded by route march to LITTES & there billeted. Good marching conditions. Distance 15 miles	[initials]
FRANCQUEHEM	14	8am	Battn proceeded by route march to FRANCQUEHEM & there billeted, good marching conditions. G.O.C. Div inspected Battn on its passing St HILAIRE and congratulated the C.O. on the good marching and turn out of Battn. Stated "the best marching Battn in the Division" also that General BAIRD had made a similar report to him. (cool sunny day with fresh breeze)	[initials]
"	15		Cleaning up	[initials]
"	16		Physical Training, Musketry, Bayonet fighting & Platoon Drill. Lectures daily. A Co, less transport, rejoined the Battn from YPRES Area.	
		4pm	C & D Cos under Major McD-Hallett (?) proceeded to LENS for work on Light Railways, their party [illegible]	[initials]
"	17		[illegible] Transport of A Co arrived from YPRES.	

L875 (?) Wt. W593/826 1,000,000 4/15 J.B.C. & A. A.D.S.S./Forms/C. 2118.

Instructions regarding War Diaries and Intelligence Summaries are contained in F. S. Regs., Part II. and the Staff Manual respectively. Title Pages will be prepared in manuscript.

WAR DIARY
or
INTELLIGENCE SUMMARY
(Erase heading not required.)

Army Form C. 2118

Place	Date	Hour	Summary of Events and Information	Remarks and references to Appendices
FRANCQUEHEM	18		Wet am. for 19th Football match D Co v Transport & HQ. Showery Wounded to-day 2nd Lt H. DAVIES. No 6/4778 6 Pte NEATE.	
"	19		Training as for 18th Concert by A Co to celebrate 3rd anniversary of raising of Batt. bright warm day Wounded in action No 22740 Pte PLANK.	
"	20		A Co training as for 19th D Co Musketry bullets, rapid and firing with gas helmet on (showery day)	
"	21		A Co Musketry D Co training battn as for 20th (bright fine day)	
"	22	8.30am	4 Hour route March A & D Cos.	
"	23	3pm	C & D Cos returned from LENS (fine bright day)	
"	24		Batt bathing, training in lewis gun. fine bright day.	
"	25		C Co Musketry remainder of Batt training as per programme. (fine bright day) Batt beat 5th South Lancashire at Rugby Football by 1 goal	
"	26		Route March to ALLOUAGNE and the day spent at Divisional Fete & Sports fine day 2nd Lt ROBERTS thrown from his horse and sustained fractured [illegible] to hospital.	
"	27		D Co Musketry remainder of Batt training as per programme. Batt played Cadet Training School at Association Football winning by 2 goals.	
"	28	8am	A & B Cos proceeded to LENS area marching to LILLIERS & then entraining C & D Cos training as per programme (fine bright day)	
"	29		C Co Musketry D Co training as per programme. (")	
"	30		Church Parade (")	

W595/826 1,000,000 4/15 J.B.C. & A. A.D.S.S./Forms/C. 2118.

CONFIDENTIAL

25th: Div: "A"

Herewith War Diary for this Bn. for month of October 1917

[illegible] Capt.
Adjt
for C.O. 6th S.W.B

1/11/17

6 S W B

Vol 26

Army Form C. 2118

WAR DIARY
or
INTELLIGENCE SUMMARY
(Erase heading not required.)

Instructions regarding War Diaries and Intelligence Summaries are contained in F. S. Regs., Part II. and the Staff Manual respectively. Title Pages will be prepared in manuscript.

6th (S) BATTALION, SOUTH WALES BORDERERS (PIONEERS)

Place	Date	Hour	Summary of Events and Information	Remarks and references to Appendices
FRANCQENEM	October 1		D. Co. Specialists C. Co. Training. Final of football against the Canadians Batt won by 2 goals (bright hot day)	[illegible]
"	2	8am	D. Co. Training C. Co. proceeded 8am to BULLY GRENAY for work in Southern Sector of line	[illegible]
"	3		D. Co. Training and baths (dull day with showers)	[illegible]
"	4		D. Co. Training. A.B.&C. Co. rejoined H.Q. from BULLY GRENAY (cold & showery)	[illegible]
"	5		Batt cleaning up and preparing for move (fine bright day) 2nd Lt THOMAS and 15 O.R. proceeded to GORRE for work on T.T.	[illegible]
ANNEZIN	6	9am	Batt proceeded by route march to ANNEZIN and billeted there for the night. (cold wet day)	[illegible]
BEUVRY	7	9.30	Batt proceeded by route march to BEUVRY & there billeted. (cold wet day)	[illegible]
"	8		Company Drill Physical training Lecture on Wiring and C.T.s bright sunny day cool	[illegible]
"	9		Work Programme until further orders. A Co. will work in the 7th Bde Area, C. Co. in 70th Bde and D in 72nd B Co in reserve to reinforce work and for use in back area. (wet day)	[illegible]
"	10		A Co. proceeded to GORRE and there billeted in the Bde area. (wet day)	[illegible]
"	11		Work as per programme B Co. ~~constructing Batt H.Q. line~~ Specialists. Capt HITCHCOX joined the Batt for duty and is posted to C. Co. (hot & stormy day)	[illegible]
"	12		Work as per programme. B Co. constructing Batt H.Q. line. (hot day)	[illegible] 26 S

1875 Wt. W593/826 1,000,000 4/15 J.B.C. & A. A.D.S.S./Forms/C. 2118.

Instructions regarding War Diaries and Intelligence Summaries are contained in F. S. Regs., Part II. and the Staff Manual respectively. Title Pages will be prepared in manuscript.

WAR DIARY
or
INTELLIGENCE SUMMARY
(Erase heading not required.)

Army Form C. 2118

Place	Date	Hour	Summary of Events and Information	Remarks and references to Appendices
BEUVRY	13		Work as per programme. One Platoon B to proceed to GORRE & there billeted (Lab Coy)	[illegible]
			Batt billeting.	
–	14		The following officers reported for duty with the Batt on the 13th inst. and posted to Coys (fine bright day)	[illegible]
			2 Lieuts J.D. SIMPSON to D, W.M. MADDOCK to A, G.B. JAKEWAY to C, R.G. BUTTERWORTH, and A.L. GOUGH to B.	[illegible]
"	15.		Col. E.V.O. Hewett proceeded to England. Command of the Bn. was taken over by Major. N.T. Fitzpatrick R.E. of 106th. Fd: Co. R.E.	
			Coys worked as per programme. C.O. visited A & D Coy: detachments.	
"			Following were wounded in action through shell fire in ANNEQUIN VILLAGE 17198 Sgt. Smith. 17176 Sgt. Lander, 16932 Pte. Hopkins, 16408 Pte. Thomas 16752 Pte. Thomas.	
			Detachment of 20 men of B Coy: billeted in ANNEQUIN for work on T.M. Emplacements.	[illegible]
"	16		Coys: worked as per programme. Further detachment of 20 men of B Coy billeted in ANNEQUIN. C.O. saw all officers at H.Q.	[illegible]
"	17.		Coys: worked as per programme.	[illegible]
"	18.		Coys. worked as per programme.	[illegible]
"	19.		Coys. worked as per programme.	[illegible]
"	20		Coys bathed. No work. 2 Lt. Hodgkin leave to U.K.	W.H.M.
"	21		Coys worked as per programme. Major Fitzpatrick proceeded on leave UK. The command of the Bn. was taken over by Major Reid Kellett.	W.H.M. W.H.M.
"	22.		Coys worked as per programme. 15 men & 1 N.C.O. from A, D, C Coys relieved 15 men of B Coy on trench tramways.	W.H.M.

C875. Wt. W593/826 1,000,000 4/15 J.B.C. & A. A.D.S.S./Forms/C. 2118.

Instructions regarding War Diaries and Intelligence Summaries are contained in F. S. Regs., Part II. and the Staff Manual respectively. Title Pages will be prepared in manuscript.

WAR DIARY
or
INTELLIGENCE SUMMARY
(Erase heading not required.)

Army Form C. 2118

Place	Date	Hour	Summary of Events and Information	Remarks and references to Appendices
Beuvry	23		Coy. worked as per programme.	W.H.H.
"	24		Coys worked as per programme.	W.H.H.
"	25		Coys worked as per programme. Capt. Stickler returned from leave to U.K.	W.H.H.
"	26		Coys worked as per programme 29170 Pte Price wounded.	W.H.H.
"	27		No work. Bath Day. 2Lt. Kelly & Pelt returned from X/Corp School. Played 1st Mons at Sailly Labourse. won 11 pts–0.	W.H.H.
"	28		Coys worked as per programme 2Lt. S. L. Hillier leave to U.K.	W.H.H.
"	29		Coys worked as per programme. 42326 Pte Cunningham wounded. ?	W.H.H.
"	30		Coys worked as per programme.	W.H.H.
"	31.		Coys worked as per programme. 29826 Pte Thomas killed in action.	W.H.H.

1875 Wt. W593/826 1,000,000 4/15 J.B.C. & A. A.D.S.S./Forms/C. 2118.

Confidential.

25th: Div: A.

Herewith War Diary for this Bn. for Month of November 1917.

L.C.W. Deane Capt.
Adjt:
for C.O. 6th S.W.B

1/32/17

ORDERLY ROOM
42

Instructions regarding War Diaries and Intelligence Summaries are contained in F. S. Regs., Part II. and the Staff Manual respectively. Title Pages will be prepared in manuscript.

WAR DIARY
or
INTELLIGENCE SUMMARY
(Erase heading not required.)

Army Form C. 2118

6/S.W.B. 1/4

Vol 27

Place	Date	Hour	Summary of Events and Information	Remarks and references to Appendices
Benvry	Nov 1	1917	Coys worked as per programme. The following Officers reported this day for duty and are posted to coys. 2Lt. Jones. J. R – 'A' Coy, 2Lt Huxley G, 'B' Coy 2Lts. James A.W, Frazer J.K, Gammon H.W 'C' Coy 2Lt. Trusler S. F. D Coy.	W.H.H.
"	2nd.		Coys. worked as per programme. 2Lt. Hodgkin returned from leave to work	W.H.H.
"	3		Back Day. D Coy worked as per programme, also ½ platoon of B. Coy and ½ platoon of C. Remainder of Corps did no work. Pte Skeld 40921 wounded. Played 1st Mons. Lost 3–1. Draft of 40 men arrived.	
"	4		Coys: worked as per programme. C.O. returned from leave & took over command from Major Rickett	[illegible]
"	5.		Coys: worked as per programme. C.O. visited Right-sector with C.R.E.	[illegible]
	6		Coys. worked as per programme. Co. visited left sector with C.R.E. Lt. Simpson, 2/Lts. Haddock, James & Gregory proceeded to join 9th S. Staffs.	[illegible]

1875 Wt. W593/826 1,000,000 4/15 J.B.C. & A. A.D.S.S./Forms/C. 2118.

27.S

Instructions regarding War Diaries and Intelligence Summaries are contained in F. S. Regs., Part II. and the Staff Manual respectively. Title pages will be prepared in manuscript.

WAR DIARY
or
INTELLIGENCE SUMMARY.
(Erase heading not required.)

Army Form C. 2118.

Place	Date	Hour	Summary of Events and Information	Remarks and references to Appendices
	7th:		Coys worked as per programme.	[illegible]
	8th.		Coys worked as per programme. D Coy resting.	[illegible]
	9th.		Coys. worked as per programme.	[illegible]
	10th.		Coys. worked as per programme. 2/Lt. H. R. MURRAY reported for duty. Draft of 11 other ranks arrived. 2/Lt. Fussler took over Regimental Transport	[illegible]
	11th.		Coys all bathed. Rugby team played & defeated 251 Tunnelling Co. R.E.	[illegible]
	12th.		3 Coys. employed on cable bury by night. 1 Coy on Bn. Stables & T.M. Emplacements.	[illegible]
	13th.		Coys continued work on cable bury etc.	[illegible]
	14th:		Coys: continued work on cable bury & T.M. Emplacements.	[illegible]
	15th.		Coys: continued work on cable bury & T.M. Emplacements.	[illegible]
	16th.		do do do do	[illegible]

2353 Wt. W2544/1454 700,000 5/15 D. D. & L. A.D.S.S./Forms/C. 2118.

Instructions regarding War Diaries and Intelligence Summaries are contained in F. S. Regs., Part II. and the Staff Manual respectively. Title pages will be prepared in manuscript.

WAR DIARY
or
INTELLIGENCE SUMMARY.
(Erase heading not required.)

Army Form C. 2118.

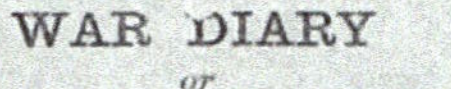

Place	Date	Hour	Summary of Events and Information	Remarks and references to Appendices
BEUVRY	17th.		Coys: continued work on cable bury & T.M. Emplacements.	[illegible]
"	18th.		Rest day. Coys: in bathed.	[illegible]
"	19th.		Coys: worked on cable bury & T.M. Emplacements.	[illegible]
"	20th.		Commenced work on tramways & continued cable bury & T.M. Emplacements. R.S.M. Sherman proceeded to Base for transfer to England.	[illegible]
"	21		Coys: worked on Tramways, & cable bury & T.M. Emplacements. 109 men of C Coy went on detachment to NOEUX-LES-MINES & were attached to 170 Tunnelling Co: for work. Lt. E.C. Amos reported for duty. Bn: played & beat 1st Corps H.Q at Rugby.	
"	22.		Coys: continued work as per programme.	[illegible]
"	23.		Work as usual. Move orders received.	[illegible]
BOMY	24		H.Q. A, B & D Coys: moved by bus to BOMY area & billetted. H.Q & B Coy in BOMY, A Coy in RUPIGNY, D Coy in LISBOURG. Transport proceeded by road, halting for night at BAS RIEUX.	[illegible]
"	25.		A Coy: moved to LILETTE. Transport arrived at BOMY.	[illegible]

2353 Wt. W2544/1454 700,000 5/15 D. D. & L. A.D.S.S./Forms/C. 2118.

Instructions regarding War Diaries and Intelligence Summaries are contained in F. S. Regs., Part II. and the Staff Manual respectively. Title pages will be prepared in manuscript.

WAR DIARY
or
INTELLIGENCE SUMMARY.
(Erase heading not required.)

Army Form C. 2118.

Place	Date	Hour	Summary of Events and Information	Remarks and references to Appendices
BOMY.	26		A Coy: moved to CAPELLE. Work continued on stables.	Lewis
"	27.		Work continued as usual on stables.	Lewis
"	28.		H.Q., & A coy: moved to billets in COYECQUES. B & D coys to billets in BEAUMETZ.	Lewis
"	29		Work continued on Stables.	
	30		Work continued on Stables. Capt. N. G. Pearson reported for duty.	Lewis

2353 Wt. W2544/1454 700,000 5/15 D. D. & L. A.D.S.S./Forms/C. 2118.

CONFIDENTIAL

25th: Div: 'A'

Herewith War diary for this Bn. for month of December 1917.

L.W. Deane.

CAPTN. & ADJT.

for O.C. 6th (S.) BN. S.W. BORDERERS (PNRS.)

6th (S) BATTALION,
SOUTH WALES
BORDERERS (PIONEERS)
No. 642.
Date 1/1/18.

Instructions regarding War Diaries and Intelligence Summaries are contained in F. S. Regs., Part II. and the Staff Manual respectively. Title pages will be prepared in manuscript.

WAR DIARY or INTELLIGENCE SUMMARY.

(Erase heading not required.)

Army Form C. 2118.

6th: S.W.B.

Vol 28

Place	Date	Hour	Summary of Events and Information	Remarks and references to Appendices
Dec: COYECQUES	1.		Bn. less C Coy: worked on stables.	LWD
MONCHY CAYEUX	2.		Bn. less C Coy: moved to MONCHY CAYEUX & there billeted. C Coy rejoined by bus from BEUVRY. 2/Lt. Dale reported for duty.	LWD
"	3.		Bn. entrained at WAVRANS at 9 P.M. & proceeded to MIRAUMENT.	LWD
	4.		Detrained at MIRAUMENT at 9 A.M. & marched to COURCELLES-LE-COMTE where it was quartered in huts.	LWD
COURCELLES	5.		Day spent resting & cleaning up.	LWD
BEAULENCOURT	6		Bn. proceeded to BEAULENCOURT by march route. 16 Lewis gunners & 4 guns attached to D.H.Q.	LWD
"	7		Day spent cleaning up, gas drill etc.	LWD
"	8		Bn. resting & cleaning up.	LWD
FREMICOURT	9		Bn. moved to camp at I.19.b.2.4 Sheet 57c. Capt. James proceeded to ALBERT.	LWD

2353 Wt. W2544/1454 700,000 5/15 D. D. & L. A.D.S.S./Forms/C. 2118.

28S
4/7

Army Form C. 2118.

WAR DIARY
or
INTELLIGENCE SUMMARY.
(*Erase heading not required.*)

• Instructions regarding War Diaries and Intelligence Summaries are contained in F. S. Regs., Part II. and the Staff Manual respectively. Title pages will be prepared in manuscript.

Place	Date	Hour	Summary of Events and Information	Remarks and references to Appendices
FREMICOURT	10.		Bn. resting & pitching tents etc: R.S.M. Slinister reported for duty.	Lwd.
	11.		Coys. employed preparing quarters in forward area.	Lwd.
	12.		A Coy: moved to new quarters at C 27C 20.	Lwd.
	13.		B.C. & D Coys. moved to new quarters at I.5.c.2.8, I 4.b.9.5 & I.4.9.7.8. respectively. All coys worked on night 13/14th: for 3rd: Div:	Lwd.
	14.		All Coys worked on new fire trench for 3rd: Div:	Lwd.
	15.		Coys. resting. Baths at VAULX. Lt. McCausland reported for duty.	Lwd.
"	16		Coys Commence work on Intermediate line in 74th Bde Area on north side of road from LAGNICOURT to D 26 C Sheet 57C	[illegible]
"	17		Coys Continue work on Intermediate line	[illegible]
"	18.		Coys Continue work on Intermediate Line	[illegible]
	19		Party from "A" Coy erect Nissen Huts at Hd Qr Camp. Coys Continue work on Intermediate line.	[illegible]

Army Form C. 2118.

WAR DIARY
or
INTELLIGENCE SUMMARY.
(Erase heading not required.)

Instructions regarding War Diaries and Intelligence Summaries are contained in F. S. Regs., Part II. and the Staff Manual respectively. Title pages will be prepared in manuscript.

Place	Date	Hour	Summary of Events and Information	Remarks and references to Appendices
FREMICOURT	20th		Coys Continue work on Intermediate Line. No. 39220 Pte	[illegible]
			SOUTHGATE W. wounded at Duty	[illegible]
"	21st		Coys continue on Intermediate line.	[illegible]
"	22nd		Coys continue on Intermediate line.	[illegible]
"	23rd		Battn Resting Stables completed	
"	24th		"A" Coy commence work on 75th Bde Hd Qrs at VAULX deep Dugouts	[illegible]
"	25th		Coys work as per programme.	[illegible]
"	26th		Coys working as per programme	[illegible]
"	27th		Coys resting. Baths at VAULX.	[illegible]
"	28th		Coys working as per programme	[illegible]
"	29th		Coy work as per programme. Draft of 100 B1 Men reported.	[illegible]
"	30th		Coys resting.	[illegible]
"	31st		Coys work on Intermediate Line.	[illegible]

2353 Wt. W2544/1454 700,000 5/15 D. D. & L. A.D.S.S./Forms/C. 2118.

Instructions regarding War Diaries and Intelligence Summaries are contained in F. S. Regs., Part II. and the Staff Manual respectively. Title pages will be prepared in manuscript.

WAR DIARY
or
INTELLIGENCE SUMMARY.
(Erase heading not required.)

Army Form C. 2118.

6th (S) Bn South Wales Borderers (Pioneers)

Vol 29

Place	Date (Jan)	Hour	Summary of Events and Information	Remarks and references to Appendices
FREMICOURT	1st		Coys working on Intermediate Line. 96 men proceeded to join 12th SWB	[initials]
"	2nd		Work continued on Intermediate Line.	[initials]
"	3rd		Coys work as per programme	[initials]
"	4th		Coys work as per programme.	
"	5th		Coys working as per programme	[initials]
"	6th		Coys Resting.	[initials]
"	7		Coys working as per programme 4 men proceeded to join 12th SWB	[initials]
"	8		CSM Ricketts awarded DCM Coys worked as usual	[initials]
"	9		Coys continue work on intermediate line. Capts J C Owen & J W Clarke, Lieut WH HANNA; Sergt Chattington, Sergt Parker mentioned in Despatches	[initials]
"	10		Coys bathed and worked as per programme	[initials]
"	11		Coys worked as per programme.	[initials]

2353 Wt. W2544/1454 700,000 5/15 D. D. & L. A.D.S.S./Forms/C. 2118.

29.S

Instructions regarding War Diaries and Intelligence Summaries are contained in F. S. Regs., Part II. and the Staff Manual respectively. Title pages will be prepared in manuscript.

WAR DIARY
or
INTELLIGENCE SUMMARY.
(Erase heading not required.)

Army Form C. 2118.

Place	Date	Hour	Summary of Events and Information	Remarks and references to Appendices
FREMICOURT	Jan 12		Coys continue work.	[illegible]
–	13		Coys resting.	[illegible]
–	14		Coys work as per programme	[illegible]
–	15		2nd Lieut Huxley proceeded to join 10th R.W.F.	[illegible]
–	16		Coys work as per programme. Following casualties in "C" Coy:- K. Pte. J. Edwards 201517; W. Pte. M. McNamara 6/16429; Pte. W. Davies 6/16412; Pte. D. Dawson 6/17229; Pte E. Nelson 6/42240; Pte. J. Gould 6/16960.	H.R.M.
–	17.		Coys. work as per programme.	H.R.M.
–	18.		Work continued by coys.	H.R.M.
–	19.		Coys. continued work as per programme. Bn. less "D" Coy. bathed	H.R.M.
–	20.		Coys. resting. "D" Coy. bathed.	H.R.M.
–	21.		Work continued as per programme. Capt. James struck off strength of Bn. on being transferred to Gen. List. 5 O.Rs. reported.	H.R.M.
–	22		Coys. continue work. 19416 L/Cpl. Hanks wounded. 1 O.R. discharged to Base.	H.R.M.
–	23		Work continued by coys. 2 O.R. sent to Labour Corps	H.R.M.

2353 Wt. W2544/1454 700,000 5/15 D. D. & L. A.D.S.S./Forms/C. 2118.

Instructions regarding War Diaries and Intelligence Summaries are contained in F. S. Regs., Part II. and the Staff Manual respectively. Title pages will be prepared in manuscript.

WAR DIARY
or
INTELLIGENCE SUMMARY.
(*Erase heading not required.*)

Army Form C. 2118.

Place	Date	Hour	Summary of Events and Information	Remarks and references to Appendices
Fremicourt	Jan 24		Coys. continued work as per programme.	HRM.
—	25		Work continued by coys.	HRM
—	26		Coys. continue work as per programme. 2 O.Rs. reported for duty. 'A' & 'B' coys. bathed at VAULX.	HRM.
—	27		Coys. rested. Remainder of Battn. bathed at VAULX.	
—	28		Coys. work as per programme. 'D' coy. start on dugouts at D 20. c.	HRM.
—	29		Work continued by coys. as per programme. 'D' coy. finished light railway at VAULX. 3 O.Rs. reported for duty.	HRM.
—	30		Work continued by coys.	HRM.
—	31		'C' Coy moved from forward position to Camp No. 5 H. 10. c. 2.5 Sheet 57c. Remainder of coys. continued work as per programme.	HRM HRM

2353 Wt. W2514/1454 700,000 5/15 D. D. & L. A.D.S.S./Forms/C. 2118.

Instructions regarding War Diaries and Intelligence Summaries are contained in F. S. Regs., Part II. and the Staff Manual respectively. Title Pages will be prepared in manuscript.

WAR DIARY
or
INTELLIGENCE SUMMARY
(Erase heading not required.)

Army Form C. 2118

ORDERLY ROOM No. 48 ... BATTN. SOUTH WALES BORDERERS

63 WB

Vol 30

Place	Date	Hour	Summary of Events and Information	Remarks and references to Appendices
	Feb.	1918		
Fremicourt	1		'C' Coy. started on dugouts for Divisional Headquarters at H.16.a.2.8.– FAVREUIL.	
			'A' Coy. working on Bgde. Headquarters dugouts at C.26.d.0.8.– VAULX, and on LAGNICOURT light railway at C.23.d.2.8. and I.4.c.7.3.	
			'D' Coy. working on dugouts at D.26.a.2.0.– Leech Avenue; D.19.c.5.1– Post 37; D.26.c.5.1. and clearing intermediate line from D.26.d.2.1 to Skipton Reserve.	
			'B' Coy. working on dugout at Post 35 and clearing intermediate line from D.26.c.2.1. to Skipton Reserve.	
–	2.		Coys. worked as per programme.	H.K.M.
			40863 Cpl. Hibbert proceeded to England to train for a commission.	
–	3		Coys. rested.	H.K.M.
			17300. Cpl. Galvin transferred to Royal Flying Corps.	
–	4		Coys. working as per programme.	H.K.M.
–	5		Coys. work as per programme.	H.K.M.
–	6		Work continued by coys. as per programme.	H.K.M.
			Capt. Cox proceeded to England on duty.	
			14317 Pte W. Walters and 40942 Pte F. Allee injured at C.26.d.0.8.	H.K.M.

305 / 5/4

Instructions regarding War Diaries and Intelligence Summaries are contained in F. S. Regs., Part II. and the Staff Manual respectively. Title pages will be prepared in manuscript.

WAR DIARY
or
INTELLIGENCE SUMMARY.
(*Erase heading not required.*)

Army Form C. 2118.

Place	Date	Hour	Summary of Events and Information	Remarks and references to Appendices
	Feb.			
Fremicourt	7.		Coys. continued work as per programme.	
			'A' and 'B' coys. bathed at VAULX.	
—	8.		Coys. continued working as per programme.	HRm
			The following have been awarded the Belgian Croix de Guerre:–	
			Capt. F. W. Clarke, Sergt. Whitehead and Pte. W. H. Walters.	
			'C' Coy. bathed at FAVREUIL.	HRm.
—	9		Coys. work as per programme.	
—	10		Coys. continue working as per programme.	HRm
—	11		Work continued by coys. as per programme.	HRm
			2/Lt. H. Davies, 4th Bn. R. W. F. brought to establishment of 6th S. W. B.	
			Battn. Headquarters, Transport and 'D' coy bathed at VAULX.	HRm
ACHIET LE GRAND	12		The Battn. less 'C' Coy and 2 Lewis Gun posts vacated VAULX area and moved to ACHIET-LE-GRAND area. Camp situated at G. 2. D. 55. on sheet 57c.	
—	13		Day spent in training and cleaning up. Improvements to Camp carried out.	HRm
				HRm

2353 Wt. W2544/1454 700,000 5/15 D. D. & L. A.D.S.S./Forms/C. 2118.

Instructions regarding War Diaries and Intelligence Summaries are contained in F. S. Regs., Part II. and the Staff Manual respectively. Title pages will be prepared in manuscript.

WAR DIARY
or
INTELLIGENCE SUMMARY.
(Erase heading not required.)

Army Form C. 2118.

Place	Date Feb.	Hour	Summary of Events and Information	Remarks and references to Appendices
ACHIET LE GRAND	14		Day spent in physical, squad, platoon, company, musketry and gas training. Improvements to the Camp carried out.	ARM
do.	15		'A' Coy. start work on D.A.C horse lines at AVESNES-LE-BAPAUME. 'B' Coy. start work on Battalion stables at G. 2. d. 5. 5. Sheet 57c. 'C' Coy. continue work on divisional dugouts at FAVREUIL. 'D' Coy. continue improving the Camp at G. 2. d. 5. 5 Sheet 57c against enemy aircraft. 14 O.R. reported for duty.	ARM.
do.	16		Coys. continue work as per programme.	ARM.
do.	17		Coys. continue work as per programme.	ARM.
do.	18.		Work continued by coys. as per programme.	ARM.
do.	19		Coys. less 'C' coy. rested Battn. less 'C' coy. bathed at COURCELLES.	ARM.
do.	20		Coys. work as per programme.	

7353 Wt. W2544/1454 700,000 5/15 D. D. & L. A.D.S.S./Forms/C. 2118.

Instructions regarding War Diaries and Intelligence Summaries are contained in F. S. Regs., Part II. and the Staff Manual respectively. Title pages will be prepared in manuscript.

WAR DIARY
or
INTELLIGENCE SUMMARY.
(Erase heading not required.)

Army Form C. 2118.

Place	Date	Hour	Summary of Events and Information	Remarks and references to Appendices
ACHIET-LE-GRAND	Feb. 20.		Battn. less 'A' & 'C' Coys. passed through gas.	ARM.
do.	21		Coys work as per programme, except 'D' Coy.	
			'D' Coy. start work on M.G. stables at G.14. b.6.7. Sheet 57C	ARM.
			9388. Sergt. A. Glenister promoted to W.O. Class I/.	
do.	22		Coys. work as per programme.	ARM
do.	23.		Work continued by coys. as per programme.	ARM
do.	24		Coys continue work as per programme.	
			'C' Coy rested and bathed.	ARM
do.	25.		Coys. work as per programme.	
			7 O.R. reported for duty.	ARM.
do.	26.		Work continued by coys. as per programme.	ARM
do.	27.		Coys. continue work as per programme.	
			10 O.R. pronounced unfit for service at the front were struck off the strength.	ARM

2353 Wt. W2544/1454 700,000 5/15 D. D. & L. A.D.S.S./Forms/C. 2118.

Instructions regarding War Diaries and Intelligence Summaries are contained in F. S. Regs., Part II. and the Staff Manual respectively. Title pages will be prepared in manuscript.

WAR DIARY
or
INTELLIGENCE SUMMARY.
(Erase heading not required.)

Army Form C. 2118.

Place	Date	Hour	Summary of Events and Information	Remarks and references to Appendices
ACHIET-LE-GRAND.	Feb. 28.		Coys. less 'B' Coy. continue work as per programme. On reorganisation of pioneer battalion to three company basis, 'B' Coy were dissolved. Officers and men transferred as from March 1st.	W.R.M.

2353 Wt. W2544/1454 700,000 5/15 D. D. & L. A.D.S.S./Forms/C. 2118.

25th Divisional Troops.

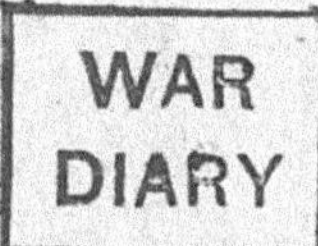

6th BATTALION

SOUTH WALES BORDERERS.

(pioneers)

MARCH 1 9 1 8

Reports on Operations attached.

4

Pioneers 345

Army Form C. 2118.

WAR DIARY or INTELLIGENCE SUMMARY.

(Erase heading not required.)

Instructions regarding War Diaries and Intelligence Summaries are contained in F. S. Regs., Part II. and the Staff Manual respectively. Title pages will be prepared in manuscript.

6 Bn S.W. Borderers

Vol 31

Place	Date	Hour	Summary of Events and Information	Remarks and references to Appendices
ACHIET-LE-GRAND. G.2.d.5.5	MAR. 1918 1.		Coys. work as under:- 'A' Coy. on horse lines for D.A.C, at AVESNES-LE-BAPAUME. H.20.d.2.3. Sheet 57c. 'C' Coy. on Divisional dugouts at FAVREUIL. H.16.a.2.8. Sheet 57c. 'D' Coy. on PIONEER CAMP horse lines at G.2.d.5.5. Sheet 57c. 2/Lt. J. H. RICHARDS. promoted to LIEUT. on completion of 18 months' commissioned service Battn. rested and St. David's Day celebrated.	
do.	2.		Battn. rested and bathed at COURCELLES.	HRM.
do.	3.		Work continued by coys. as per programme.	HRM.
do.	4.		Coys. continue working as per programme.	HRM.
do.	5.		Part II orders - vide London Gazette 1.1.1918, Lieut. Col. N. T. FITZPATRICK, M.C., R.E. awarded D.S.O. 8 ORs. classified as unfit for further service at the front sent to BASE today. Work continued by coys. as per programme.	HRM. 3/S

4353 Wt. W2544/1454 700,000 5/15 D.D. & L. A.D.S.S./Forms/C. 2118.

Army Form C. 2118.

WAR DIARY
or
INTELLIGENCE SUMMARY.
(*Erase heading not required.*)

Instructions regarding War Diaries and Intelligence Summaries are contained in F. S. Regs., Part II. and the Staff Manual respectively. Title pages will be prepared in manuscript.

Place	Date	Hour	Summary of Events and Information	Remarks and references to Appendices
ACHIET-LE-GRAND	MAR. 6.		Coys. continue work as per programme except as under:-	
			2 Platoons 'D' Coy. work on horse lines at G. 2. d. 5. 5.	
			2 ——— start work with 'A' Coy. at H. 20. d. 2. 3.	WRM.
do.	7		Work continued by coys. except as under:-	
			1 Platoon 'D' Coy. with 'A' Coy. at H. 20. d. 2. 3.	
			1 ——— on M. G. Battn horse lines at ACHIET-LE-PETIT.	
			2 Platoons 'D' Coy. on horse lines at G. 2. d. 5. 5.	
do.	8.		Work continued by coys. as on 7th inst.	WRM.
			2/Lt. W. L. BOWEN reported for duty and posted to 'D' Coy.	
do.	9.		Coys. work as per programme of 7th inst.	WRM.
do.	10.		Work continued by coys. as for yesterday.	WRM.
do.	11.		Battn. less 'C' Coy. rested and bathed at COURCELLES.	WRM.
			5 ORs. reported for duty.	

2353 Wt. W2544/1454 700,000 5/15 D. D. & L. A.D.S.S./Forms/C. 2118.

Army Form C. 2118.

Instructions regarding War Diaries and Intelligence Summaries are contained in F. S. Regs., Part II. and the Staff Manual respectively. Title pages will be prepared in manuscript.

WAR DIARY
or
INTELLIGENCE SUMMARY.
(Erase heading not required.)

Place	Date	Hour	Summary of Events and Information	Remarks and references to Appendices
ACHIET-LE-GRAND.	Mar. 11 con.		'D' Coy. together with coy. transport moved forward to camp at FAVREUIL H. 10. c. 2. 4 Sheet 57c.	WRM.
do.	12		'A' Coy. together with coy. transport moved forward to camp at LEBUCQUIERE I. 29. b. 40. 85. Headquarters at I. 30. a. 5. 5. Sheet 57c. 'C' Coy. continue work on divisional dugouts at FAVREUIL. 'D' Coy. start with 2 platoons on same work, and 2 platoons hutting at H. 10. c. 2. 4 Sht. 57c. The following officers were promoted tempy. Lieuts. vide 'London Gazette' 4/3/18 :- Ty. 2/Lts. G. H. TAYLOR, A. G. PEARCE, and A. D. ROBERTS.	WRM.
FAVREUIL do.	13		Battalion Headquarters vacated camp at G. 2. d. 5. 5. and marched to FAVREUIL area H. 10. c. 2. 4. Work continued by coys. as per programme. 'A' Coy. start digging trenches and putting up wire for	

2353 Wt. W2544/1454 700,000 5/15 D. D. & L. A.D.S.S./Forms/C. 2118.

Instructions regarding War Diaries and Intelligence Summaries are contained in F. S. Regs., Part II. and the Staff Manual respectively. Title pages will be prepared in manuscript.

WAR DIARY
or
INTELLIGENCE SUMMARY.
(Erase heading not required.)

Army Form C. 2118.

Place	Date	Hour	Summary of Events and Information	Remarks and references to Appendices
FAVREUIL	MAR. 13	con.	defence of BEAUMETZ J.13.14.19.20. central.	HRM
do.	14		Coys. continue working as per programme.	HRM.
do.	15.		Work continued by coys. as per programme.	HRM.
do.	16.		Work continued by coys. as per programme.	HRM.
do	17.		Battn. less 'A' Coy and 2 shifts comprising 100 O.Rs. bathed at FAVREUIL	
			Coys. work as per programme.	
			1 OR. reported for duty, and taken on strength	HRM.
do.	18.		Work continued by coys. as per programme.	
			Remainder of 'C' and 'D' coys. bathed at FAVREUIL.	
			1 OR. struck off strength on proceeding to England.	HRM.
do.	19.		Coys. continue work	HRM
do.	20		Coys. worked as per programme.	
			1 OR. 40702 Pte E. Ogden wounded	HRM.

2353 Wt. W2544/1454 700,000 5/15 D. D. & L. A.D.S.S./Forms/C. 2118.

Instructions regarding War Diaries and Intelligence Summaries are contained in F. S. Regs., Part II. and the Staff Manual respectively. Title pages will be prepared in manuscript.

WAR DIARY
or
INTELLIGENCE SUMMARY.
(Erase heading not required.)

Army Form C. 2118.

Place	Date	Hour	Summary of Events and Information	Remarks and references to Appendices
SAPIGNIES ETC.	MAR. 21/28.		Attached is the history of the operations of the Battalion between 21st and 28th March.	
			The following are the casualties sustained in above operations:—	

	Officers	ORs.
Killed	1	9.
Wounded	2	33
Missing	–	11

KILLED:—

No.	Rank.	Name	Date.
	2/Lt.	S.N. Hillier	25/3/18
~~L/Cpl~~ 42237	L/Cpl	H.T. Monks	23/3/18
6/16385	Pte	J. Corcoran	—
6/16982	–	W. J. Dowd.	—
40089	–	J Cater	24/3/18
29189	–	A. Evans	—
6/17207	–	J. Brothwood	25/3/18
40895	–	J. M. Hogg	—

2353 Wt. W2514/1454 700,000 5/15 D. D. & L. A.D.S.S./Forms/C. 2118.

Army Form C. 2118.

Instructions regarding War Diaries and Intelligence Summaries are contained in F. S. Regs., Part II. and the Staff Manual respectively. Title pages will be prepared in manuscript.

WAR DIARY
or
INTELLIGENCE SUMMARY.
(Erase heading not required.)

Place	Date	Hour	Summary of Events and Information				Remarks and references to Appendices
SAGIGNIES ETC.	MAR. 21/28		No.	RANK.	NAME	DATE.	
			6/14488	Pte	M. Ryan	25/3/18	
	Con.		42413	—	C. F. Lloyd	—	
			WOUNDED:-				
			~~LIEUT.~~	LIEUT.	W. H. Hanna	24/3/18	
				—	A. G. Pearce	—	
			40122	Pte.	W. H. Roberts	21/3/18	
			6/14558	Cpl.	G. Smith	22/3/18	
			29463	Pte	W. Evans	—	
			260336	—	G. A. Anderson	—	
			6/16753	—	G. Sargent	23/3/18	
			6/16952	—	J. T. Jones	—	
			42273	—	G. H. Holder	—	
			6/19996	—	M. Acton	—	
			39251	—	E. T. Stanley.	—	
			39245	—	T. J. Rogers	—	
			260296	—	F. Hynds	—	

2353 Wt. W2544/1454 700,000 5/15 D. D. & L. A.D.S.S./Forms/C. 2118.

Army Form C. 2118.

Instructions regarding War Diaries and Intelligence Summaries are contained in F. S. Regs., Part II. and the Staff Manual respectively. Title pages will be prepared in manuscript.

WAR DIARY
or
INTELLIGENCE SUMMARY.
(Erase heading not required.)

Place	Date	Hour	Summary of Events and Information				Remarks and references to Appendices
			No.	RANK.	NAME.	DATE	
SAPIGNIES ETC.	MAR. 21/28 Con.		6/17433	Pte	H. Corbett	23/3/18	
			40880	–	W. Gannon	24/3/18	
			200942	–	W. P. Rees		
			39203	–	R. Oyston	25/3/18	
			39261	–	T. Drinkwater	–	
			45866	–	A. Dickenson	–	
			8952	C.S.M.	J. Cheese	–	
			6/17592	Cpl	A. Sully	–	
			40862	Pte	J. Beckett.	–	
			6/15243	–	J. R. Clark	–	
			39151	–	E. Edwards.	–	
			29282	–	D. W. Williams	–	
			35823	–	T. Barkley	–	
			6/19232	–	N. Binns	–	
			6/17127	–	W. Green	–	
			6/16932	–	D. Hopkins	–	
			29308	–	– Jackson	–	
			39208	–	E. Jones	–	

2353 Wt. W2544/1454 700,000 5/15 D. D. & L. A.D.S.S./Forms/C. 2118.

Instructions regarding War Diaries and Intelligence Summaries are contained in F. S. Regs., Part II. and the Staff Manual respectively. Title Pages will be prepared in manuscript.

WAR DIARY
or
INTELLIGENCE SUMMARY
(Erase heading not required.)

Army Form C. 2118

Place	Date	Hour	Summary of Events and Information	Remarks and references to Appendices
SAPIGNIES ETC.	MAR. 21/28 con.			

No.	RANK.	NAME.	DATE.
6/14112	Pte	W. Jones	25/3/18
6/14048	–	W. Pugh	—
6/17544	–	S. Suter	—
6/16815	–	E. Manley	—

MISSING

No.	RANK.	NAME.	DATE.
42314	Pte	R. Macdonald	25/3/18
6/16918	–	G. Green	–
6/14522	–	E. J. Elliott	–
6/14343	–	E. Williams	–
260306	–	F. Matthews	–
30316	–	H. H. Cooke	–
29203	–	A. Dean	–
40889	–	A. Hughes	–
6/16845	Cpl	R. Taylor	–
40168	Pte	W. G. Evans	–
33442	–	– Perkins	–

WRM

1875 Wt. W593/826 1,000,000 4/15 J.B.C. & A. A.D.S.S./Forms/C. 2118.

Instructions regarding War Diaries and Intelligence Summaries are contained in F. S. Regs., Part II. and the Staff Manual respectively. Title Pages will be prepared in manuscript.

WAR DIARY
or
INTELLIGENCE SUMMARY
(Erase heading not required.)

Army Form C. 2118

Place	Date MAR.	Hour	Summary of Events and Information	Remarks and references to Appendices
PERNOIS	28.		Battn. arrived in billets in PERNOIS at 2·30 a.m. and rested remainder of day.	HRM.
do.	29		Battn. rested	HRM.
do.	30.		Battn. spent the day cleaning up and adjusting deficiencies caused through operations 21st/28th March. Battn. paraded at 12 midnight and moved off for CANDAS at 12·30 a.m. (31st).	HRM.
ROMARIN	31		Battn. marched from PERNOIS to CANDAS, arriving at latter place about 3.30 a.m. Entrained at CANDAS at 11 a.m. and detrained at CAESTRE at 9 p.m. Lorries conveyed battn. from CAESTRE Station to camp at T. 26. c. 7. 5 ROMARIN. Sheet 28. Transport complete arrived here at 4 a.m. (1st).	HRM.

1875 Wt. W593/826 1,000,000 4/15 J.B.C. & A. A.D.S.S./Forms/C. 2118.

Report on Operations of
6th Battalion South Wales Borderers
(Pioneers)
21st to 28th March 1918.

6th S. W. B.
Report on operations 21st – 28th
March 1918
p. 1. l. 19. "H. 29. b. 9. 3." is
a mistake for "B. 29. b. 9. 3."

28. 7. 25. H R Davies

REPORT ON OPERATIONS OF 6th. S. W. BORDERERS (PIONEERS). BETWEEN 21st. and 22th. MARCH 1918.

....

1. On the morning of 21st. Battalion Headquarters and C & D Coys were situated in FAVREUIL WOOD working on the Divisional Dugouts whilst A Company, lent ot C.E., IV Corps was situated at LE BUCQUIERE and working on the defences of BEAUMETZ.

According to Divisional Plans it was never anticipated that the Battalion would take part in operations on the 21st, so work proceeded as usual, the two night shifts on the dugouts came off at 6 a.m. on 21st. and A Company carried on at BEAUMETZ.

About 6 a.m. on 21st. Headquarters 6th. Division decided to occupy the FAVREUIL Dugouts; all work was stopped and Headquarters with C Company moved into Camp 5 at H.10.c.?.5. whilst D Company moved into Camp 12 in H.16.central.

At 4.30 p.m. on 21st. G.S.O.1 6th. Division gave me orders to rendezvous with C. & D Coys at once in H.9 central for work on Army Line whilst A Company was to stand fast in LEBUCQUIERE.

At 5.30 p.m. I met the C.R.E., 25th.Division at H.9. central and there received orders to move up to improve and man the ARMY LINE - my right flank was to join the R.E. on the BAPAUME - VRAUCOURT Road at H.6.c.?.6., whilst MY LEFT was to be at H.30.b.9.3.

We moved up at once but on arrival at H.5.d a dense ground mist had set in, I had never seen this section of the Army Line and on finding a wire belt coming down to the last tree in H.6.a I took this for the Army Line and dug in behind it, forming a front line of two four platoon posts and a support line of four platoon posts.

At about 11 p.m.we finished work and I met the C.R.E. who pointed out that I had taken up the wrong line position and the entire LINE had to be advanced and re-dug about 800 yards further North. This work was completed about 4 a.m.

The Battalion was in position in touch with 106 Field Company R.E. on the right and with some H.L.I. on the left. No attack developed and at 9 a.m. on 22nd. we stood down for some rest as the men were rather tired, especially those who had been working through the night of 20-21st.

At 8 a.m. on 22nd. the C.R.E. returned to Divisional Headquarters leaving me in charge so when the fog lifted at 9 a.m. I reconnoitred the front with Major Deane and we found the real Army Line still further in advance of the positions we had taken up.

At 11 a.m. on 22nd. the Battalion moved forward again in position on the real Army Line which was a continuous trench 3 feet deep; again we dug in and I told the R.E. on the right to move up also; I could find nobody on the left flank . The line ran almost due north and South there was movement of our own troops about a quarter of a mile North so the North flank was considered safe.

The R.E. on the right could not move up owing to heavy shelling so they held their original positions and were in touch on their right.

At about 2 p.m. on 22nd a Brigade of 41st Division re-inforced us on the Army Line - the garrison filled the ~~sough~~ TRENCH to overflowing and according to orders received from C.R.E. 25th. Division at 4 p.m. the Battalion was relieved from the Army Line and commenced to dig a continous support line about 200 yards in rear.

The situation seemed very obscure, Major Deane went to H.Q. 41st. Division at FAVREUIL and on hearing of the manning of the Army Line by 41st. Division, the 25th. Division ordered the Battalion and the R.E. to withdraw to the horse lines behind SAPIGNIES.

The Battalion and R.E. were clear of the line about 6 p.m. and I passed FAVREUIL at the rear of the column, I received orders to make sure that 41st Division were established in Army Line before I withdrew. I knew that the 41st. were established, all the Pioneers and R.E. were on their way to SAPIGNIES so I went to H.Q. 41st. Division and reported the fact.
The Brigade Major of the 41st. Division Brigade was satisfied that his Brigade was established and I reported by wire to C.R.E. C. & D Coys 6th. S.W.B. and R.E. arrived at the bivouac at H.7 a. about 8 p.m. on 22nd and turned in.
Meanwhile "A" Company at LE BUCQUIERE was standing to and awaiting order from 21st. till 4 p.m. on 22nd. when ~~oooo~~ it was ordered to join the Battalion on the Army Line - A Company started off but just received the orders to proceed to H.7.a in line and rejoined the Battalion at H.7.a. late on 22nd.

At 6 a.m. on 23rd. the bivouac was heavily shelled , at about 7 a.m. I received orders from G.S.O.3 25th. Division to take up a position EAST of SAPIGNIES - ~~ERVILLERS~~ guarding the Sapignies Bihucourt Road from an attack from MORY.

We moved out at once and by 11 a.m. on 23rd. we were entrenched on a *lin* line from H.9 b central to H.3.a central order of battle being 130th.105th. 106th.Coys.R.E. on the right with 6th. S.W.B. on left. The right flank seemed obscure although there were troops in FAVREUIL WOOD; to combine protection and enfilade fire right up the valley in H.4.c. and H.28.c. & a I put the 130th. Field Coy.R.E. on the spur in H.9.b. whilst the left of our position was in touch with details of 119th.? Brigade 41st.Division.

The remarkable fact during the day, 23rd., was that we could not observ any movement to our front; both sides appeared to shell MORY, whilst our line appeared well in front of BEUGNATRE.

Night of 23/24th. passed quietly except for shelling, and on morning of 24th. the 6th.S.W.B. and R.E. were brigaded with 75th. Infantry Brigade - B.G.C., 75th. Inf. Brigade came to Battalion Headquarters in H.3.c. centra went round the dispositions and decided to further secure the right flank with the 11th.Cheshires, whilst the 8th. Borders and 2nd. South Lancs came in on the left, extending the line into H.2.a. in front of BEHAGNIES. The 8th. Borders and 2nd. South Lancs came into line during the afternoon of 24th. whilst 11th. Cheshires came up at dusk.

During the afternoon of 24th. the position on the left seemed very quiet, whilst there was a prolonged action East of BEUGNATRE. We knew nothing of what was happening; we heard that the Guards had got MORY, which appeared to secure our left, but all during the afternoon troops were streaming away from FAVREUIL towards MONUMENT CORNER. This was put down to a relief as the shelling was still East of BEUGNATRE, and at dusk we still saw our troops in H.10.d., and out guns in action just North of MONUMENT CORNER.

About 7 p.m. on the 24th. I received orders from the 75th. Inf.Brigade that /-

that we were to be relieved by a Brigade of the 41st. during the night of 24/25th. and that the 6th.S.W.B. and R.E. were to move into a line East of LOGEAST WOOD.

By 11 p.m. our position in H.3.b. seemed critical, machine gun fire was coming from MONUMENT CORNER and enemy Very Lights were going up near ERVILLERS; I heard that the 41st were not coming up, and went to Bde.H.Q. of 120th. Brigade in SAPIGNIES. There we had a conference, the C.O. of the 9th. Lanc. Fusiliers, 74th.Brigade, luckily arrived and I found that the right flank was a line running from SAPIGNIES to BIHUCOURT; I could find no news of any troops on the left except that ERVILLERS, and accordingly we decided to withdraw the line West of the main road (which was being machine-gunned from both flanks); the line decided on was to run between WATERLOT FARM and the road through SAPIGNIES and joining the Right flank in H.8.d. I came out to re-adjust the line and found that the 41st. had arrived and that a battalion was in process of taking over a shortened line just in front of BEHAGNIES and SAPIGNIES.

The line was new to the incoming Battalion and we decided to line the 6th.S.W.B. on the line required by 41st.

All three Companies lined up; "A" Coy on the right were relieved and proceeded to the rendezvous in G.12.b. but no trace could be found of the companies due to relieve the left flank of the Brigade line.

It was then found that the troops due to relieve the left flank had taken over the original 2/S.Lancs and Border Line and with the C.O. of the 7th. Lanc. Fusiliers it was agreed that the two Companies of the 6th.S.W.B were to withdraw into SAPIGNIES, that this Battalion was to find a Lewis Gun post in the gap which we knew existed and that the 2 Companies of 6th.S.W.B. were to remain in reserve in SAPIGNIES under authority of B.G.C., 121st. Brigade, 41st. Division.

Major DEANE carried out this operation just in time to prevent these 2 Companies being mown down by Machine gun fire. Lieut. PEARCE and two Lewis Gun teams were pushed into the gap, and we went to review the situation.

By this time it was broad daylight on 25th., the enemy were attacking SAPIGNIES from three sides and it was decided to form a line behind SAPIGNIES.

A Battalion of 41st. Division were in H.1.a. and b., the 6th.S.W.B. were strung out in line from their right to H.7.b., some troops in trenches in an ineffective hollow on the West edge of SAPIGNIES were pulled out and re-enforced a line running South from the SAPIGNIES - BIHUCOURT Road touching on to the SAPIGNIES - BIEFVILLERS Line, about 200 stragglers down the BIHUCOURT Road were put in position on the threatened South flank Major DEANE went off to try to inform artillery of the line and en route posted a battery of Machine guns in BIHUCOURT to fire into SAPIGNIES.

The enemy attack on the Southern slopes of SAPIGNIES HILL was repulsed then our line was advanced a bit, but the gain was only of short duration because apparently BIEFVILLERS went.

By this time Canadians were in line South of BIHUCOURT, we appeared cut off from the North and the 6th.S.W.B. took up a line on high ground in in G.6.central with our left linked up with Manchesters and our right in touch across the valley with Lancashire Fusiliers.

By this time I had lost all touch with 120th. Brigade and wondered what we should do; leaving Major Deane in Command I made for Pioneer Camp at C.2.c., then into ABLAINZEVILLE where I foun from G.O.C. 75th. Infantry Bde. that we were to come into Divisional reserve. I went back intending to extract the companies at dusk or at the first opportunity; on arrival at C.6 central I found no trace od Major Deane and only a few men of "C" Coy.

6th. S.W.B. had been seen going towards ACHIET LE GRAND so I withdrew with the dozen men I found to LOGEAST WOOD.

Major Deane's report is attached.

Meanwhile the Companies which had been relieved in front of SAPIGNIES went back to the LOGEAST LINES and were ordered to commence digging on the right of 7th. infantry Brigade.

At 9.15 a.m. these companies received orders to proceed into Divisional reserve on the ACHIET LE PETIT - BUCQUOY Road whence they proceeded to PUISEUX to take up a defensive flank position on the South East side of the Church to defend the village from an attack from MIRAUMONT - the Companies were in position about 11 p.m.

After his operation Major Deane brought his men out to LOGEAST CAMP where he left them according to orders whilst he came on to Bde. Headquarters at BUCQUOY. There we met having with us about 40 men, not knowing where we were supposed to go, where the Battalion H.Q. with transport lines had gone to or where the men who had been relieved from SAPIGNIES had gone.

Whilst we were there the 75th. Infty.Bde got orders to proceed towards HEBUTERNE, I heard that the Divisional H.Q. were at COLINCAMPS and understood that the latter was our destination.

A runner was despatched ordered the party at LOGEAST to rejoin at COLINCAMPS and we proceeded to COLINCAMPS with our party.

On arrival at PUISEUX the SERRE Road seemed to be occupied by the enemy so we followed the traffic into HEBUTERNE on the North side of which we joined the Headquarters and Battalion Transport at about 1 a.m. on 26th. finding them on the point of moving to SAILLY AU BOIS where we arrived about 3 a.m. on 26th.

The detachment at LOGEAST got my message late on 25th. and made for COLINCAMPS whilst the detachment at PUISEUX after the Brigade had passed through was ordered to withdraw at 1 a.m. on 26th. and rejoin the Battalion.

At 7 a.m. on 26th. the PUISEUX party rejoined the Battalion at SAILLY AU BOIS but there was no trace of the LOGEAST Party, which did not rejoin the Battalion until 1 a.m. on 27th. as the Battalion was passing through COUIN; we were now encamped with Battn.Headquarters 2 Companies and Transport on the SAILLY - FONQUEVILLERS road just north of SAILLY.

At 7.30 a.m. on 26th. Adjutant R.E. arrived and told me that the Battalion would shortly receive orders to take up a position North of FONQUEVILLERS and I got packed up ready to move.

At about 8 a.m. there seemed to be a general retirement Westwards from HEBUTERNE and ~~SERRE~~ GOMMECOURT, troops and transport streamed over the hill, I did not know whether this was our front line coming back or not, enemy shells were bursting on the ridge between HEBUTERNE and SAILLY. We were massed on the East Slope of the BAYENCOURT Ridge and had machine guns come into action West of HEBUTERNE we should have suffered heavily.

I sent the transport to SOUASTRE and took up a position between SAILLY and BAYENCOURT my right flank in touch with outpost position of 51st. about a quarter of a mile South of the B in BAYENCOURT and my left flank in touch with a Battalion which had taken up a position West of the SAILLY - FONQUEVILLERS Road.

We dug in on this position but by 12 noon nothing developed so leaving Major Pearson in charge I went to SOUASTRE to make enquiries; there I met G.S.O 2 25th. Division, told him of my dispositions and decided to remain there. At that moment I got orders from C.R.S., 25th. Division telling me that the HEBUTERNE - GOMMECOURT front was intact and that the Battalion was to take up a position in front of HANNESCAMPS guarding the ESSARTS - POMMIER Road.

I rejoined the Battalion, informed neighborring units of the situation, told them I was marching to a flank and moved off to HANNESCAMPS where I arrived about 5 p.m. and got finally dug in with my right on R.S. and left on MONCHY Road about 9 p.m. We were in touch with our transport at POMMIER, cookers came up and the men were just standing down for a rest when at 11.30 p.m. I got orders to move the Battalion and all R.S. at once via BIENVILLERS to COUIN.

At 2.10 a.m. on 27th. the Battalion passed the starting point at BIENVILLERS, marched via SOUASTRE - COUIN and COIGNEUX to ROSSIGNOL Farm where we arrived at 8 a.m. on the 27th.

Meanwhile "B" Company started off from LOGEAST WOOD at 6 p.m. on 25th., marched to BUCQUOY and got instructions from 75th. Brigade to rejoin the Battalion at COLINCAMPS; the company arrived at COLINCAMPS about 3 a.m. on 26th. to find that there was no trace of the Battalion at COLINCAMPS but that it was supposed to be at FONQUEVILLERS. Again the company started off but on arriving at BAYENCOURT they heard that the whole 25th. Division had gone to ACHEUX. At ACHEUX there was no trace of the Division and were informed that the Division H.Q. were at MARIEUX, so they set of to MARIEUX. At MARIEUX they were ordered to go to COUIN and report there to the Division. On arrival at Couin late on the 26th. night they could still find no trace of the Divisional H.Q. or the Battalion but passers by said that we were at POMMIER. Again the company set off for POMMIER but on arrival at SOUASTRE the Battalion was said to be marching south so the men were left at SOUASTRE whilst 2 Officers scouted to the North, got in touch with the Battalion at BIENVILLERS and we picked up this company on our way through SOUASTRE about 5 a.m. on the 27th.

At last at 8 a.m. on 27th. was fairly complete except for various lost parties and we had food and about 3 hours sleep at ROSSIGNOL Farm.

At 2 p.m. on 27th. the Battalion marched with 7th. Brigade Group from COIGNEUX via AUTHIE and MARIEUX into bivouac 1 mile west of PUCHEVILLERS arriving about 10.30 p.m.

At 10.30 a.m. on 28th. the Battalion marched with 7th. Bde. again via TALMAS & HAVERNAS into billets at PERNOIS where we arrived about 2.30 p.m. on 28th.

"C". COMPANY.

	FROM.		TO.					
	PLACE.	TIME.	PLACE.	TIME.	DISTANCE.	FOOD.	SLEEP.	WORK.
21st.	H.9.a.	5 p.m.	Army Line.	6 p.m.	$1\frac{1}{2}$	Nil.	Nil.	Dug and manned 2 positions.
22nd.	Army Line.	5 p.m.	H.7.a.	7 p.m.	$2\frac{1}{2}$	Tea & Dinners on arrival.	6 hrs.	Dug and manned 1 position.
23rd.	H.7.a.	7 a.m.	SAPIGNIES LINES.	7.45 a.m.	1	Bully.	4 hours.	Dug & manned 1 position.
24th.						Bully.	Nil.	Being relieved.
25th.	SAPIGNIES LINE.	4 a.m.	PUISIEUX via ACHIET and BUCQUOY.	1 a.m. on 26th.	12	Nil	Nil	Took up flank position.
26th.	PUISIEUX	6 a.m.	SAILLY.	8 a.m.	5	Breakfast.		Took and manned
	SAILLY.	8 a.m.	BAYENCOURT.	9 a.m.	1			
	BAYENCOURT.	12 Noon.	HANNES CAMPS.	4 p.m.	4	Tea.	Nil.	position.
27th.	HANNES CAMPS.	2 a.m.	COIGNEUX.	8 a.m.	8	Dinners.	3 hours.	
	COIGNEUX.	2 p.m.	PUISEUX.	9 p.m.	11	Tea and Breakfast.	6 hours.	
28th.	PUISEUX.	10.30 a.m	PERNOIS.	3 p.m.	11			Six positions dug and manned.
				Total.	57 miles.		19 hours.	

"A" Company:-

22nd.	BEAUMETZ.	4 p.m.	H.7.a.	8 p.m.	8	Dinners.		Dug and manned 3 positions.
			Then as for "C" Coy.	Total.	61 miles.			

"D" COMPANY.

DATE.	FROM. PLACE.	TIME.	TO. PLACE.	TIME.	DISTANCE.	FOOD.	SLEEP.	WORK.
			Same as "C" Company till the 25th.					
[illegible]th.	SAPIGNIES LINES.	4 a.m.	LOGEAST WOOD.	5 p.m.	4	Nil.	Nil.	Dug & manned 3 positions
	LOGEAST	6 p.m.	BUCQUOY.	8 p.m.	3	"	"	
	BUCQUOY.	8 p.m.	COLINCAMPS.	3 a.m. 26th.	7.	"	"	
[illegible]th.	COLINCAMPS.	3 a.m.	ACHEUX.	5 a.m.	4	"	"	
	ACHEUX.	5 a.m.	COUIN, via MARIEUX.	6 p.m.	10.	"	"	
	COUIN.	6 p.m.	SOUASTRE.	2 a.m., 27th.	2½	"	"	
[illegible]th.	SOUASTRE.	1 a.m.	CONCHEUX.	8 a.m.	3½	Rejoined the Battalion.		
		And then on with Battalion.						
				Total.	87 Miles.			

From the morning of the 21st. to evening of the 28th. "A" Company marched 61 miles; "C" Coy. 657 miles; and "D" Coy. 87 miles, whilst the Transport marched 65 miles and outspanned at 12 different camps.

Each Company dug and manned at least 5 positions; no man in the Battalion had more than a total of 18 hours sleep whilst many had far less, and during the whole time the men in the Companies had the equivalent of 3 square meals.

The Battalion marched into PERNOIS on the 28th. with the Band playing and the men singing, all ranks full of spirit, but only wanting food and sleep. Every animal was fit, though tired, and we did not lose an animal through galls or foot trouble.

During the operations 1 man in the Battalion reported sick, whilst up to the 27th. inclusive 4 men fell out on line of marchand on the 28th. 16 fell outwithin one mile of PERNOIS; on the morning of the 29th. 2 men reported sick at the Battalion Sick parade.

W Kilpatrick

Lieut.Colonel, R.E.,

30/3/18. Commdg:6th.(S).Bn.S.W.Borderers (Pioneers).

Report on Operations by "D" Company

6th S.W.B. 25th March.

--

REPORT ON OPERATIONS CARRIED OUT BY "D" COY. 6th.BN. SOUTH WALES BORDERERS ON 25th. INSATNT.

-:-:-:-:-:-:-:-:-:-

About 10 a.m. on the 25th. instant I was left by the C.O. to take up a position with "D" Company on the BEHAGNIES - BIHUCOURT ridge.

The situation at this time was as under:-

The enemy had entered SAPIGNIES and had worked his way down the BIHUCOURT ridge to a point about K.

His main line of attack appeared to be about K L and he showed no inclination to attack North of the BIHUCOURT - SAPIGNIES road.

I took up an entrenched position at A.B. I was seen going into this position from the road about K and was heavily machine-gunned and shelled with low bursting shrapnel. I at once decided that the position was untenable and that I was doing no good by staying there so I withdrew to a position in a sunken road at C.D. I then had behind me a battalion of Manchesters and some scattered troops dug in on a line MN.

The enemy then appeared to be advancing on a line O P, so seeing that I was of no use at C D, I withdrew and worked my way across to E F, where there was a poor field of fire and already a strong line of infantry who had fallen back.

I carried on and took a position at G H, where I dug in with a good field of fire and a belt of wire in front of me. There was a line of posts (I J) in front of me held with Lewis Guns of 42nd. Division.

At this point I was asked by a Colonel of the 42nd. Division to assist him in driving the enemy out of the wood Q as his trenches were being enfiladed at R S. I decided that this was the proper course and that the wood must be denied to the enemy.

The position I J was meanwhile under M.-G. fire from the left, but I managed to get my Company across the open in one rush into the line I J without casualties. Here we re-organised and improved the position with a view to jumping off from there and clearing the wood. One L.-Gun kept the near side of the wood clear and all was ready to continue the advance into the wood when I received orders that tanks had been detailed for the duty. The tanks crossed my position at J and to a certain extent cleared the wood before returning.

The enemy then showed at point T, where we met him with heavy rifle fire and drove him off. He then advanced to the edge of the wood but he was again driven back by rifle and M.-G. fire.

He then appeared to settle down and give up the idea of advancing throu the wood.

The line I J had become congested with various odd troops meanwhile, and I decided that there was no further work for the pioneers in this trenc

I therefore withdrew my men one by one with a view to strengthening the position in front of the main German attack somewhere about U V. I succeeded in safely withdrawing the Company to a point W, where we assemble I then found that I had a very weak company, several men having been detached and mixed up in the general advance on I J and the previous positions.

I ascertained that the positions round U J were held by two brigades of the 61st.(?)Division, and as the men had been fighting for 4 days and nights on end with no sleep and little food, I withdrew throught ACHIET - LE-GRAND where I suffered heavy casualties from shell fire directed at the railway.

(Sd) L.G.W.Deane, Major.

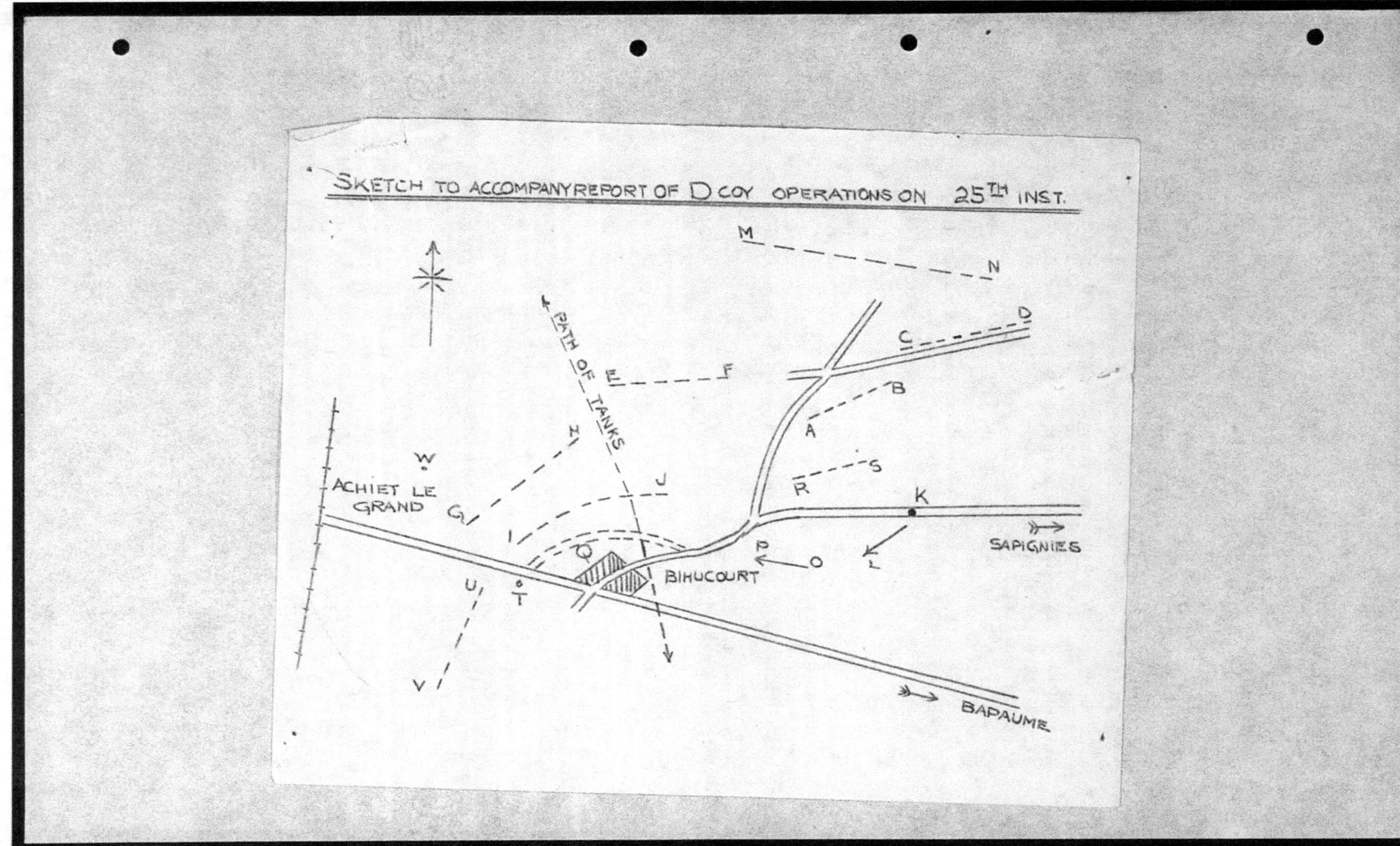
SKETCH TO ACCOMPANY REPORT OF D COY OPERATIONS ON 25TH INST.
PATH OF TANKS
ACHIET LE GRAND
BIHUCOURT
SAPIGNIES
BAPAUME
A
B
C
D
E
F
G
H
I
J
K
L
M
N
O
P
Q
R
S
T
U
V
W

25th Divisional Troops

WAR DIARY

6th BATTALION

THE SOUTH WALES BORDERERS

Pioneers

APRIL 1 9 1 8

Attached :- Report on Operations 9th-15th

Instructions regarding War Diaries and Intelligence Summaries are contained in F. S. Regs., Part II. and the Staff Manual respectively. Title Pages will be prepared in manuscript.

R/25

WAR DIARY
or
INTELLIGENCE SUMMARY
(Erase heading not required.)

Army Form C. 2118

1st Bn. S. W. Borderers.

Vol 32

Place	Date	Hour	Summary of Events and Information	Remarks and references to Appendices
	APRIL	1918		
ROMARIN	1		Day spent resting and cleaning up 3 O.Rs. from base taken on strength	H.R.M.
do.	2		Battn. carry through gas parades, rifle drill, etc. 14 O.Rs. reported for duty and taken on strength of 'D' Coy.	H.R.M.
do.	3		Battn. trained – training consisting of musketry, bayonet fighting, physical training, gas, signalling, squad drill, etc	H.R.M.
do.	4		'A' and 'C' Coys. moved to the CATACOMBS at HYDE PARK CORNER T.19.b.4.7. Sheet 28 S.W. for work on the Corps and secret lines. 'D' Coy. took over and have to maintain the railways in divisional area. Transport remain at BONANZA LINES B.8.c. Sheet 36 12 O.Rs. reported for duty and have been taken on	

33.S
23 pp.

1875 Wt. W593/826 1,000,000 4/15 J.B.C. & A. A.D.S.S./Forms/C. 2118.

Army Form C. 2118

Instructions regarding War Diaries and Intelligence Summaries are contained in F. S. Regs., Part II. and the Staff Manual respectively. Title Pages will be prepared in manuscript.

WAR DIARY
or
INTELLIGENCE SUMMARY
(Erase heading not required.)

Place	Date APRIL	Hour	Summary of Events and Information	Remarks and references to Appendices
ROMARIN	4 con		the strength of coys as follows:-	
			'A' Coy. 4 ORs.	
			'C' – 2 ORs.	
			'D' – 3 ORs.	
do.	5		'A' and 'C' Coys. start work on Corps line repairing trenches erecting shell hole defences and wiring.	H.K.M.
			'D' Coy start on divisional railways with one platoon, remaining three carrying on training as laid down on the 3rd.	
			Tempy. Lieut (A/Captn.) D. H. STICKLER promoted to Tempy. Captn. 9/12/17 vide Supplement London Gazette 21/3/18.	
do.	6		'A' and 'C' Coys. work as for previous day. 'A' Coy. take over railways in divisional area from 'D' Coy.	H.K.M.
			'D' Coy. start sapping at RAVELSBERG S.17.d.9.8. Sheet 28 S.W with 2 platoons, remaining 2 carry on training	

Instructions regarding War Diaries and Intelligence Summaries are contained in F. S. Regs., Part II. and the Staff Manual respectively. Title Pages will be prepared in manuscript.

WAR DIARY
or
INTELLIGENCE SUMMARY
(Erase heading not required.)

Army Form C. 2118

Place	Date APRIL	Hour	Summary of Events and Information	Remarks and references to Appendices
ROMARIN	6 con		'D' Coy. and Headquarters bath at PALMERS BATHS T 26a 2.9. Sheet 28 SW.	
			Following Tempy. 2/Lieuts. promoted Tempy. Lieuts from dates shown against their names:-	
			Tempy 2/Lieut E.W.S. KITE 8/10/17	
			Tempy 2/Lieut. W.T. DAVIES 7/9/17	
			vide Supplement London Gazette 4/4/18.	
do	7		Coys. work as detailed on previous day.	AKM.
			'A' Coy. repair track	
do.	8		Coys. work as per programme.	AKM.
			Draft of 133 N.C.Os. and men joined the Battn. and posted temporarily to Headquarter Coy.	
do.	9		'A' and 'C' Coys. bath at RED LODGE T.18.d.6.4 Sheet 28 S.W.	AKM.
			The draft of 133 ORs. posted as follows:-	
			'A' Coy 42 ORs.	
			'C' " 45 ORs.	
			'D' " 46 ORs.	AKM

1875 Wt. W593/826 1,000,000 4/15 J.B.C. & A. A.D.S.S./Forms/C. 2118.

Instructions regarding War Diaries and Intelligence Summaries are contained in F. S. Regs., Part II. and the Staff Manual respectively. Title Pages will be prepared in manuscript.

WAR DIARY
or
INTELLIGENCE SUMMARY
(Erase heading not required.)

Army Form C. 2118

Place	Date APRIL	Hour	Summary of Events and Information	Remarks and references to Appendices
WIPPINHOEK	9/15	2PM/4AM.	Attached is an account of the operations of Batn. from 9th – 15th April. Casualties on following sheets.	HKK.

1875 Wt. W593/826 1,000,000 4/15 J.B.C. & A. A.D.S.S./Forms/C. 2118.

Instructions regarding War Diaries and Intelligence Summaries are contained in F. S. Regs., Part II. and the Staff Manual respectively. Title Pages will be prepared in manuscript.

WAR DIARY
or
INTELLIGENCE SUMMARY
(Erase heading not required.)

Army Form C. 2118

Place	Date	Hour	Summary of Events and Information	Remarks and references to Appendices
			Following are the casualties sustained in operations 9th/15th April:—	
			10th April.	
			Killed:–	
			6/17619 C.S.M. D.G. PARKER. — 6/17176 SGT. W. LANDER – M.M.	
			6/16997 SGT. A. HEMMINGS. — 26027 PTE. C. BAKER.	
			260302 PTE. E. LEE. — 6/14553 – L. PHILLIPS.	
			6/16546 – J. BROWN — 6/17557 – J. CHARLTON.	
			6/13769 – A. C. PRICE. — 29802 – B. PRINCE.	
			35502 – W. WALTERS – B.C. de G. — 37841 – C. MALAM.	
			40696 – J. LATHAM. — 6/42308 – W. S. MARSH.	
			41732 – H.O. DUFFIL — 40882 – G. HEAD.	
			40904 – W.C. MARTIN. — 30251 – A.L. FORD.	
			39421 – F.T. GREENWAY. — 6/42391 – H.E. CROXTON.	
			Wounded:—	
			6/17058 SGT J. WILKINSON. — 6/19697 SGT W.J. ASHMAN.	
			6/16757 – W.J. SHEPHERD – M.M. — 6/19138 – B. SANKEY.	
			6/17496 – G. CARPENTER. — 6/17302 – A. CLARKE.	
			6/17212 – J. REES. — 6/17153 – A. WILLIAMS.	
			6/17436 L/SGT. R. WHEELER – M.M. — 40709 A.L/SGT D. SHOTTON.	

1875 Wt. W593/826 1,000,000 4/15 J.B.C. & A. A.D.S.S./Forms/C. 2118.

Instructions regarding War Diaries and Intelligence Summaries are contained in F. S. Regs., Part II. and the Staff Manual respectively. Title Pages will be prepared in manuscript.

WAR DIARY
or
INTELLIGENCE SUMMARY
(Erase heading not required.)

Army Form C. 2118

Place	Date	Hour	Summary of Events and Information	Remarks and references to Appendices
	APRIL 10th con.		Wounded con.	

6/17567	CPL	A.J. THOMAS — M.M.	6/19702	CPL	E. ADDISON
6/16466	–	H.R. BERRY	6/19381	–	J. COLES
27380	–	E.G. EMMETT	23120	–	S. WILLIAMS.
40090	L/CPL	F. DAVIES	40851	L/CPL	A. BAINBRIDGE
6/42234	–	B. LIDDINGTON	39385	–	G. F. SWEET.
201385	PTE.	J. BOUND	48896	PTE	A. COX
6/17195	–	W. DAVIES	2562	–	A. S. LLEWELLYN
39271	–	W. JENNINGS.	40156	–	J. YOUCKS
6/19137	–	W. SANKEY.	40080	–	R. BRADLEY.
39001	–	G. CHAPPELL.	6/16292	–	J. WILLIAMS
6/17581	–	A. GUEST	40679	–	G. DAVIES
30192	–	F. FITTON.	40086	–	F. CHAMBERS
6/17516	–	A. GRIFFITHS.	6/16356	–	W. HEMMINGS
29306	–	J.W. JEPSON.	40899	–	J. LENG.
6/19038	–	T. JONES — M.M.	6/19235	–	G. BARBER.
6/17485	–	W. MOYLON.	6/16887	–	W. GRIFFITHS.
6/17504	–	G. POWIS	35632	–	R. J. PARRY.
6/17493	–	R. STANLEY.	6/19136	–	J. SANKEY.
40734	–	J. TOMKINSON.	6/16782	–	T. SAMUELS.
29218	–	J. WEATHERBY.	33559	–	A. FRANKLIN
29239	–	T. WHITTAKER.	42293	–	C. GREEN
			6/17016	–	J. HORROBIN — M.M.

1875 Wt. W593/826 1,000,000 4/15 J.B.C. & A. A.D.S.S./Forms/C. 2118.

Army Form C. 2118

Instructions regarding War Diaries and Intelligence Summaries are contained in F. S. Regs., Part II. and the Staff Manual respectively. Title Pages will be prepared in manuscript.

WAR DIARY
or
INTELLIGENCE SUMMARY
(Erase heading not required.)

Place	Date	Hour	Summary of Events and Information	Remarks and references to Appendices
	APRIL 10th con		Wounded con.	
			31361 PTE. C.E. JONES — 40905 PTE. F. MILLS	
			41058 - R. LEATHER. — 360344 - R.E. BLATCHLEY.	
			29170 - C.E. PRICE — 6/16458 - W. H. HARRIES	
			6/17540 - T. SIMMONDS — 6/17258 - H. DAVIES	
			6/16452 - G. THOMAS — 40165 - P. POWELL	
			6/17561 - J. WILLIAMS — 41742 - H. FIELDING.	
			29280 - L. WASTELL — 39224 - J. TROY	
			25840 - A. WALTERS — 29448 - R. BOURNE	
			39184 - E. WOZENCROFT — 41043 - C. FELL	
			40425 - C. TAYLOR. — 5/18962 - W. J. DRAPER	
			6/19674 - G. WIDDICK. — 29815 - W. H. POLLY	
			6/10799 - J. CALLAGHAN. — 29751 - W. BEER	
			6/17469 - W. WESTON — 6/16760 - W. HOLLIDAY —— D.C.M.	
			6/42303 - J. McNAUGHTON. — 6/17259 - F.G. WHITE.	
			40423 - E. THORPE	
			6/42306 - T. H. PARR	
			30163 - H. E. MARTIN	
			30151 - R.E. CADDY	
			41422 - J. B. COGGINS	
			40911 - J. NIXON	
			40082 - J. C. BYWATER.	
			41743 - G. FREE	
			Missing.	
			6/17449 CPL R. COOMBES	
			40008 - W. E. NAUGHTON	
			40016 L/CPL. F. LEAH.	
			42969 PTE J. O. HUGHES	
			41741 - W. F. ELSTON	
			40681 - T. GREENHALGH	

1875 Wt. W593/826 1,000,000 4/15 J.B.C. & A. A.D.S.S./Forms/C. 2118.

Instructions regarding War Diaries and Intelligence Summaries are contained in F. S. Regs., Part II. and the Staff Manual respectively. Title Pages will be prepared in manuscript.

WAR DIARY
or
INTELLIGENCE SUMMARY
(Erase heading not required.)

Army Form C. 2118

Place	Date APRIL	Hour	Summary of Events and Information	Remarks and references to Appendices
	10th con		Missing con.	
			29604 PTE. C.J. BOROUGHS — 40710 PTE. J. SUMPTER.	
			29472 - J. SMITH — 41716 - F. CREAM.	
			41001 - W. GRANDORGE — 40081 - W. BROUGHTON.	
			6/42438 - G. BARTRAM — 6/19033 - C.N. BEVAN	
			26639 - S. BOSWELL — 41729 - E.C. DAVIES	
			37749 - A. GOWER — 30180 - A. GADSDON	
			23555 - C.A. HARRISON — 40790 - H. BEALE	
			29247 - W.H. MEYER. — 6/16981 - N. BURTONSHAW	
			6/17529 - W. REYNOLDS — M.M. — 6/16806 - J. DAVIES	
			45582 - F. ROWLEY. — 29241 - A.R. HARRISON	
			39200 - H. ROGERS — 40111 - W. C. JONES	
			40714 - R. STANSFIELD — 6/17207 - B. REYNOLDS	
			40932 - R. TURNBULL — 26385 - D.T. OWEN	
			40547 - T. WOLSTENHOLME — 42408 - A.G. HEATH.	
			41694 - S. ANKERS. — 48811 - D. BEBBINGTON	
			41709 - R. BLACKBURN — 48956 - W. L. DONNELLY	
			48866 - E.C. BROOME — 48910 - F.G. EDWARDS	
			48872 - R. BLAKE — 48914 - W.T. FRANCIS	
			48889 - G. CLEMONT — 48935 - P.G. GRIFFITHS	
			48892 - W. A. CRITCHLEY. — 48932 - J. HIGGINBOTTOM	
			41714 - W. CONNOLLY — 40181 - J. MITTON	
			48901 - J. DAVIES. — 39233 - S. WHIPP	

1875 Wt. W593/826 1,000,000 4/15 J.B.C. & A. A.D.S.S./Forms/C. 2118.

Instructions regarding War Diaries and Intelligence Summaries are contained in F. S. Regs., Part II. and the Staff Manual respectively. Title Pages will be prepared in manuscript.

WAR DIARY
or
INTELLIGENCE SUMMARY
(Erase heading not required.)

Army Form C. 2118

Place	Date	Hour	Summary of Events and Information	Remarks and references to Appendices
	APRIL 10th Con		Wounded and missing	
			48860 CPL. J. R. HACKLEY — 260267 PTE. C. J. O'NEILL	
			40431 PTE. J. DIXON — 29393 – E. BATTERLEY	
			40690 – W. HOPWOOD — 260270 – F. STANTON.	
			29133 – E. J. WARNE.	
			11th April	
			Killed	
			6/19223 C.S.M. J. RANSOME — MM. — 6/17124 PTE. J. TONKS.	
			6/17320 PTE. J. QUICK	
			Wounded.	
			6/16552 SGT. J. HORTON — 6/17122 L/SGT. B. TONKS.	
			6/17347 — A. J. QUINTON — 6/17330 CPL. W. ANDREWS	
			48858 CPL. C. H. OLD — 21154 – E. SWANTON	
			40853 L/CPL. J. WALTON. — 6/42305 PTE. T. ASPINALL	
			6/42230 PTE. A. ARSCOTT — 6/16817 – G. MORGAN.	
			45874 – J. BUFTON — 6/17178 – C. FITZGERALD	
			40099 – E. GREEN — 41731 – J. G. DAVIES	
			40917 – E. RENDER. — 41326 – S. RANDALL	
			6/18845 – G. WARBRICK. — 41744 – G. FLETCHER.	
			42399 – F. T. CLARKE — 39278 – F. COOKE.	
			6/14707 – W. S. JONES. — 40867 – R. GOWAN	
			26063 – A. COLES — 42323 – J. FAGAN	
			31166 – G. GARDNER.	
			39270 – R. ELLIS	

1875 Wt. W593/826 1,000,000 4/15 J.B.C. & A. A.D.S.S./Forms/C. 2118.

Instructions regarding War Diaries and Intelligence Summaries are contained in F. S. Regs., Part II. and the Staff Manual respectively. Title Pages will be prepared in manuscript.

WAR DIARY
or
INTELLIGENCE SUMMARY
(Erase heading not required.)

Army Form C. 2118

Place	Date	Hour	Summary of Events and Information	Remarks and references to Appendices
	APRIL 11th Con.		Wounded con.	
			6/42243 PTE. B. HOOPER — 29061 PTE. M.G. SMITH.	
			45979 - R. HARGREAVES — 6/13337 - J. HORMAN	
			42271 - W.T. PEARCE. — 39664 - E. JONES.	
			Missing.	
			22066 SGT. B. CRONIN — 6/16849 PTE. F. PAYNE	
			41970 PTE. J. JONES — 42400 - W.F. CLARKE	
			360243 - S.C.J. ROBINSON — 39209 - E. WARNER	
			360269 - J.F. WILLIAMS — 6/19382 - T. KAVANAGH	
			260344 - W.F. ROWSON — 41739 - W. EDGE.	
			31804 - A. STAPLETON — 41720 - C. CORK	
			40160 - E. HENSHALL — 40737 - F. HALLIDAY	
			41726? - T.W. COWLEY — 6/17519 - E. JONES	
			6/17341 - A. PINK. — 41698 - W. BISHOP	
			41704 - W. BILSBOROUGH. — 41699 - S. BAILEY	
			41705 - C. BATES.	
			Wounded & missing.	
			39186 PTE J. ALLFORD — 40923 PTE. L.T. SPOORS	
			40132 - S. PORTER — 41740 - W.T. EGERTON	
			40726 - W. GREEN. — 6/16972 - P. WILLIAMS	
			41719 - A. CARR	
			12th April.	
			Killed	
			40686 PTE. W HUGHES	

1875 ~~Wt. W593/826~~ 1,000,000 4/15 J.B.C. & A. A.D.S.S./Forms/C. 2118.

Instructions regarding War Diaries and Intelligence Summaries are contained in F. S. Regs., Part II. and the Staff Manual respectively. Title Pages will be prepared in manuscript.

WAR DIARY
or
INTELLIGENCE SUMMARY
(Erase heading not required.)

Army Form C. 2118

Place	Date	Hour	Summary of Events and Information	Remarks and references to Appendices
	APRIL 12th Con.			

Wounded

6/17009	SGT.	P. BURGE	29623	L/SGT.	C. H. ALLEN
6/19898	CPL.	R. KNIGHTHALL	6/17144	L/CPL.	J. GOOCH
260318	PTE.	W. SWAIN — MM.	40855	PTE	W. ANDERSON
6/44506	-	E. HAMPTON	42341	-	L. BAYARD
40907	-	A. MIDDLEMISS	31029	-	G. BARKER.
30327	-	W. A. COOKE	30340	-	J. HART
42435	-	L. FARMER	209147	-	W. MARTIN
35331	-	P. GREEN	6/16318	-	J. THOMAS
6/17199	-	F. W. THOMPSON	31170	-	W. BAINES
6/11667	-	G. THOMPSON	45559	-	T. W. FLETCHER.
			40936	-	J. FOWELL

Missing.

48855	SGT.	J. PRICE	201458	PTE.	B. PRICE
41737	PTE.	L. EVANS	6/18390	-	C. A. STAGG.
31373	-	N. FLYNN	29219	-	F. TAGELL.
41728	-	R. T. DAVIES			

13th April

Killed.

6/77030	CPL.	E. DREW	201458	PTE	B. PRICE
39212	PTE.	W. ENTWHISTE	6/18390	-	C. A. STAGG.
40944	-	W. WAKEFIELD	29219	-	F. TAGELL
42264	-	C. V. HOULDING.			

Wounded.

260258	SGT.	J. A. ROBINSON	6/16796	L/CPL	H. A. MORGAN
38544	PTE.	A. E. HEAP	40897	PTE	G. KENDALL
			6/17188	-	F. MOORE
			40919	-	J. B. RILEY

1875 Wt. W593/826 1,000,000 4/15 J.B.C. & A. A.D.S.S./Forms/C. 2118.

Instructions regarding War Diaries and Intelligence Summaries are contained in F. S. Regs., Part II. and the Staff Manual respectively. Title Pages will be prepared in manuscript.

WAR DIARY
or
INTELLIGENCE SUMMARY
(Erase heading not required.)

Army Form C. 2118

Place	Date	Hour	Summary of Events and Information	Remarks and references to Appendices
	APRIL 13th con.		Wounded con.	
			40902 PTE. G. LUMLEY — 6/16798 PTE S. SAMUELS	
			38665 - H. GRIFFITHS. — 6/17286 - E. THOMAS	
			39181 - G. A. MORGAN — 6/16929 - J. J. JAMES	
			40112 - F. G. OLIVER — 39678 - J. D. MASSIE	
			6/18364 - T. DOWLING	
			40898 - W. KIDD	
			6/16933 - T. A. MORGAN	
			Wounded & Missing.	
			40787 PTE. A. T. PERKINS.	
			Missing	
			29232 PTE. E. LEWIS — 6/17110 PTE R. WATT	
			14th April.	
			Missing	
			34545 PTE F. HERBERT — 29793 PTE E. BAILEY	
			41697 - J. BRENNAN — 40130 - G. HARRIS	
			41702 - D. J. BARRETT — 40892 - W. HAWTHORNE	
			41708 - W. BANCROFT — 29770 - T. JONES	
			41710 - A. G. BROWN — 41075 - R. LLOYD	
			48882 - A. BROWN — 41495 - W. MOSESON	
			41213 - J. CLAYTON — 39521 - H. W. PARKER	
			41731 - A. E. CLOUGH — 48435 - J. E. SAMUEL	
			— 6/11896 - J. WATKINS	
			Wounded.	
			26336 CPL. P. DAVIES — 227381 PTE F. LEWIS	
			42045 PTE. W. CONNINGHAM — 37719 - W. SAVILLE	
			— 40752 - J. H. TROUSDALE	
			— 29741 - R. WILLIAMS	

1875 Wt. W593/826 1,000,000 4/15 J.B.C. & A. A.D.S.S./Forms/C. 2118.

Instructions regarding War Diaries and Intelligence Summaries are contained in F. S. Regs., Part II. and the Staff Manual respectively. Title Pages will be prepared in manuscript.

WAR DIARY
or
INTELLIGENCE SUMMARY
(Erase heading not required.)

Army Form C. 2118

Place	Date	Hour	Summary of Events and Information	Remarks and references to Appendices
	APRIL 14 con.		Wounded con.	
			6/16356 PTE. J. JONES — 6/16446 PTE R. N. PRICE — 33206 - G. DAVIES	
			15th April.	
			Wounded	
			48910 PTE. G.B. EDGAR — 41071 PTE. A. JONES	
			260292 - J. C. FIGURES — 40120 - T. PEERS	
			48917 - W. FORSHAW — 207682 - T. SANDERS	
			30183 - M.T. GRIFFITHS — ? - J. LUKE.	
			Missing	
			42395 PTE. A. R. BORRIDGE	
			Unknown date	
			Wounded.	
			6/13670 SGT. A. J. EVANS — 40919 PTE. J. B. RILEY	
			44613 L/CPL. W. ROBERTS — 29412 - A. JONES	
			200106 PTE. W. L. WEAVER. — 6/17484 - E. SMITH	
			6/13812 - S. T. JONES — 41321 - W. C. BROCKWAY.	
			Wounded & missing.	
			48859 CPL. J. CHAPMAN. — 260263 PTE. T. E. BROWN.	
			Missing.	
			24165 CPL. W. EASTHOPE — 6/16406 PTE. A. ATTWOOD	
			24932 L/CPL W. HAMILTON — 48870 - W. F. BEVAN	
			29652 PTE R. A. LEWIS — 48885 - J. BAKER	
			48864 - A. R. ALDRIDGE — 48883 - J. L. BEARCROFT	
			237932 - J. ASPINALL — 42390 - J. BRYAN	
			45821 - J. BATH	
			48878 - H. BURNIC	

1875 Wt. W593/826 1,000,000 4/15 J.B.C. & A. A.D.S.S./Forms/C. 2118.

Instructions regarding War Diaries and Intelligence Summaries are contained in F. S. Regs., Part II. and the Staff Manual respectively. Title Pages will be prepared in manuscript.

WAR DIARY
or
INTELLIGENCE SUMMARY
(Erase heading not required.)

Army Form C. 2118

Place	Date	Hour	Summary of Events and Information	Remarks and references to Appendices
	APRIL UNKNOWN DATE.		Missing con.	

No.	Rank	Name	No.	Rank	Name
6/14427	PTE.	R. SCOTT	48898	PTE.	J. CUTTANCE
42253	-	H. STACKDEN	48888	-	E. CONWAY
39179	-	A. FOLMAN	28979	-	J. DAVIES
48867	-	H. BABY	48899	-	J. CROMPTON
42274	-	C. OPPREY	48907	-	A. DUTTON
6/17183	-	S. PEARSON	?	-	? FAWCETT
21989	-	R. YEOMAN	6/16384	-	W. GRIFFITHS
39204	-	E. McDONOUGH	6/16360	-	J. GOULD
6/13644	-	C. MEREDITH	48929	-	J. GIBSON
360321	-	J. FIBBALS	42249	-	M. HUMBER
89030	-	A. WILLS	40156	-	G. HOWELL
48879	-	A. BIBLEY	40112	-	G. KNIGHT
			40149	-	E. ROBERTS
			40151	-	E. ROBERTS.

Following are the officers casualties

Rank	Name	Killed	Wounded	Missing	Sick	Date	
Lt. Col.	N. T. FITZPATRICK. DSO. MC. RE.		W.			14th April	
						13th —	(at duty)
Maj.	N. G. PEARSON MC.		W.			10th —	
Capt.	J. C. OWEN MC.		W			10th —	
—	D. JENKINS MC.		W.			10th —	
—	F. A. HITCHCOX				S	9th —	
Lieut.	C. M. RIGG		W			10th —	
—	E. W. S. KITE		W.			10th —	

1875 Wt. W593/826 1,000,000 4/15 J.B.C. & A. A.D.S.S./Forms/C. 2118.

Army Form C. 2118

WAR DIARY
or
INTELLIGENCE SUMMARY
(Erase heading not required.)

Instructions regarding War Diaries and Intelligence Summaries are contained in F. S. Regs., Part II. and the Staff Manual respectively. Title Pages will be prepared in manuscript.

Place	Date APRIL	Hour	Rank	Name	Killed	Wounded	Missing	Sick	Date	Remarks and references to Appendices
	con.									
			Lieut.	J. H. RICHARDS. MC.		W			11th April	
			–	G. H. TAYLOR.		W			11th –	
			–	W. T. DAVIES	K				13th –	
			–	W. H. HANNA		W			13th –	
			2/Lieut.	T. R. JONES		W			10th –	
			–	R. G. BUTTERWORTH		W			10th –	
			–	A. L. GOUGH		W			10th –	
			–	L. PETTS MC.		W			11th –	
			–	I. K. FRASER		W			11th –	
			–	A. JENKINS			M		13th –	
			–	F. A. JAKEWAY.				S	11th –	

1875 Wt. W593/826 1,000,000 4/15 J.B.C. & A. A.D.S.S./Forms/C. 2118.

Instructions regarding War Diaries and Intelligence Summaries are contained in F. S. Regs., Part II. and the Staff Manual respectively. Title Pages will be prepared in manuscript.

WAR DIARY
or
INTELLIGENCE SUMMARY
(Erase heading not required.)

Army Form C. 2118

Place	Date	Hour	Summary of Events and Information	Remarks and references to Appendices
			SUMMARY OF CASUALTIES.	

OFFICERS.

DATE.	K.	W.	W a M.	M.	S.
9th					1
10th		7			
11th		4			1
12th					
13th	1	2		1	
14th		1			
TOTAL	1	14		1	2

18

OTHER RANKS.

DATE	K.	W.	W a M.	M.	S.
9th					
10th	20	89	7	50	
11	3	32	7	21	
12	1	21		7	
13	7	17	1	2	
14		9		17	
15		8		1	
U		8	2	38	
TOTAL	31	184	17	136	

366

386

HRM

1875 Wt. W593/826 1,000,000 4/15 J.B.C. & A. A.D.S.S./Forms/C. 2118.

Instructions regarding War Diaries and Intelligence Summaries are contained in F. S. Regs., Part II. and the Staff Manual respectively. Title Pages will be prepared in manuscript.

WAR DIARY
or
INTELLIGENCE SUMMARY
(Erase heading not required.)

Army Form C. 2118

Place	Date APRIL	Hour	Summary of Events and Information	Remarks and references to Appendices
WIPPIN HOEK.	15	4 AM.	Battn. was relieved by 1st Leicesters and moved off to Bgde. concentration area at DRANOUTRE M: 35. d. Sheet 28 SW. Food was given all ranks and battalion rested until mid day.	
			At 1 P.M. orders were received to move to WIPPIN HOEK L. 28. b. Sheet 27 NE. arriving there about 6 P.M.	ARM:
do.	16		Battn. rested and cleaned up.	ARM:
GODEWAERS-VELDE	17		At 11.30 A.M. orders were received to concentrate in divisional area at Q. 17. d. Sheet 27 near GODEWAERSVELDE Battalion moved off at 2 P.M. and reached Q. 17. d. at about 5 P.M.	
do.	18		Battn. rested.	ARM:
do.	19		Battn. carried out the following training – musketry, bayonet fighting, physical training, gas, squad drill etc.	ARM:
			The following ORs. have been awarded the Military	

1875 Wt. W593/826 1,000,000 4/15 J.B.C. & A. A.D.S.S./Forms/C. 2118.

Instructions regarding War Diaries and Intelligence Summaries are contained in F. S. Regs., Part II. and the Staff Manual respectively. Title Pages will be prepared in manuscript.

WAR DIARY
or
INTELLIGENCE SUMMARY
(Erase heading not required.)

Army Form C. 2118

Place	Date APRIL	Hour	Summary of Events and Information	Remarks and references to Appendices
GODEWAERSVELDE	19 con		Medal – refce D.R.O. 3604 :–	
			6/17436 A/Sgt. R. WHEELER 6/17111 Pte. J. ATHERTON	
			6/19038 Pte. T. JONES 6/42242 A/Sgt. A. JOHNSON	
			44495 Sgt. T. GREEN 6/17529 Pte W. REYNOLDS	
			6/17176 – W. LANDER 6/17080 – S. WATERS	
			6/13670 – A.J. EVANS 31131 – J. HOWELLS	
			6/17458 Pte. F. BURSTON 6/17016 – J. HORROBIN (Bar to M.M.)	
			260318 – W. SWAIN. 6/17528 – A. PEARCE	
do.	20		Battn. trained as detailed for yesterday.	ARM
do.	21		Battn. had orders to move to DIRTY BUCKET CORNER CAMP A.30.d.15.85. Sheet 28 via ABEELE – WIPPINHOEK – HOOGEGRAS. Transport was met at K.27.c (27 N.E.) on the line of march. Arrived at A.30.d.15.85 about 3 P.M.	ARM:
FLAMATINGAE	22		Battalion carried out training as laid down on 18th April.	ARM.
			The following officer has been awarded the Distinguished Service Order – refce D.R.O. 3608 :–	
			A/Major L.C.W. DEANE, M.C.	

1875 Wt. W593/826 1,000,000 4/15 J.B.C. & A. A.D.S.S./Forms/C. 2118.

Instructions regarding War Diaries and Intelligence Summaries are contained in F. S. Regs., Part II. and the Staff Manual respectively. Title Pages will be prepared in manuscript.

WAR DIARY
or
INTELLIGENCE SUMMARY
(Erase heading not required.)

Army Form C. 2118

Place	Date	Hour	Summary of Events and Information	Remarks and references to Appendices
	APRIL			
FLAMATINGHE.	22 con		The following officers have been awarded the Military Cross – refce. D.R.O. 3608:– T/Lieut. A. G. PEARCE. T/Lieut. H. DAVIES. T 2/Lieut. L. PETTS. The u/m OR. has been awarded the Distinguished Conduct Medal – refce. D.R.O. 3608:– 6/16760 Pte. W. HOLLIDAY	
do.	23		Battn. trained as per programme.	HRM.
do.	24		3 ORs. reported for duty – 2 sent to 'A' and 1 to 'D' Coy. Lieut. ~~Colyer~~ COLYER of Army School reported to act as instructor ~~of~~ to battn. Training carried out as per details.	HRM:
do.	25		Battn. trained as per programme.	HRM.
PROVEN	26		Battn. commenced training as per programme, but orders to move were received at 1P.M. Battn. moved at 2.45 P.M. and arrived at E. 14. d. 5.3	HRM.

1875 Wt. W593/826 1,000,000 4/15 J.B.C. & A. A.D.S.S./Forms/C. 2118.

Instructions regarding War Diaries and Intelligence Summaries are contained in F. S. Regs., Part II. and the Staff Manual respectively. Title Pages will be prepared in manuscript.

WAR DIARY
or
INTELLIGENCE SUMMARY
(Erase heading not required.)

Army Form C. 2118

Place	Date APRIL	Hour	Summary of Events and Information	Remarks and references to Appendices
PROVEN	26 con.		Sheet 27 NW at about 7 p.m.	
			A/Capt. T.H. DAVIES reported for duty and posted to 'A' Coy.	AKM.
do.	27		Battn. trained as per programme.	
			Lieut COLYER left battn and rejoined Army School of Instruction	
			'A' Coy and Headquarters bathed at COUTHOVE CHATEAU (main POPERINGHE/PROVEN road)	
			Orders received at 2 a.m. for two companies ('A' and 'C') to move up to G.27.C. 3.5 Sheet 28 for work under brigade instructions.	
			These 2 coys. start digging a line at LA CLYTE N.Y. b/d Sheet 28SW at 10 p.m.	
do.	28		Coys. work as per brigade instructions and instructions received via brigade from French military authorities.	
			'D' Coy. carry out battalion scheme of training.	
			'D' Coy and details of 'A' and 'C' Coys. bath at COUTHOVE CHATEAU.	AKM.
do.	29.		Work and training as for yesterday.	
			'C' Coy. lost 1 OR killed and 7 ORs. wounded	AKM.

1875 Wt. W593/826 1,000,000 4/15 J.B.C. & A. A.D.S.S./Forms/C. 2118.

Instructions regarding War Diaries and Intelligence Summaries are contained in F. S. Regs., Part II. and the Staff Manual respectively. Title Pages will be prepared in manuscript.

WAR DIARY
or
INTELLIGENCE SUMMARY
(Erase heading not required.)

Army Form C. 2118

Place	Date	Hour	Summary of Events and Information	Remarks and references to Appendices
LES CISEAUX	APRIL 30		'C' Coy was relieved by 'D' Coy at 10 A.M. Orders received at 1.30 A.M. to move to K.27.d.7.9. Sheet 27 N.E. Battn. less 'A' and 'D' Coys. moved off at 9.30 A.M. Arrived at K.21.c at 12 noon as camp at K.27.d.7.9. was occupied by Glam. T. Army Troops (R.E.) Coy. Battn. then moved to K.32.b.3.7.	HRm.

1875 Wt. W593/826 1,000,000 4/15 J.B.C. & A. A.D.S.S./Forms/C. 2118.

[...]PERATIONS carried out by 6th.Bn.So.Wales Borderers (Pioneers) - between 9th. and 15th. April 1918.

....

On April 9th. at 2 p.m. orders were received to concentrate the Battalion at CANTEEN CORNER CAMP with a view to its probable participatic in impending operations.

"A" Company under Major N.G.Pearson and "C" Coy under Captn J.C. Owen were accordingly withdrawn from the CATACOMBS and joined H.Qrs. and "D" Coy under Captn D.Jenkins at CANTEEN CORNER Camp.

At 10 p.m. orders were received for the Battalion to move forthwith and to take up a position together with the 3 Field Coys.R.E. along the line of the LYS from VANNE to B.18.b.8.0. as a defensive flank. The Battalion moved at once under Lt.Col.N.T.Fitzpatrick and took up the required position.

Patrols were sent out to the river and as far S.W. as PONT DE NIEPPI The position was maintained until early on the morning of the 10th. No enemy were seen.

At 7 a.m. on the 10th. Lt.Col.Fitzpatrick received orders from 75th. Infantry Brigade to assemble the Battalion and 3 Field Coys. R.E. at CHAPE CHAPELLE ROMPUE with a view to counterattacking between LYS FARM and RESERVE AVENUE where the enemy had broken through. Under heavy shell fire barraging all the roads, the assembly was completed and Col.Fitzpatrick with Captn.J.C.Owen and "C" Coy. pushed forward to view the situation before launching his counter attack.

He reached LYS FARM and found the situation had been restored by troops on the spot and that the main attack was developing rapidly on PLOEGSTEERT VILLAGE.

Meanwhile I remained at LE BIZET with the 2 remaining Companies and the R.E. Companies. At 10 a.m. I received orders for Col.Fitzpatrick which I accepted and/on acted as I was quite out of touch with Col.Fitzpatrick and time was short.

The order was from 75th. Bde. ordering the withdrawal of the Battn. and the 3 R.E.Coys to GRAVIER Area as the enemy was in possession of PLOEGSTEERT and was threatening the ROMARIN Road.

I withdrew the 2 remaining Coys and the R.E. Coys to GRAVIER Area and sent runners to find Col.Fitzpatrick and "C" Coy to inform them of the move.

The withdrawal was carried out under heavy artillery fire - the REs sufferin many casualties.

I then took up a position in the Army Line east of ROMARIN with with the R.E. Coys on my right, and reported to 75th. Bde. where I saw the Brigadier and explained the sitiuation.

At this point Col.Fitzpatrick rejoined the Battalion. "C" Coy. remained somewhere in the neighbourhood of LE BIZET having failed to get my orders of withdrawal.

Brigade ordered the line forward about noon and the 2 Coys and R.E. Coys moved forward in open order.

No opposition was met and the line finally settled down from REGINA CAMP on the left to B.12.a.88 on the right.

Captn.Owen withdrew "C" Coy back to the right of the lineand continued it to B.12.b.central. The right was in tough with 8th.Borders and the left with 2n[...]. S. Lancs. The whole line dug in.

At 4.30 p.m. -

At 4.30 p.m. orders were issued to Major Pearson by Col. Allso, commanding 2/S.Lancs. ordering the Battalion to re-capture PLOEGSTEERT Village, working in conjunction with details of R.E's, Australians and 2 Coys S.Lancs. - the attack to commence at 5.30 p.m.

LE BIZET was meanwhile occupied by the enemy and the attack could be enfiladed by him.

At.5.30 p.m. following a M.G.barrage and a short T.M. barrage on the village the attack went forward in short rushes. It was immediately met with sweeping M.G. fire both from PLOEGSTEERT and the neighbourhood of LE BIZET.

Casualties were heavy but the attack pushed forward in a most determined manner to within 200 yards of the village, when owing to enfilade M.G. fire from the right and intense fire from the village the remnants of the attacking troop were compelled to fall back.

The enemy also put down an artillery barrage on the outskirts of the village during the latter stages of the attack. The report that the village was only lightly held by M.G's was entirely disproved as large numbers of enemy infantry were seen and the M.G. fire was intense. Moreover the T.M.barrage preceding the attack was practically useless as only 48 shells were available for the mortars.

Several officers were among the casualties during this attack including Captains Owen and Jenkins (2 Coy.Commanders).

Lieut.E.C.Amos took over command of "C" Coy. Lieut.W.H.Hanna the command of "D" Coy.

The enemy kept pushing on and a general withdrawal took place - the Battalion holding a line from REGINA CAMP to DOU DOU FARM held by Major Pearson and "A" Coy and a switch running back from DOUDOU FARM South to Army Line held by "C" & "D" Coys under Lieut. Amos. This line was heavily shelled all night and at 9.30 a.m. on the 11th. touch was lost on the left and troops were seen falling back - heavy M.G. fire opened on our right and immediate front and the Battalion was driven slowly back to the Army Line east of ROMARIN - holding the trench south of the road from B.4.a.9.8.

At this point touch was lost for a while with the Coys and Major Pearson took control of all he could find.

Enemy was seen in LE DON and ROMARIN Camp. Touch was regained and the line fell back to a line 800 yards west of ROMARIN west of ROMARIN Camp on the North side of RUE DE SAC. At 2 p.m. orders were issued from 75th.Bde. for the Battalion to retake ROMARIN and the Army Line.

The Battalion was to attack with Suffolks and R.Scots on the right, south of RUE DE SAC.

The Battalion was disposed as follows :-

"D" Coy. under Lieut.Hanna astride the CONNAUGHT Road in T.27.c, "C" Coy under Lieut. Amos in the centre and "A" Coy under Major Pearson on the right with R.E. in support.

The attack was successfully launched - the troops S. of the road entered the Village first but could not get across the ROMARIN - BRUNE GAYE Road and "A" & "C" Coys got a footing in the village.

"D" Coy. held the road junction at T.28.c.2.5. but the enemy M.G. fire from the Army Line was too much for the attack and no further progre[ss] could be made.

At 4 p.m. Col.Fitzpatrick went forward and a second effort was made to take the village but it proved unsuccessful owing to lack of support from the right.

~~Lieuts. Potts and Richards -~~

~~Lieut. Petts and Richards were wounded in this attack.~~

At dusk, acting under orders of the 75th.Bde. the Battalion moved back and dug itself in South of CONNAUGHT Road in T.26.d. with 8th.Borders in support, 2/S.Lancs. on the left and R.E. on the right.

Early on the 12th. the enemy searched all this ground with heavy artillery fire but did not attack until 2 p.m. when he broke through on the right and came through in several waves.

The line on the low ground had to withdraw and this was immediately done to the general line of the KORTEPYP Road where trench was gained on the right with 2nd. Worcesters .

This position was held all night. At 1 a.m. reinforcements arrived and were pushed down the road to DE SEULE to gain touch with the right front. At 6 a.m. in a heavy fog the enemy broke through the Division on our right and the line fell back on NEUVE EGLISE where a party of the Battalion hung on till 6 p.m.

The remainder withdrew with 75th. Bde line to the high ground East of CRUCIFIX CORNER, RAVELSBERG.

At 6 p.m. the enemy again attacked and the party left in NEUVE EGLISE was forced to fall back on the high ground with the Battalion.

The Battalion then took up a position S.18.b.central to S.18.b.9.9. with 8th. Borders on left and 9th. Cheshires on right. This line was held all night.

Early on 14th. Col.Fitzpatrick was wounded by M.G. fire whilst moving "D" Coy forward to command the valley in S.13.b. where an attack seemed pending.

I took command of the Battalion from that point.

The line was heavily shelled all day but stood fast.

Orders were received at 10.30 p.m. that the Battalion would be relieved by 1st. Leisters during that night. The relief was successfully carried out and I withdrew the remnants of the Battalion at 4 a.m. at 4 a.m. to the 75th. Bde. rendezvous at KOUDEKOT Camp.

Casualties during these operations amounted to 1 Officer killed, 1 Officer missing, 14 Officers wounded.

33 O.R. killed, 200 O.R. wounded, 118 missing, 29 O.R. wounded and missing.

27/4/18.

Major,
Commdg.6th.(S).Bn.S.W.Borderers (Pioneers).

P. 25.

Army Form C. 2118.

Vol 33

WAR DIARY
or
INTELLIGENCE SUMMARY.

Instructions regarding War Diaries and Intelligence Summaries are contained in F. S. Regs., Part II. and the Staff Manual respectively. Title pages will be prepared in manuscript.

(Erase heading not required.) 6th (S) Bn South Wales Borderers (Pioneers)

Place	Date	Hour	Summary of Events and Information	Remarks and references to Appendices
	MAY	1918		
LES CISEAUX	1		The u/m. officers reported and posted to coys. shown against their names:-	
			Tempy 2/ Lieut A. BRYAN 'A' Coy.	
			- - F. T. KITCHEN 'A' -	
			- - W. RAVENSCROFT 'C' -	
			- - F. SHERRING 'C' -	
			- - G. CARLYLE 'D' -	
			- - J. W. RENDRICK 'D' -	
			The following N.C.Os. have been awarded bars to their Military Medals:-	
			44495 Sgt. J. GREEN, M.M.	
			6/17154 Cpl. J. ELSDON, M.M.	
			The following ORs. have been awarded the Military Medal:-	
			6/16470 Sgt. T. CHATTINGTON.	348

D. D. & L., London, E.C. (A8001) Wt W1771/M2031 750,000 5/17 Sch. 52 Forms/C2118/14

Army Form C. 2118.

Instructions regarding War Diaries and Intelligence Summaries are contained in F. S. Regs., Part II. and the Staff Manual respectively. Title pages will be prepared in manuscript.

WAR DIARY
or
INTELLIGENCE SUMMARY.
(*Erase heading not required.*)

Place	Date	Hour	Summary of Events and Information	Remarks and references to Appendices
	MAY			
LES CISEAUX	1 con.		6/17106 Cpl. J. FELLOWS	
			6/17159 – B. BISHOP	
			6/17152 L/Cpl. E. DAVIES	
			6/17353 Pte. L. YOUNG.	
			6/17203 – R. MAYBURY	
			6/16794 – B. J. LEWIS	
			6/14504 – D. THOMAS	
			6/19225 – J. CASSIDY	
			11622 – A. GALLENT	
			229147 – W. MARTIN.	
			The u/m. OR. was wounded at LA CLYTE:-	
			22178 Pte. A. MAINWARING – 'D' Coy.	
			'A' and 'D' Coys. carry on work at LA CLYTE under brigade instructions, and 'B' teams of these 2 coys. train as per programme.	

D. D. & L., London, E.C. (A5004) Wt W1771/M2031 750,000 5/17 Sch. 52 Forms/C2118/14

Instructions regarding War Diaries and Intelligence Summaries are contained in F. S. Regs., Part II. and the Staff Manual respectively. Title pages will be prepared in manuscript.

WAR DIARY
or
INTELLIGENCE SUMMARY.
(*Erase heading not required.*)

Army Form C. 2118.

Place	Date MAY	Hour	Summary of Events and Information	Remarks and references to Appendices
LES CISEAUX	1 con.		'C' Coy. left LES CISEAUX at 2 P.M. and relieved 'A' Coy. at G. 26. c. 3. 5 Sht. 28 at 4.30 P.M. — 'A' Coy. returning to LES CISEAUX at 9.30 P.M.	
			'C' and 'D' Coys. work under brigade, night 1st/2nd May.	ARM.
do.	2		The u/m. ORs previously reported as missing rejoined battn. from 34th Division this day:- 40149 Pte E. ROBERTS. 40151 - E. ROBERTS. Coys. work and train under brigade and battn. schemes respectively	
do.	3		Bn. trained. 'C' and 'D' Coys. work as per programme.	ARM.
			'D' Coy returned to LES CISEAUX from LA CLYTE at 9.30 P.M. in accordance with instructions received.	
			'D' Coy lost 1 O.R. wounded.	
do	4		'C' Coy returned from LA CLYTE at 6.30 P.M. in accordance	

D. D. & L., London, E.C. (A8004) Wt W1771/M2031 750,000 5/17 Sch. 52 Forms/C2118/14

Army Form C. 2118.

Instructions regarding War Diaries and Intelligence Summaries are contained in F. S. Regs., Part II. and the Staff Manual respectively. Title pages will be prepared in manuscript.

WAR DIARY
or
INTELLIGENCE SUMMARY.
(Erase heading not required.)

Place	Date MAY	Hour	Summary of Events and Information	Remarks and references to Appendices
LES CISEAUX	4 Con.		with instructions received.	
			48629 L/Cpl W. MASSIE – 'C' Coy – wounded.	
			'A' and 'D' Coys train as per programme.	
			Orders received at 10.30 PM for Battn to move to WYLDER.	R
WYLDER	5.		Capn F.M. McCAUSLAND and 2/Lt H.R. MURRAY left at 9 AM in advance of battn. to billet.	
			Battn paraded at 11 AM to reach STEENVOODE CHURCH at 11.30 AM (divisional schedule)	
			Bn. reached WYLDER at 6 PM.	R
do.	6		Bn. trained	R
do.	7		Bn. trained.	
do	8		3 O.Rs. reported and taken on strength of Coys as follows :– 2 – 'D' Coy; 1 – 'C' Coy.	
WYLDER	"		Orders received for Battn to move to SOISSONS area – entraining at WAAYENBURG – X13.C 3.3 Sheet 19.	R

D. D. & L., London, E.C. (A8004) Wt W1771/M2031 750,000 5/17 Sch. 52 Forms/C2118/14

Instructions regarding War Diaries and Intelligence Summaries are contained in F. S. Regs., Part II. and the Staff Manual respectively. Title pages will be prepared in manuscript.

WAR DIARY
or
INTELLIGENCE SUMMARY.
(Erase heading not required.)

Army Form C. 2118.

Place	Date MAY	Hour	Summary of Events and Information	Remarks and references to Appendices
WYLDER	8 Con.		2 officers and 100 men of 'D' Coy reported at WAAYENBURG STATION at 3·PM to act as loading party 2/Lt H.R. MURRAY and billetting party proceeded on first train from WAAYENBURG at 6·45 PM	
~~VÉZILLY~~ R. WYLDER	9		Transport paraded at 7·AM and reached entraining station ready to be loaded at 11·45 AM. Bn. paraded and moved off from WYLDER at 9·30 AM. reaching WAAYENBURG at 12·45 PM – via BAMBECQUE, OOST CAPPEL and ROUSBRUGGE. Entrained at 2·45 PM. Loading party detailed by 'D' Coy left WAAYENBURG by the 9·45 PM train.	R. R.
	10		Billetting party detrained at FÉRE at 2·30 AM and reached VÉZILLY, via COULONGES at 5 AM. Ref. Sheet 22:- SOISSONS	R.
	11		'A' and 'C' Coys and details of Headquarters detrained at FÉRE at 1 AM and reached VÉZILLY at 6 AM.	R.

D. D. & L., London, E.C.
(A8004) Wt W1771/M2031 750,000 5/17 Sch. 52 Forms/C2118/14

Instructions regarding War Diaries and Intelligence Summaries are contained in F. S. Regs., Part II. and the Staff Manual respectively. Title pages will be prepared in manuscript.

WAR DIARY
or
INTELLIGENCE SUMMARY.
(Erase heading not required.)

Army Form C. 2118.

Place	Date	Hour	Summary of Events and Information	Remarks and references to Appendices
	MAY 11		Remainder of 'D' Coy unloaded at detraining station and marched up with loading party detailed by that Coy arriving at VÉZILLY at 11.30 AM.	
VÉZILLY	do		Bn. less D. Coy. paraded with 74th Inf. Brigade and was inspected by G.O.C. Division at COHAN.	
			The following officers have been awarded the MILITARY CROSS vide D.R.O. 11th May:–	
			Temp. Capt. A.C. MANN RAMC. att. 6th S.W.B.	
			" " D.H. STICKLER	
			" Lt. E.C. AMOS	
			The u/m W.O. has been awarded the Distinguished Conduct Medal vide D.R.O. 11th May:–	
			6/17090 C.S.M. J. PEARSON.	JR.

D. D. & L., London, E.C. (A8004) Wt W1771/M2031 750,000 5/17 Sch. 52 Forms/C2118/14

Instructions regarding War Diaries and Intelligence Summaries are contained in F. S. Regs., Part II. and the Staff Manual respectively. Title pages will be prepared in manuscript.

WAR DIARY
or
INTELLIGENCE SUMMARY.
(Erase heading not required.)

Army Form C. 2118.

Place	Date MAY	Hour	Summary of Events and Information	Remarks and references to Appendices
VÉZILLY	12		Bn. rested and cleaned up.	
			The following Tempy. Sec. Lieuts. have been promoted Tempy. Lieuts. on completion of 18 months Commissioned service:–	
			Tempy. Sec. Lt. W. L. BOWEN att'd 6th S.W.B.	
			— — — W. J. KENDRICK — — —	[illegible]
do	13		All Coys. and specialists train under Battn. Scheme. – squad & rifle drill, bayonet fighting, physical training, signalling, Lewis gun etc. Short route marches. Lectures given in afternoon on wiring, communication etc.	
			Tempy. Maj. L.C.W. DEANE DSO. MC. appointed Act/Lt Col. to command this Bn.	[illegible]
do	14		Training as per programme.	[illegible]
do	15		Training as per Bn. programme	[illegible]
do	16		3 NCOs reported and taken on strength	
			Bn. trained as per programme	[illegible]

D. D & L., London, E.C. (A8004) Wt W1771/M2031 750,000 5/17 Sch. 52 Forms/C2118/14

Army Form C. 2118.

Instructions regarding War Diaries and Intelligence Summaries are contained in F. S. Regs., Part II. and the Staff Manual respectively. Title pages will be prepared in manuscript.

WAR DIARY
or
INTELLIGENCE SUMMARY.
(Erase heading not required.)

Place	Date	Hour	Summary of Events and Information	Remarks and references to Appendices
	MAY			
VÉZILLY	17		Battn. trained as per programme	
			The u/m officers reported today:-	
			Temp. major A. REID-KELLETT M.C.	
			— 2/Lt. L. PETTS MC and posted to 'D' Coy.	
			— — RAVENSCROFT and posted to 'C' Coy	
			16 ORs. reported from Base and taken on strength of Coys as follows:- 'A' Coy. 3: 'C' Coy. 6: 'D' Coy. 7.	R.
do	18		Bn. trained.	R.
do	19		Bn. rested	R.
			Church of England and Non-Conformist services in morning.	R.
do	20		Bn trained	R.
do	21		Bn trained as per programme	R.
do	22		Bn. trained.	
			Warning order to move received at 4.30 P.M. followed by move orders at 11.30 PM.	R.

D. D. & L., London, E.C. (A8004) Wt W1771/M2031 750,000 5/17 Sch. 52 Forms/C2118/14

Army Form C. 2118.

Instructions regarding War Diaries and Intelligence Summaries are contained in F. S. Regs., Part II. and the Staff Manual respectively. Title pages will be prepared in manuscript.

WAR DIARY
or
INTELLIGENCE SUMMARY.
(Erase heading not required.)

Place	Date MAY	Hour	Summary of Events and Information	Remarks and references to Appendices
VEZILLY	23		Battn moved by march route to MAGNEUX	
	24		Bn trained	
			The U/m Officers reported for duty and taken on the strength and posted to Coys as follows	
			2ND LT J. T. PARRY — "A" Coy.	
			2ND LT J. SOUTHWARD — "C" Coy	
			Maj. J. H. MORGAN having reported for duty is taken on the strength of Battn as from 23RD instant and assumes the duties of Second-in Command of the Battn as from this date.	
			10. O.Rs reported from the Base and posted to Coys. as follows:- A. Coy. — 5. C — 2. D — 3.	JK.

D. D. & L., London, E.C.
(A8004) Wt W1771/M2031 750,000 5/17 Sch. 52 Forms/C2118/14

Instructions regarding War Diaries and Intelligence Summaries are contained in F. S. Regs., Part II. and the Staff Manual respectively. Title pages will be prepared in manuscript.

WAR DIARY
or
INTELLIGENCE SUMMARY.
(Erase heading not required.)

Army Form C. 2118.

Place	Date	Hour	Summary of Events and Information	Remarks and references to Appendices
	MAY			
MAGNEUX	25		Battn. trained as per programme	RC.
	26		Battn. rested.	
			A Coy. H.Q. Coy. & Transport paraded for Divine Service at 11-AM	
			AWARDS	
			Under authority granted by His Majesty the King, the Field Marshal Commanding-in-Chief has granted the following award.	
			The DISTINGUISHED SERVICE ORDER	RC.
			Maj. N.G. PEARSON South Wales Borderers	
			The following Officers have been mentioned in despatches London Gazette dated 23rd May 1918	
			Lt. Col. L.C.W. DEANE D.S.O. M.C.	
			A/CAPT S.E. RUMSEY M.C.	
			2/Lt S.F. TRUSLER	
			also the ~~4/~~ N.C.O.	
			6/19227 Sgt G. Hemmings.	Kings

D. D. & L., London, E.C. (A8004) Wt W1771/M2031 750,000 5/17 Sch. 52 Forms/C2118/14

Instructions regarding War Diaries and Intelligence Summaries are contained in F. S. Regs., Part II. and the Staff Manual respectively. Title pages will be prepared in manuscript.

WAR DIARY
or
INTELLIGENCE SUMMARY.
(Erase heading not required.)

Army Form C. 2118.

Place	Date MAY	Hour	Summary of Events and Information	Remarks and references to Appendices
MAGNEUX	26		Warning orders received at 8 PM followed by move orders at 10.30 PM	[initials]
LOISY EN BRIE	31st		Att. Report of Operations of this Bn between dates May 26 & May 31st.	[initials]
			Casualties to Officers during these operations are as follows:-	
			Lt. Col. L.C.W. DEANE DSO. MC. Killed 29.5.18	
			2 Lieut. F.T. KITCHEN Wounded & missing 28.5.18	
			Lieut. H. DAVIES missing 28.5.18	
			2nd Lieut. G. CARLYLE Missing 28.5.18	
			2nd Lieut. H.R. MURRAY missing 30.5.18	
			2nd Lieut J.T. PARRY Wounded 28.5.18	
			Capt. A. CASE Wounded at duty 30.5.18	
			Lieut. J.W. KENDRICK do do 30.5.18.	
			Casualties to O.Rs. from 28-5-18 to 31-5-18:-	
			KILLED 18.	
			WOUNDED 103	
			MISSING 101	
			[signature] Capt. for Maj. Comdg. 6th LWB Rmrs	[initials]

D. D. & L., London, E.C. (A8004) Wt W1771/M2031 750,000 5/17 Sch. 52 Forms/C2118/14

Reference Map Soissons 1-100,000

REPORT OF OPERATIONS CARRIED OUT 6TH BN. SOUTH WALES BORDERERS (PIONEERS) between 26th and 31st MAY 1918.

On the 26th May the Battalion were lying in billets at Magneux and at 8 p.m. on the 26th orders were received to stand by and move at an hours notice in battle order accompanied by Battalion Transport. Packs were accordingly dumped. Move orders were received and the Battalion moved at 10.30 a.m. to Romain where orders were received to continue the march to Vaux-Varennes at which point Battalion came under the orders of G.O.C., 7th Brigade.

The march from Magneux to Vaux-Varennes occupied five hours as there was considerable movement of troops and transport on the road and the enemy had heavily shelled the back areas with gas shells and it was at some points on the march necessary to march in gas helmets.

On arrival at Vaux-Varennes at 3 a.m. on the 27th the Battalion rested in huts while I, who had taken over duties of Second in Command, reported the arrival of Battalion to G.O.C. 7th Brigade at Brigade Headquarters at Guyencourt.

The Battalion was ordered by the 7th Brigade to move at once and occupy the second position on the right of 7th Brigade from the Chalons-la-Vergeur Cormicy Road to the boundary of the 9th Corps Area at a point 600 yards due West of Trigny. The Transport remained at Vaux-Varennes.

At 8.30 I took D Company commanded by Lieut. Davies and C Company commanded by Lieut. Amos and occupied this position from the Vaux-Varennes Cormicy Road to a point approximately 400 yards due East of Hermonville. A Company, commanded by Capt. Stickler, marched independently and occupied the high ground to the North East of Trigny on Hill 220.

Along this line, which was approximately four miles in length, there was a fairly good traversed trench two feet in depth and strongly wired in front.

From the Chalons-la-Vergeur Cormicy Road to immediately South of the Tile Works the line ran in thick wood, but from the Tile Works round Hermonville ~~and round Hermonville~~ to the East and back to St. Joseph's Farm near Chateau Hervelon the trenches were in the open and for a considerable distance on the forward slope of the hill and under direct observation of the enemy. Battalion Headquarters were in Farm St. Joseph and communication by visual signalling was established between the Battalion Headquarters and Transport Lines.

The maps supplied were not very helpful in locating the line to be held and little time was available in reconnoitring the positions, but by mid-day the men were all in position and O. C. D. Company sent out patrols to establish connection on the right of the 7th Brigade. I returned to Battalion Headquarters and reported to Lieut. Colonel Deane what had been done.

At 4 p.m. orders were received from 7th Brigade that the left Company should side step to the left to take over a gap formerly occupied by the 10th Cheshires who had been withdrawn

REPORT ON MOVEMENT OF TRANSPORT

26.5.18. -to- 31.5.18.

- - - - - - - -

On Sunday, 26th May, the Battalion was resting at Marneux when orders were received about 10 p.m. to move forward through Coulonges and Bouvancourt to a hutment camp at Vaux Varennes, where the Battalion with Transport arrived at about 3 a.m. on the 26th. On this march, a little gas from enemy shelling was experienced and Box Respirators were worn.

About 9 a.m. on the 26th the Companies moved up to the line leaving the Transport in rear of Battalion Headquarters at Vaux-Varennes under Capt. McCausland, ~~[illegible]~~. About 6 p.m. the same date, Major Morgan joined the Transport, having arrived from Marneux where he had been left to hand over billets and he then took over command.

At this time the Camp at Vaux-Varennes was being shelled and one horse had been wounded by machine gun fire from enemy aeroplanes, so Major Morgan decided to move in the direction of Montigny through Pevy and about 9 p.m. the same evening the convoy halted in a small wood about half a mile South of [illegible] in Montigny. Here the animals were fed and the men rested until about 1 a.m. on the 27th when it was again decided to move in the direction of Jonchery.

Traffic in Jonchery was very congested and the Transport was halted for about one hour at the entrance to the town the time being about 5 a.m., and at 6 a.m. the Transport moved on through the town and then turned South on to the Jonchery Vandeuil Road. There was a very steep uphill gradient to climb on this road and the traffic was even more congested than ever, different transports having double banked one another, and pontoon wagons having blocked the road, machine gun fire was soon drawn from the enemy aircraft, and afterwards continuous shelling from enemy artillery. The shelling was very good most of the shells either hitting or landing very close to the road. Three of our G.S. wagons, two limbers and one cooker were knocked out here. These had to be abandoned. All the animals and men were saved except No. [illegible] Evans, [illegible] and his two mules, and this man is still missing.

From here the Transport moved right on to Aougny via Savigny, Crugny and Arcis le Ponsart and arrived at 5.30 p.m. Here, the animals and men were rested, watered and fed after having moved about twentysix kilometres in eleven hours.

About 8.30 p.m. on the same evening of the 27th, orders were received from the 25th Division to move on to Goussancourt via Villers Agron, a distance of about 8 kilometres. The men were very tired and there was an endless column of British and French transport and traffic in both ~~each~~ directions which made progress very slowly.

to reserve and C. C. D. Company proceeded to carry out this order but found that a half Company of the Lincolns had already taken up a position formerly occupied by the Cheshires and therefore it was only necessary to side step a very short distance.

At 7 p.m. I visited this part of the line and found that troops in the front line consisting of 1st and 2nd Lincolns and 7th Leicesters were retiring through the second position. I stopped them and reorganised them to form defensive flank facing North in which direction I was informed the enemy were advancing. In all I collected about One hundred and eighty men from these three units and sent an Officer of the 2nd Lincolns to proceed to their Brigade Headquarters to endeavour to arrange rations for these men as I was informed by their Officers that they had had no food or water for some considerable time. I had almost completed reorganisation when the enemy appeared advancing up the Northern slope of the hill and commenced sniping and machine-gunning those not already occupying the trenches.

An 18 pounder of the 25th Divisional Artillery, which had been placed immediately in front of these trenches, was firing at the enemy over open sights and the team retired when the enemy got within 100 yards. Upon seeing the trench strongly held, the enemy retired, and the gun team returned to their gun and recommenced firing.

At 8.30 p.m. the enemy again advanced against the hill but was driven back by fire of Company Lewis guns and rifle fire of the Composite Units and made no further attempt that night. Between 9 and 10 p.m. the men of the 1st and 2nd Lincolns and Leicesters retired from the position leaving D Company to hold the trenches alone.

After reorganising the left flank I returned with the Company Commander along the trench to the right and encountered a further forty men of the 7th Leicesters under 2nd Lieut. Knight. These men were also portion of the front line garrison and I placed them under the command of Lieut. Davies and instructed him to place them in the second position to assist in the defence of the hill. I also encountered a Vickers gun and Section of 21st Divisional Machine Gunners and as they had no ammunition I guided them to Battalion Headquarters intending to obtain ammunition for them and make use of the gun with the Companies holding out on the right.

I visited a Battery of 18 Pounders that was in action near St. Auboeuf and explained to them the situation and the Battery at once commenced barraging the Northern end of the wood immediatbly North of Hill 180.

At 7 a.m. on the morning of the 28th, scouts reported that the enemy had worked right round the left flank of the Company and were in possession of the French Dump some distance in rear on the Chalons-la-Vergeur and St. Aboeuf Road. It was then decided that the Company should be withdrawn to a position further in rear the Lewis Gunners being used to cover the retirement. The enemy were swarming in the wood and offered excellent targets to the gunners who caused considerable casualties, as the guns were so placed to command all the numerous tracks leading through the woods.

Approaching St. Aboeuf it was found that the enemy were in possession of this place and accordingly a detour was made to the South East in the direction of Hermonville and retirement effected in that way. Unfortunately two Officers and about forty other ranks were cut off in the wood and entirely surrounded, and were lost sight of.

The enemy having now reached the Bouvencourt-Hermonville Road, it was deemed advisable to withdraw C Company from East of Hermonville, and A Company who had the previous evening moved from the high ground North West of Trigny to the second position immediately North of Farm St. Joseph to form a defensive flank from the Farm St. Joseph Westward immediately in front of Chateau Hervelon. As fast as the men could be withdrawn I guided them to new position. Portions of A C and D Companies under the command of Capt. Stickler remained between Chateau Hervelon and Farm St Joseph. On their immediate left was a number of Zouaves with machine guns, and the remainder of the Battalion were occupying position on the Zouaves left facing North.

I saw a considerable number of men streaming back just to the East of Chateau Hervelon and accordingly placed the left detachment of the Battalion under 2nd Lieut. Perry of A Company and endeavoured to intercept these stragglers and bring them in to assist in the defence of the left flank. I succeeded in intercepting nearly two hundred men of various units, chiefly Northumberland Fusiliers (Pioneers) of the 21st Division, and guided them round behind the left flank. Before I could get them into position their Commanding Officer arrived and I explained the position to him and he deployed his men on our left.

I reconnoitred the flank to the left in the direction of Vaux-Varennes and Bouvencourt and found that there was a gap of nearly One thousand yards between the left of the Northumberland Fusiliers and the next British Unit on that flank. Enemy could be seen advancing over Hill 200 in great strength from the direction of Chalons-la-Vergeur and further to the North West from the direction of Guyencourt. Enemy transport was seen coming down the road from Guyencourt towards Vaux-Varennes.

The units on the left eventually retired and finally the Northumberland Fusiliers moved back to a trench along the high ground running West from Trigny to Prouilly. A Company and Machine Gun Detachment of the 3rd Zouave Regiment hung on for another two hours but the left flank was turned and eventually all had to retire and take up positions in conformity with the Northumberland Fusiliers and other units including French Units who were preparing to hold this ground.

During all this time, D Company, who had been cut off in the wood North West of Hermonville had been steadily fighting their way back and inflicted considerable casualties on the enemy with Lewis Gun fire, these Lewis Guns being skilfully handled by the teams. This Company, with the exception of those previously mentioned as being captured, succeeding in extricating themselves and retiring to the Trigny-Prouilly line. The detached section of A Company which had been holding out between the Farm St. Joseph and Chateau Hervelon retired and took up position on Hill 220 to the North of Trigny.

The Battalion had by this time been transferred to the 64th Brigade of the 21st Division and the whole line appears to have been under the orders of French Commander. The line

X. A Coy surprised a patrol of the enemy prowling and succeeded in capturing one of them and killing the remainder. This prisoner was taken to French Headquarters and it is understood gave valuable information as to the enemy's dispositions.

running over Hill 220 West of Trigny and along the high ground to Prouilly was held until 2 a.m. on the morning of the 28th, all the time being persistently shelled and trench mortared by the enemy. X

At 1.30 a.m. general retirement was ordered and the Battalion retired and took up position along the Reims-Jonchery Railway with its left the Tile Works, C Company holding the line of the railway, D Company being in support and A Company in reserve in trenches dug by them on the forward slope of the hill 300 yards South of Reims-Jonchery Road, Battalion Headquarters being in a Quarry about 400 yards on the left rear of A Company's position.

At 10 a.m. orders were received that the Battalion was transferred to the 62nd Brigade and ordered to evacuate its positions and proceed via Rosnay to reinforce the line in front of Hill 202. Commanding Officer ordered me to withdraw the Battalion while he proceeded to confer with the G. O. C. 62nd Brigade as to the new position.

The order was carried out in the following manner. C Company front line were ordered to file along the Railway to the left and into the wood in which the Tile Works were situated and file South and East round the Edge of the wood and rendezvous in the wood immediately West of the "R" in Rosnay. D Company in support were ordered to advance to the front line as soon as C Company were clear and follow same route and A Company were to act in a similar manner as soon as D Company got clear. Unfortunately the enemy got on to the manouvre and put up a terrific barrage of 5.9's. It was therefore deemed inadvisable that A Company should move in the wake of the other two Companies. Accordingly orders were sent to Capt. Stickler to filter his men back in two's straight into the wood in rear of his position. This occupied about four hours as the shelling was extremely heavy the whole manouvre being carried out in full view of the enemy. Happily the casualties were extremely light.

By 3.30 the whole Battalion had arrived at the rendezvous and awaited the instructions of the Commanding Officer. At 4 p.m. information was received that the Commanding Officer had been killed at the Cross Roads by Rosnay Church. I proceeded to the spot in company with the Medical Officer and found that the Commanding Officer's body had been carried to a house near by and he was quite dead, therefore no information was available as to new position to be taken up his map case containing maps and orders having been stolen.

I assumed command and instructed the Adjutant who had come from the Transport Lines to find the Battalion, to proceed to Brigade Headquarters which were reported to be in Mery Premicy and report what had occurred.

At 5.30 p.m. instructions were received to proceed to Hill 202 and report to Colonel Guise of the Lincolns or Colonel Sawyer of the Leicesters. I immediately proceeded to Hill 202 which I found was held by French machine guns and the Officer in charge informed me that this was now the front line and that all English troops had retired. I proceeded to the farm to the East of Hill 202 where I found the Officer commanding the French Battalion holding this portion of the front and the Adjutant of the 6th Leicesters who informed me he had eighty men still holding on.

I placed myself at the disposal of the French Commanding Officer who informed me that he had plenty of French troops and was able to deal with the situation and as my men were very tired he would be satisfied if I brought the Battalion up within 800 yards and placed them in the wood to get sleep and a rest.

I returned to the rendezvous and found that in my absence information had been conveyed to the Battalion that the enemy were almost into Rosnay Village and Captain Stickler whom I had left in command, accordingly moved the Battalion to the high ground immediately astride the Rosnay Mery-Premicy Road and commenced digging in.

I moved the whole line back in order to get a good field of fire and commenced digging in on this line together with Composite Company of the 21st Division.

While the Battalion were digging in the Medical Officer called for volunteers and entered Rosnay Village to evacuate the wounded who had been abandoned in the dressing station there. There were in all five cases which were successfully evacuated and the wounded were carried to Mery-Premicy.

About half an hour later, Colonel Morris and eighty men of the 4th South Staffords arrived and on hearing that it was our intention to hold out on this line, decided to remain and assist also. Shortly afterwards, while I was reconnoitring the left flank with Colonel Morris, the Composite Company of the 21st Division assembled on the road and retired in the direction of Mery-Premicy.

At 1 a.m. on the 29th the Intelligence Officer of the 62nd Brigade arrived at the position and informed me that G. O. C., 45th French Division was satisfied with the position and that all British Units might retire for rest and reorganisation. In compliance with this order I assembled the Battalion on the road and marched them to Mery-Premicy where, I had been informed, we would be supplied with water and rations.

I reported to 62nd Brigade on arrival there and was instructed to proceed to Marfaux. I waited at Mery-Premicy for an hour in order to obtain promised rations and water but only fifty rations were available and no water.

I bivouaced the Battalion at 3 a.m. in the wood immediately South of Aubilly on the Aubilly and Bligny Road, resuming the march to Marfaux at 7.15 a.m. and arriving at Marfaux at 10 a.m. I rested the Battalion in a field close to the Marfaux-Pourcy Road 400 yards South East of Marfaux.

Immediately on arrival there, 62nd Brigade informed me that a lorry had arrived from the 25th Division with 850 rations for the Battalion.

At 10.45, orders were received from the 62nd Brigade that the whole Brigade were moving at 11.30 to Foret de Epernay South of the Marne River. I accordingly distributed as many of the rations as possible and gave eighty rations to the 4th South Staffords, One hundred to the Brigade for stragglers and forty to a machine gun Company of the 21st Division who had had no rations for some considerable time. The oats and forage of course had to be left behind as we had no Transport.

A halt for three hours was made in the Bois de Courtin three kilometres to the South of Nanteuil. At 5.30 the march was resumed, progress being extremely slow owing to the enormous volume of traffic moving along the road.

After proceeding one kilometre along the road I decided that the slow rate of progress and the dust was making the men very exhausted and accordingly left the main road and followed overland tracks through Montorgueil keeping about one kilometre to the West of the main road the whole way to Damery.

[illegible] nearly four hours [illegible]

In the morning we were found by 2nd Lieut. [illegible] to find the Battalion. I instructed him to return to the Transport Lines [illegible] the Battalion. [illegible] by the [illegible] Brigade.

[illegible]

At 20.00 [illegible] the Battalion marched to [illegible] north of Villers-[illegible] where one Company was billeted in barns and two Companies in huts, where they rested for the night.

At 1[4] [illegible] following day orders were issued that the Battalion should rejoin the [illegible] Division and accordingly marched to Loisy-en-Brie, [illegible] at Loisy-en-Brie [illegible]

[illegible] attached herewith [illegible] report of [illegible] Section A. Company of the [illegible] Battalion, Machine Gun Corps, which Section was attached to the Battalion during these operations.

It is regretted that [illegible] Officer were lost with his map case and other notes in possession of the [illegible] to find the Transport Lines, [illegible] by the enemy.

On the march from [illegible] I made a point of collecting all stragglers of the [illegible] Division and succeeded in collecting over fifty men, and on arrival at Loisy-en-Brie these stragglers were [illegible] to their own units in the Division.

The [illegible] by the Battalion during the [illegible] is shown on the attached [illegible].

A record of the Transport is also attached herewith.

The men were very footsore at the conclusion of the march and they suffered from lack of sleep but finished full of spirit.

(Signed) A Reid-Kellett
Major
6th South Wales Borderers.

Reference Map SOISSONS 1 - 100,000.

\- - - - - - - - - - - -

Report of Operations carried out by:-

No 3 Section "A" Company, 25th Battn, Machine Gun Corps.

1\. The section (4 guns) reported to the C.O. 6th S.W.B. at VAUX-VARRENNES at 7.30 a.m. on Monday 27/5/1918.

2\. I was told to reconnoitre the sector, CHALONS-LA-VERGEUR HERMONVILLE - TRIGNY and place guns in position.

3\. At 12.15 p.m. I reported to C.O. 6th S.W.B. at Ferme St Joseph (2 Kilometres S.W. of H in HERMONVILLE) that the guns were in position at the following places:-

LEFT SUBSECTION GUNS. (2).
400 S.W. of C in CHALONS-LA-VERGEUR.

RIGHT SUBSECTION GUNS. (2).
½ Kilometre E of S in VAUX-VARENNES. (in stone quarries)

LEFT SUBSECTION GUNS. I visited the left subsection guns at 5.15 p.m. and found them all correct. At 5 a.m. on Tuesday 27/5/1918, I attempted to reach the positions but failed as they had been cut off by the advance. Two men of "A" Coy 25th Battn, M.G.C. (who joined me on the 30/5/1918) reported that they had seen the guns in action at 10.30 p.m. Monday and were still intact at 9 a.m. Tuesday.

The supply of S.A.A. with each gun at the positions was 24 belts (6,000 rounds) also 1 box of S.A.A. (1,000 rounds).

The above is all the information I have at present regarding the above two guns.

RIGHT SUBSECTION GUNS. 2 Horses and 1 mule of the limber were killed on Monday evening, leaving only 1 mule and the limber Early on Tuesday morning I received information that the 6th S.W.B. were withdrawing to take up new positions South of FERME ST JOSEPH, and then chose 2 gun positions about 200 N of FERME ST JOSEPH and ordered the guns to withdraw to these positions at once. The limber was overturned on the road by a shell and the guns, etc were strewn over the road. One gun managed to get clear away, but was put out of action by Machine gunfire from the crest. By this time the enemy was machine gunning from the crest and swarming the road. The remaining gun and kit was captured. The Gun teams now joined the 6th S.W.B. as infantry and remained with them throughout the retirement.

(Sgd) R. Watson, 2/Lieut.

"A" Coy, 25th Battn, M. G. C.

In the field.

1/6/1918.

Marneux to Vaux-Varennes - - - - - - - - - - - - - - 11 Kilometres

Vaux-Varennes to Chalons-le-Vergeur - - - - - - 3 "

Chalons-le-Vergeur to the Vesle at Tile Works - 11 "

Tile Works to Rosnay - - - - - - - - - - - - - - [illegible] "

Rosnay to Aubilly - - - - - - - - - - - - - - - - 6 "

Aubilly to Marfaux - - - - - - - - - - - - - - - - [illegible] "

Marfaux to Foret de Gernay - - - - - - - - - - 10 "

Foret de Gernay to Soulieres - - - - - - - - - 10 "

Soulieres to Loisy-en-Brie - - - - - - - - - - - 4 "

Total marched - - - [illegible] Kilometres.

www.ingramcontent.com/pod-product-compliance
Lightning Source LLC
Chambersburg PA
CBHW082009220426
43670CB00014B/2585

* 9 7 8 1 4 7 4 5 1 3 4 2 5 *